WOMEN'S MARKET HANDBOOK

About the Author

Carol Nelson is General Manager, Creative Director of Cohn & Wells, Chicago, a full-service, international direct marketing agency. She's a recognized speaker on advertising and marketing, having addressed audiences all over the world, including Australia, Switzerland, England, Hong Kong, as well as the United States.

Formerly, Nelson was the Creative Director for Frequency Marketing, Inc., Cincinnati, Ohio, and an advertising consultant and copywriter. Her writings have appeared in a number of marketing magazines including *Direct Marketing*.

WOMEN'S MARKET HANDBOOK

Understanding and Reaching Today's Most Powerful Consumer Group

CAROL NELSON

guest foreword by

FRANCES LEAR

 **Gale Research Inc.** • DETROIT • WASHINGTON, D.C. • LONDON

GALE RESEARCH INC. STAFF

Peg Bessette, Developmental Editor

Lawrence W. Baker, Senior Developmental Editor

Jane Hoehner and *Kelle S. Sisung,*

Contributing Editors

Editorial Assistants: Laurel S. Burke,

Julie Carnagie, Erin L. Diniak,

Scott F. Heil, Kristine M. Lewis,

K'Ailene McGlothen, Todd E. Zornik

Mary Beth Trimper, Production Director

Evi Seoud, Assistant Production Manager

Shanna Heilveil, Production Assistant

Cynthia Baldwin, Art Director

Mark C. Howell, Cover and Page Designer

Barbara J. Yarrow, Graphic Services Supervisor

Willie F. Mathis, Camera Operator

Benita L. Spight, Data Entry Supervisor

Gwendolyn S. Tucker, Data Entry Group Leader

Constance Wells, Data Entry Associate

The Graphix Group, Typesetting

Library of Congress Cataloging-in-Publication Data
1. Marketing. 2. Advertising. 3. Women consumers. I. Title.
HF5415.N3495   1993
658.8'348—dc20

93-30264
CIP

To my mother, Margo,
the source from whom all energy seems to flow.

Contents

Foreword

State-of-the-art marketing and product development are creative pursuits, but for three decades both have been replaced by computer technology; and—just as dramatically—by a consumer who is like no woman before her. A man cannot know this woman. He may know her as his wife, or his daughter, or his sister, or his colleague, but he does not know her as his customer.

The entire emphasis in American life—and in marketing strategy—is changing because women are changing. We are involved in the big picture: the quality of life, solutions to social issues, the national—and global—economy; and we are finding our way out of the traditions that bind us through our *discretionary buying power,* and *independent buying decisions.*

One woman of 40 is entering law school in Los Angeles; another woman of the same age is starting a business in Dallas; and still another woman of 40 is becoming a senior VP in an advertising agency in Chicago. All three women have the same basic needs. All three women have additional and different needs: from clothes, to automobiles, to financial services, to take-out food. The woman going back to school is most often targeted by marketers within an 18-to-24 age segment. Does marketing for business products and services to entrepreneurs in their twenties differ from marketing to entrepreneurs in their fifties? At what age does a woman buy a car? Lipstick? Insurance? Go skiing? Wear sneakers? Start a business? Have a baby? My friend Barbara, who is 52, just adopted her second child. My younger daughter buys the same brand of cosmetics that I buy. My elder daughter has a more expensive car than mine. I have never shopped for my grandson, because this grandmother—and others like me—are too busy to shop. The lifestyles and product needs of women no longer reflect their ages. Not all traditional demographics fit the contemporary woman. Income? Yes. Employment? Yes. Age? No.

How to market to women? *De-age* products. Target the stage of a woman's life. There are only two: Under thirty is preparation for life; over thirty is living life.

Consumerism in the '90s can only be understood when women are understood. A male trend watcher at a major agency wrote, "We have to speak to women from a woman's perspective." How does a man do that? No survey, no focus group, can deliver our perspective because there isn't one. We are not a collective. We are individuals, and we are spelling out new priorities and marketing imperatives. Successful enterprise depends upon listening to the customer, satisfying her product needs, and responding to her demand for corporate social responsibility. Products count less to many of today's consumers than a company's good citizenship.

How to market to women? *Listen to management women.* Industry cannot know what women want without the input of women. To raise consumer confidence, to beat the competition, the marketer needs credibility with the consumer. My mother believed product promises. I don't. Nor do my children. Selling hope in a jar was yesterday's lore, thought up by a man. Successful advertising begins with an honest image, and ends with a believable message. We are in need of new icons in advertising: women with vitality, housewives with sex, women who indeed have a brain in their heads, who care about the world around them, who think about making money and loving and being loved, not just about clean bathrooms and the comparative porosity of paper towels.

Since management women *are* the consumer, listening to them is the most direct, and least costly, route to successful marketing to other women. Effective selling and product development requires insight and experience from both men and women. *Creative collaboration between men and women colleagues, each with equal access to decision making,* is the future winning corporate culture. Otherwise, consumer confidence will remain low; basic goods will last from year to year; fashion advertising in magazines will still be for the trade only, out of touch with the consumer; beauty products will be targeted to the crib. Television commercials that portray women as air-heads will offend rather than entice; financial advertisers will continue to believe that an absence of creativity contributes to their credibility. Automotive advertising will remain off target until it addresses—in understandable terms—women's main concerns: safety, reliability.

I don't think women should break the glass ceiling. Instead, we should sit on top of it next to the men who are already there.

FRANCES LEAR, FOUNDER *LEAR'S*

Preface

What do women want?

If you're asking "What kind of question is that?" you just might be a puzzled marketer.

Okay, what *do* women want?

Sigmund Freud declared the question unsolvable . . . an eternal mystery. Freud wasn't spending advertising dollars. We are. Is the question still unsolvable?

Today's marketers (and that includes women as well as men who try to reach this target group) don't have time for rhetorical questions. They need concrete answers.

Current background research—including lifestyle and demographic information presented in clear charts and tables and statistics on behavior—will give marketers the foundation to begin building clear sales arguments. Yet, according to a recent study by Grey Advertising, the great majority of women believe that too often, advertising "doesn't respect them in terms of the people they really are."

In light of this documented complaint, one truth is painfully obvious . . . despite the availability of updated statistics, advertisers *still* aren't telling women what they want to hear.

Tables, charts, and lifestyle segments offer intelligent marketers the raw material to build. But a heap of raw material, without an accompanying plan, doesn't parallel a blueprint for custom-designing an advertising message. Marketers need to know how to combine changing market trends with basic psychologically targeted communication.

Does a need actually exist for a book such as this one? Let's quote pioneer feminist and publisher Frances Lear:

> A new consumer—an agent of change—is requiring industry to rewrite marketing and advertising concepts and strategies, to redo images, to bring relevance and honesty to product claims, and above all else, to respect the consumer. *Marketing to women* is the slogan; the task for industry is to develop the art.

Lear may go too far in suggesting that marketers adopt a separate set of standards when targeting women. Do women really want a separate set of standards? Or do they just want advertisers to recognize them as a viable target?

The advertiser who does—or who wants to—recognize this target is in turn the target of this book.

As recently as the early 1980s, marketers were of two types: They either took a "unisex" approach, ignoring gender, or they took a militant approach, assuming women objected to being treated as separate marketing targets.

Today's marketer faces a bewildering assortment of expert profiles of who women are and what they really want. As a result, a horrifying amount of advertising is either wasted—hopelessly off-target—or it actually offends the woman at whom it's aimed by being unwittingly patronizing or sophomoric. Result? No sale, and sometimes outrage and boycott.

To be effective, the revolution in marketing communications has to parallel the revolution in women's lives. Advertisers baffled by the knowledge that they can no longer treat women as a homogenous group must learn to adapt their messages to a diversity of women. From gentle earth-mother to corner-office powerhouse . . . from bedroom to boardroom . . . from scout leader to majority leader . . . these subgroups might represent several women, or just one woman who can move seamlessly from role to role during the course of a single day.

Yet even the giants are stumbling. As often as not they make bizarre, insensitive, and costly mistakes in their weak attempts to communicate with and market their products to women.

These costly mistakes are unnecessary because there are principles that enable an astute marketer—of any size, selling any product or service—to aim a message smack into the center of this huge, but ever-moving target.

What do women want? What *do* women want?   How about an acknowledgement of their societal role-change?

Women show up in far more roles in today's ads than they did just five years ago. Astute companies now seek not only to avoid offending women sensitized to exploitation by a generation of feminism, but to target them as likely buying prospects and woo them as customers.

And that's the difference we're talking about today. This book reports, analyzes, and delivers an action-plan based on a logical look at how women are changing—and how they're reacting to our advertising. If we as aggressive marketers are going to increase our share of this booming market, we'd better make sure that women react *favorably* to our targeted sales appeals.

From automobiles to Apple computers, from fashion to Fords, the marketing future of thousands of products and services hinges on what women want and how they react to our communications.

Does sex still sell? The answer to this question, and to a thousand others that pop up when we market to women, is "Yes, but . . ."

"Yes, but . . ." is what this book is about; it gives the forward-thinking marketer the answers to all those necessary "Yes, but . . ." objections.

Acknowledgments

I've been lucky enough to have some extraordinary people to thank for helping me put this book together.

Without the humor, wit, and persistence of Gale Research's Greg Michael, this book would still be a collection of notes and presentations. Without the patience, can-do attitude, and thoughtful suggestions of my editor, Peg Bessette, the manuscript would have been incomplete.

I owe thanks to Martin Cohn of Cohn & Wells for sharing his marketing insights and communication experience with me. Thanks to Kris Madson, also of Cohn & Wells, for searching out many of the advertising examples pictured in these pages.

Much gratitude goes to Kathleen Eardly, Managing Editor of *Colloquy* Newsletter for her invaluable research. She can find mounds of information, articles, and data on anything, and distill it all down to succinct, often humorous summaries.

I'm deeply obliged to the pre-eminent advertising communications pro, Herschell Gordon Lewis of Communicomp, for giving his time so freely. His incisive reviews, suggestions, arguments, comments, and criticism made this book. Many thanks to Communicomp's Margo Lewis, who can spot an inconsistency in the blink of an eye, for the gift of her time, and the help in managing my own.

Finally, heartfelt thanks to my husband, Rocky James, for his unwavering support both for this book and for me.

CHAPTER 7

- Does Sex Still Sell? What a Question!

- The Need for Niche-Targeting

- Is It Politically Correct? Can It Be Politically Correct?

- Confusing? Yes, But . . .

"In Europe a woman decides early on what type she will be — mother, doctor, cook, or siren. Women [in America] want to be all of these and also run Wall Street."

—ALISTAIR COOKE

Does Sex Still Sell?

Yes, But . . .

Sex had *better* sell, or all those beauty aid products, perfumes, seductive fashions, Danielle Steele novels, and Chippendale dancer calendars will wind up on remainder shelves.

Does sex still sell? What a question!

But . . .

The simplistic sex-approach of a generation ago is laughable in the mid/late 1990s. The woman no longer clings onto the man straddling the Harley-Davidson; she has her own.

This applies to both sides of the gender-street. The pretty girl in a bikini holding an automobile tire—what does that have to do with the way the tire performs?

No, sex isn't "old-hat," but it's both tired and dangerous. Remember the Swedish Bikini Team that a beer company tried to foist onto the consciousness of television viewers in 1992? Not only was the campaign a failure; it caused such an outcry and threats of boycott that the company wound up apologizing as it hastily withdrew its leggy embarrassments.

Add to that the fear of AIDS, the charging-out-of-the-closet gay militancy, and the ongoing fragmentation of the marketplace. Sex? Except for specifically sexually oriented items, advertisers who in years past depended on this once-powerful motivator now have more valid marketing ploys.

The Need for Niche-Targeting

Ask an old-time beer salesman who his targets are. (First of all, the word "his" is used advisedly. Who in years past ever heard of a female beer salesman — I mean, salesperson?)

He'll give you the traditional answer: blue-collar workers, college students, bleacher bums at baseball games — not the demographic top-of-the-line. Even premium beers, he'll tell you, aim themselves downward, not upward, on the socioeconomic ladder.

Now, suppose you've reached saturation within your targeted group.

In fact, suppose this group is drinking less beer, which means your market isn't just static — it's shrinking — as are the waistlines of health-conscious beer-drinkers. Do you fold your tent or sell out to a more stalwart competitor (as some brewers have done)? Do you try to extend your line (as some brewers have done)? Do you, with exquisite and scalpel-like precision, recognize potential beer-drinkers and mount hyper-targeted appeals to them (as some brewers have done)?

As subsequent chapters of this book will delineate, hypertargeting has been the marketing solution for any number of products and services. A "one size fits all" strategy doesn't work in a me-myself-I

Does Sex Still Sell? Yes, But . . .   CHAPTER ONE

5

society. Sears discontinued its venerable big catalog because the sun is setting over the era of generalized marketing.

Certainly no contemporary marketer is surprised by market fragmentation. We don't just ask for a Coke. We ask for a liter bottle, a 12-pack or six-pack; we then choose from Classic Coke, Coke II, clear cola, caffeine-free Coke, Diet Coke, Cherry Coke, Diet Cherry Coke . . . with more to come.

Beer? Sure. We don't just ask for a Miller Beer. It's Miller Genuine Draft, Miller Lite, Miller Premium, Miller Dry. The original Miller High-Life — "the champagne of bottled beers" — an elegant slogan for its time, but is it still around?

Rolling Stone carried a peculiar beer ad, placed on two sequential horizontal half-pages (see figure 1-1). The first half-page had this hand-drawn reverse legend:

■

If men are
only interested
in one thing,
why do they
like beer so much?

■

The second horizontal half-page, in full color bleed, shows a bottle of Bud Dry, with a full glass of beer in the foreground. Imprinted at the rim of the glass is lipstick from a woman's lower lip. The legend accompanying this illustration:

■

Why ask Why?
Try Bud Dry.

The one beer
Cold-Filtered for
smooth, draft taste.
And Dry Brewed
for no aftertaste.
For refreshment that's
beyond question.

■

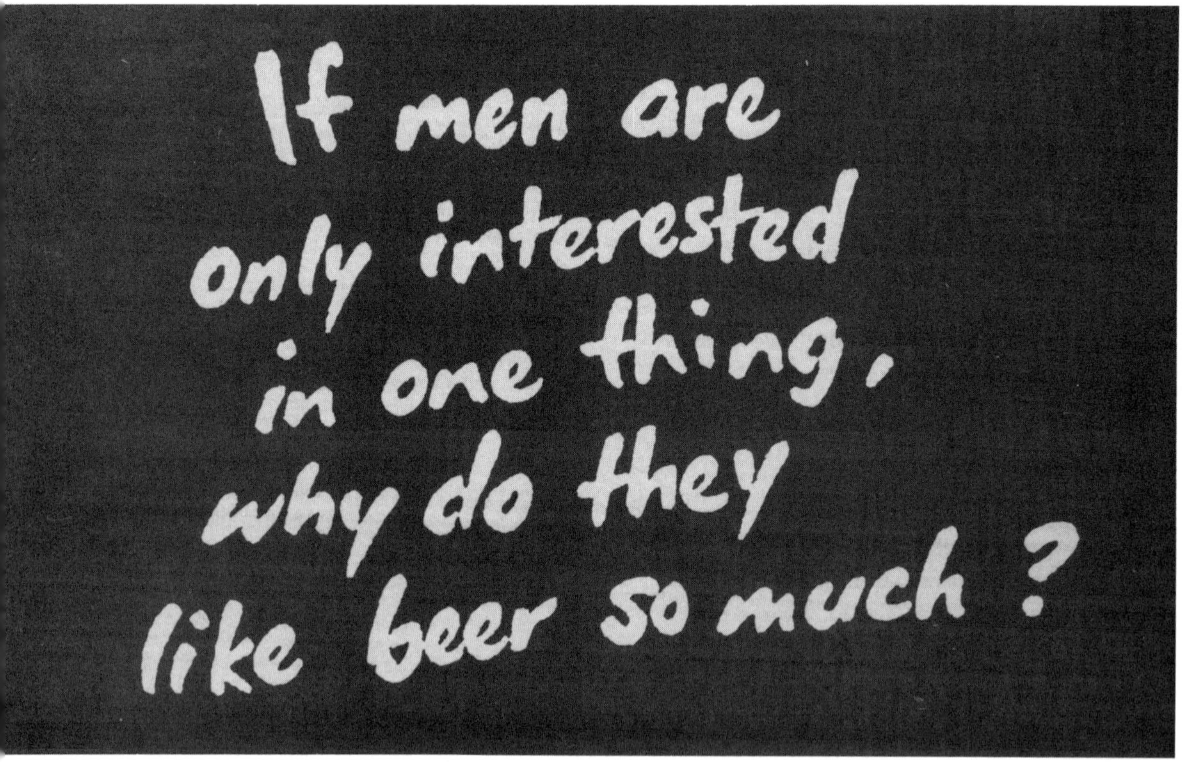

Figure 1-1.
Does sex still sell?
Apparently the advertiser
of this beer thinks so,
although the targeting
as well as the message
is muddy.

Many readers—even those used to the plethora of cryptic ads in *Rolling Stone*—will just note the picture of the Bud Dry bottle and flip the page. Others may wonder: What does this message mean?

If men are only interested in one thing, why do they like beer so much?

One interpretation, based on the lipstick on the glass, is that this marketer believes sex does sell beer. Yes, the message is muddy, and yes, this might *not* be what it tried to say. But one thing is as clear as the lipstick on the glass: the lip prints symbolize an awareness of "the other sex" as a beer-drinking target.

Less obscure is almost any television commercial for beer in the mid-1990s. *Never* is the target purely masculine. Even those touch-football games that wind up with a beer-drinking party include women in the cast (and not *always* in their bikinis).

Marketing astuteness is just one component of the 1990s market-

Is It Politically Correct? Can It Be Politically Correct?

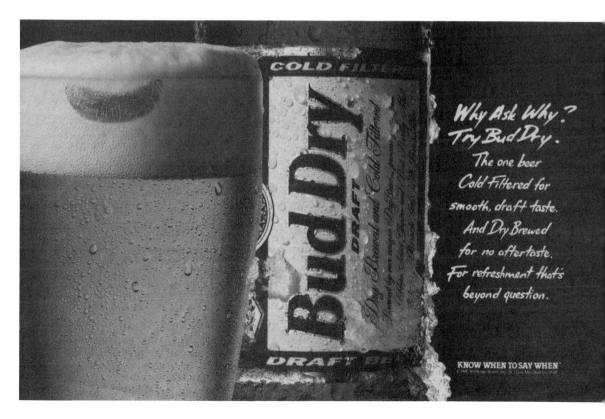

ing mix. Political correctness, that deadly but ever-present ingre-
dient, is a governor on the creative throttle.

So a commercial that omits women will have some militants
demanding a boycott, just as so many other militant women cry,
"Why are you targeting women?" A lose/lose situation?

As we approach the twenty-first century advertisers have weath-
ered so many slings and arrows that they have become numb to
attacks. They expect to annoy *somebody*, no matter what they say.
Some splinter-group will claim exclusion or over-inclusion. *Some*
splinter-group will interpret a comment as an insult.

So political correctness is a theory, not an achievement, because a
universally accepted message—one with any force behind it, at
least—just isn't possible.

Good or bad?

The knee-jerk reaction is, "Oh, isn't this terrible! No matter what
we say, someone will hate us for it."

The marketer who doesn't want to develop ulcers has to ignore
the negative consequences of market fragmentation and enjoy its
fruits instead. So a positive marketing philosophy begins to
emerge.

*Matching a targeted message to a targeted medium and a targeted audience
will attract more new buyers than it repels.*

The proper way to look at this little rule of marketing is that readers who don't match the intended profile aren't your targets anyway. You'll reach them by generating yet another type of message,
one that is politically correct for *them*.

Does Sex Still Sell? Yes, But . . .   CHAPTER ONE

9

And isn't that proof? Politics makes strange bedfellows.

Aiming our marketing communications at women by depending on a single message based on a single "women are women" attitude—a blanket approach regardless of the advertising medium in which a message appears—is lazy and unprofessional.

Confusing?
Yes, But . . .

Yes, in practice, what we're selling may dictate ignoring differences both *between* genders and *within* the gender. But today's marketers must also have a sense of human psychology, knowing when those differences are germane . . . and when their intended buyers *don't* want the differences emphasized.

If I can transmit only one concept as you begin the voyage through these pages, it's this:

The more persuasively we communicate, the more we'll sell. So we have to know and recognize three distinct components: 1) who our target-groups are; 2) where to find them; 3) the most effective way to approach each of these groups after we've found them.

Easy? No. Possible? Absolutely.

☐ 1. If your product or service is more than 10 years old, make sure you change with the times. Have you done your historical homework? How were women portrayed in your product category 20 years ago? 10 years ago? 2 years ago?

Marketing
Checklist—Chapter 1

☐ 2. Women are sensitive to "one-size-fits-all-genders" advertising. If you're marketing a traditionally "male" product, have you repositioned it to target women?

☐ 3. Women are also sensitive to not being recognized as individuals. Have you resisted the urge to address 51 percent of the population as generalized "female," without recognizing fragmentation of the marketplace?

☐ 4. The woman of the '90s responds to advertising that appears to be talking to her alone. Have you aimed your sales benefits specifically to your target audience?

☐ 5. The woman of the '90s responds to hard information. Does your message give answers to what your target audience wants to know? Or is it "fluffy," without benefits or information?

☐ 6. Do you know exactly:
   a. Who your target group is?
   b. Where to find her?
   c. The most persuasive way to approach her?

☐ 7. The woman's market of the '90s comprises diverse groups. Not everyone will be happy with the way you target your message. After you've created, tested, and run your campaign, have you kept your courage, despite the realization that someone, somewhere will be unhappy with it?

CHAPTER 2

"Without a

doubt, time

is the

new currency

of the '90s."

— BARBARA FEIGIN,
GREY ADVERTISING

The New Currency: Time

Will the Woman of the '90s

Spend It with You?

What *do* women want?

The answer may surprise you.

More than half the women polled in 1992 by the highly respected research group Yankelovich Monitor responded that being able to take a day off whenever they wanted to was more valuable to them than having a million dollars.

The Yankelovich survey found that the typical woman's priorities (if a "typical" woman exists) have shifted dramatically in the '90s. Instead of the '80s icons—a pair of Gucci shoes or an Hermès scarf—what she now lists as most important are "family, a good, steady job, friendships, and enjoying life."

"Shop 'til you drop?" If you still believe this, your marketing education ended in the 1980s.

According to Yankelovich, when a '90s woman has free time, she's more likely to spend it at home than in a store. A recent *Wall Street Journal* Study agrees: *women no longer shop for fun.*

Think about that: women no longer shop for fun. What a change from the 1980s! According to the *WSJ* study, three of every five women now classify shopping as a negative experience. And an astonishing one of three female consumers would rather do housework than shop.

Think in terms of advertising to this marketplace. That last statistic may account for all the midnight calls to L'Eggs customer service, which claims to sell 60 percent of all its panty hose by direct mail and phone order. (And it may explain why many of the catalog marketers—who neglected to expand their 8:00 A.M.–5:00 P.M. Eastern Standard Time hours—have been bested and even driven out of business by their more astute, more time-sensitive competition.)

The advertiser who is surprised by this mild time revelation needs a quick update.

Finding the Woman on the Move Every day of their lives, most women move through several different scenes, playing several different roles within them. In fact, according to a Federal Highway Administration study, women are running around—actually, driving around—like crazy. According to the study, women drivers made more car trips per day in 1990 than men (an average of 3.13 vs. 3.04). Women travel from home to work. Their days are punctuated by trips to nursery school, Girl Scout troop meetings, piano lessons, and their own MBA night classes thrown in for good measure.

With all that driving, is it any wonder that women now buy half of all new cars in the U.S.? That translates to around $65 billion in sales every year. (See Chapter 4 to find out how the car makers are doing).

Women hit the front doorstep at a dead run. And with all that running, shoe manufacturers have to make sure they're running in the right shoes.

As the woman of the '90s keeps moving, how can we advertisers find her? When we *do* find her, how can we get her attention amid everyone else's clamoring? And once we finally have her attention, how do we convert that attention into a sale?

To quote Laurel Cutler, Chairman of FCB/Leber Katz, "Never underestimate the tiredness of the American woman." Yes, she's tired. She's busy. She's distracted. And we have to keep one important point in mind as we try to reach her: She's not looking for us or our message.

So our advertising has to be everywhere every day. We phone her. We fax her. We mail her. We grab her attention as she commutes to and from work. And we always make sure our message is relevant to her in every situation. That means we spend a lot of time getting to know her.

Who are these '90s women and how do they spend their leisure time? Most will answer immediately: *"What* leisure time?"

An Abbreviated Intro to the Woman of the '90s

Self magazine asked women of all ages: If you had an extra hour in every day, what would you do with it? Here's what they said:

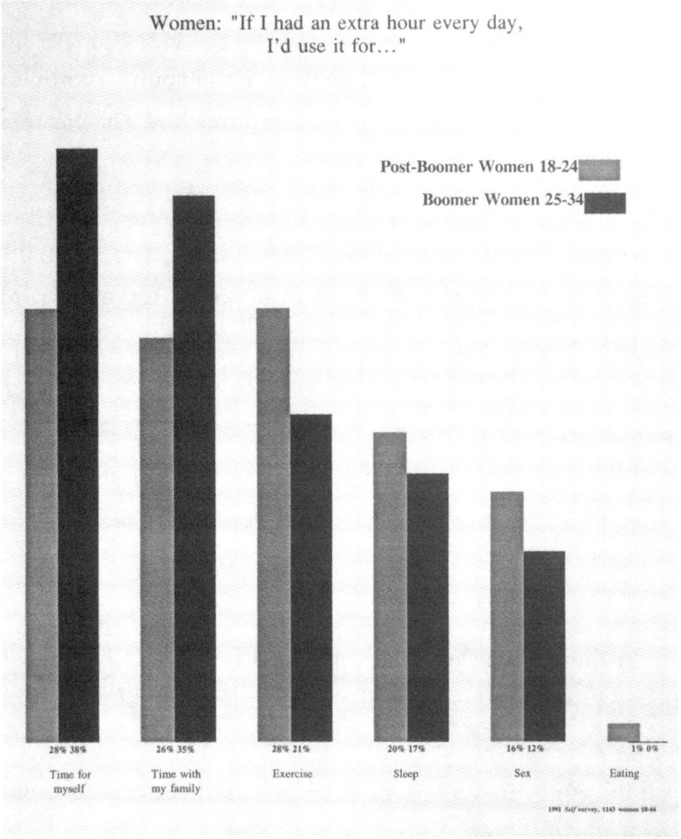

Women: "If I had an extra hour every day,
I'd use it for..."

Post-Boomer Women 18-24
Boomer Women 25-34

| 28% 38% | 26% 35% | 28% 21% | 20% 17% | 16% 12% | 1% 0% |
| Time for myself | Time with my family | Exercise | Sleep | Sex | Eating |

1991 Self survey, 1163 women 18-44

Figure 2-1.
Here's how women aged
18-34 would spend a
precious extra hour
every day.

Of course lack of time isn't a problem strictly limited to women. According to a periodic Roper women's poll and *ADWEEK* magazine, women's leisure hours lagged behind men's an average of seven hours a week across all groups polled, with wives in two-earner households getting shortchanged the most. According to *ADWEEK,* some 45 percent of women believed they had enough leisure time in 1975. In 1990: only 35 percent did.

Hyatt Hotels and Resorts survey reports that women are more likely than men to say that vacations are necessary to their well-being. Yet a recent study by researchers Erdos and Morgan finds that it's men—not women—who are "getting away from it all":

Just one-third of those who took more than five leisure trips a year were women.

Jagdish Sheth, professor of marketing, UCLA: "Women used to have time but no money. Today, it's the opposite. If they have any money to spend, they surely can't find the time to spend it. *And that's created a new way to market to women.*"

It also may explain the marketing transformation of a company like Avon, which has changed to accommodate the time-starved woman of the '90s.

Household Labor and Child Care Time Allocation

Adjusted mean time spent in hours per week in household labor and child care, by gender, wife's employment status, and presence of children.

Wife's Employment Status	Women			Men		
	Homemaker	Part-time	Full-time	Homemaker	Part-time	Full-time
Preschool-age children in household						
Household labor	33.4	30.3	15.0	9.4	13.1	8.2
Child care	19.1	10.2	5.2	4.8	5.2	2.8
Number of respondents	16	16	9	12	8	13
School-age children in household						
Household labor	35.6	28.7	18.9	12.5	12.3	11.7
Child care	3.5	3.3	2.7	1.7	1.9	1.1
Number of respondents	12	23	14	14	18	26
No children in household						
Household labor	31.0	32.9	14.6	14.7	13.3	13.6
Number of respondents	36	11	10	25	11	27
All households						
Household labor	35.6	28.7	18.9	11.6	14.0	12.1
Child care	7.0	3.7	2.1	2.1	1.8	1.0
Total households	64	50	33	51	37	66

Source: Beth Anne Shelton, "The Distribution of Household Tasks," *Journal of Family Issues* 11:2 (June 1990, Table 2, p. 115-135. Primary source: data made available by the Inter-University Consortium for Political and Social Research, State University of New York at Buffalo. Data collected from 620 respondents and 376 of their spouses.

**From the Doorbell
to the Mailbox**

A few decades ago, "Ding-dong. Avon calling" was cutting-edge marketing material. Back then, sample-case-toting women sales representatives—Avon Ladies—made in-home sales calls to women during the daytime. But Avon sales began to falter during the late 1970s and through the 1980s. Why? Because as women entered the work force, Avon sales representatives could no longer find them at home during the day. And during evening

*Figure 2-2.
Avon advertising
acknowledges and uses a
woman's lack of time to sell
its products four different
ways: by phone, by fax, by
mail, and, the old-fashioned
Avon-calling way, by rep.*

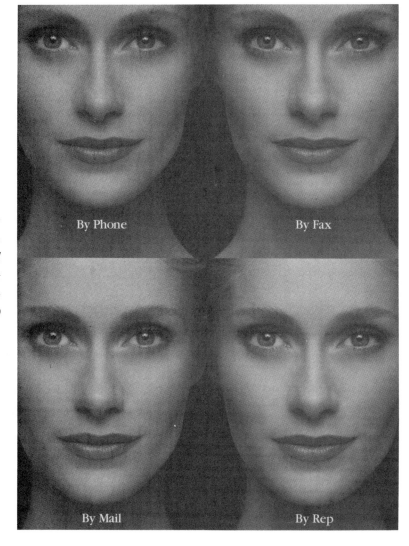

hours, too many other details left too little time for working women to spend browsing over the saleswomen's lipsticks and powders.

The Avon Lady became a symbol of the provincial '50s stay-at-home housewife . . . not a very appealing image to the new working woman.

Announcing four ways to be beautiful.

It's not a new brush. Or a new blush.

It's a whole new way to shop Avon.

Now you can order foundation by phone. Nails by mail. And your favorite fragrance by fax.

In your office. In your car. In your kitchen, with a cookie at 2 a.m.

Call 1-800-858-8000,

and we'll send you our new Avon catalogue.

It's filled with our complete selection of Avon Color, the smartest most wearable color cosmetics you can buy at any price. Plus our truly exceptional skincare. Jewelry. And gifts.

Just order by phone or fax or mail, and we'll send

your order right out, direct to you.

Or, if you prefer, you can order from your Avon Representative.

You'll find her name and number right on your catalogue.

So find out just how beautiful shopping can be.

It's never been so simple to look so great.

AVON

THE SMARTEST SHOP IN TOWN

© 1992 Avon Products, Inc. NY, NY

Instead, during the late '70s and '80s, Avon took great pains to revamp its image with ads that touted change with the times. "Look How Good You Look Now" replaced the old and tired, but familiar, "Avon calling." Graphics were dramatically updated.

But advertising is just one component of the marketing mix. What if, although the image had changed with the times, nothing else had? What if the only way a woman could order an Avon product was in person through an Avon sales representative? That would mean even though the promotional approach is smartly modern, the sales technique—sitting in the living room, going through a sales pitch—is mired in the tar pits.

How to attract the "new" woman without alienating the coexisting "traditional" woman?

Figure 2-2 is the '90s version of the Avon lady. The headline says:

Figure 2-2a.
The Avon catalog is the
1990s version of
"The Avon Lady"
who used to sell
door to door.

■

Announcing four ways to be beautiful.
By Phone. By Fax. By Mail. By Rep.

■

The copy explains it's "a whole new way to shop Avon." Here's an advertiser who has responded to the time plight of the '90s woman. Avon now offers chances to order cosmetics " . . . in your office. In your car. In your kitchen with a cookie at 2 a.m." with the 24-hour convenience of a toll-free phone line. And for those who prefer the old-fashioned way, the Avon lady's still around.

When a customer calls the toll-free number, the professional saleswoman on the phone explains that Avon has, in fact, changed the way customers can order. But she emphasizes that there might be a time when a woman would want the option of choosing personal service from a sales rep. So calling the Avon order number gets you more than a catalog, it gets you options. The operator immediately gives you the phone number of your local sales rep and emphasizes that she can be called anytime. And, presumably, between the time a prospect orders her catalog and the two weeks before it's delivered . . . she will call that rep.

"Women are moving faster than the speed of light," says Gaile Blanke, senior vice president of Avon, "and, as the world's largest women's company, we have to provide them with unified support. With us it's a sacred trust. And even if it weren't, we'd have no choice. Not if we want to stay alive."

What if Avon hadn't adapted itself to the new society, instead waiting for the old society to return? "Ding dong" would have become "Ding dong gone," because the "traditional" woman no longer represented the sole potential target.

Fragmentation of the marketplace: That's the mid–late 1990s!

Fragmentation of the Marketplace

Figure 2-3 shows how insurance was advertised in 1957. The headline asks:

■

How does your life insurance
look on today's balance sheet?

■

It's subtitled:

■

A reminder for men who are making progress . . .

■

The copy goes on to read:

■

A man who provided for his future needs and
family security several years ago may find that
his situation has since changed.

■

Figure 2-3.
A typical 1950s insurance
sales approach. The
subtitle reads, "A reminder
for men who are making
progress."

"How does your life insurance look on today's balance sheet?"

A reminder
for men who are making progress
from
LEONARD SPACEK
Managing Partner, Arthur Andersen & Co.

"NO PRUDENT INVESTOR would base his appraisal of a company on a financial report that was several years old. We know that conditions can change quickly. That's why up-to-date figures are so necessary.

"We would do well to exercise the same care in appraising our personal financial condition—particularly life insurance. A man who provided for his future needs and family security several years ago may find that his situation has since changed. It is quite likely that he will have set up new goals and taken on new responsibilities—perhaps without realizing the need for added life insurance protection.

"If you suspect that this might have happened to you, the first thing to do is to consult a qualified life insurance agent. He will be glad to analyze your needs. His skill and experience will enable him to show you the easiest way to bring your life insurance back into balance with today's conditions."

A CENTURY
OF SAFEGUARDING TOMORROW

BIRTHS, deaths, marriages, taxes are all reasons why you should review your life insurance program at least every two years. You'll find real assistance when you call upon a Northwestern Mutual agent. He is well trained to advise you. His company, now celebrating its 100th year, is one of the world's largest . . . and offers the new Quantity-Earned Savings (QES) for lower-than-ever net cost on all types of policies, $5,000 and up.

A NORTHWESTERN MUTUAL POLICYHOLDER. *Mr. Spacek's life insurance policies with this company are an important part of his personal estate.*

The NORTHWESTERN MUTUAL *Life Insurance Company*
MILWAUKEE, WISCONSIN

TIME, SEPTEMBER 16, 1957

That's similar to the way the situation has changed in selling insurance. Compare this 1957 relic with a recent ad for life insurance (figure 2-4). The headline reads:

■

Working Women need life insurance, too.

■

"Working women need life insurance, too. So I bought $160,000 of IEEE Members' Life Insurance..."

"...We're both paying for our home, our car, and our living expenses. So, naturally, we both want to protect what we have...and what we're working for."

As a member of our group, you can easily make sure your family's insurance protection is on a par with your needs. And thanks to our group's buying power, you can get life insurance at low-cost, affordable group rates.

Our term life insurance can protect your entire family—you as a member, your spouse and eligible children. And you can request coverage by mail.

Check how much insurance you really need now, and protect your future. Call or write the Administrator for enrollment forms.

UP TO $540,000 IN
TERM LIFE INSURANCE PROTECTION
IS AVAILABLE TO IEEE MEMBERS.
Plus these other group insurance plans:
Major Medical Expense Insurance
Excess Major Medical
In-Hospital Insurance
Disability Income
High-Limit Accident Insurance
Medicare Supplement

Figure 2-4.
A targeted insurance sales
approach in the 1990s. The
copy reads, "We're both
paying for our home, our
car, and our living
expenses. So, naturally, we
want to protect what we
have ... and what we're
working for."

And, incidentally, working women can now buy it by calling a 24-hour toll-free number to talk to a consultant.

And they're doing it. *ADWEEK* magazine reports a Grey Advertising study that shows a rapidly increasing number of women are doing midnight shopping . . . calling discount brokerages, com-

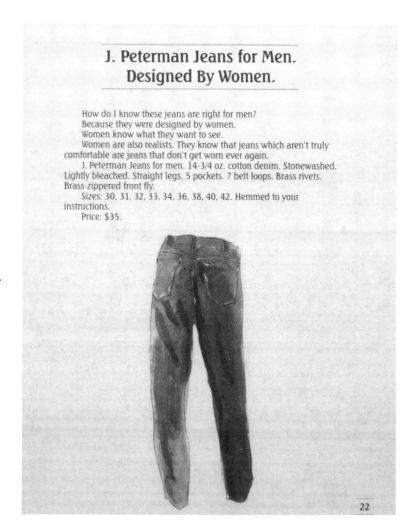

Figure 2-5.
How to sell a pair of
men's jeans to women.

puter on-line videotext services, and they're phoning in late-night investments. Direct marketing is taking over the women's market.

But according to *ADWEEK* magazine, convenience isn't the only powerful motivator responsible for direct marketing's popularity. Other factors contribute to the appeal of buying by phone or mail. Take catalog shopping, for example. Researcher Judy Langer finds that many catalog marketers count on filling the emotional need of their customers who feel they're giving themselves a gift when they order from a catalog. Even though customers have ordered, they don't know exactly when their order will arrive, so when it comes, Langer says, it's like receiving a present.

Figure 2-5 shows a page from a catalog with the headline:

■

J. Peterman Jeans for Men.
Designed by Women.

■

That's a good way to get attention for these jeans. Getting attention is an admirable door-opener; but how to sell them? The copy goes on to read:

■

How do I know these jeans are right for men?
Because they were designed by women.
Women know what they want to see.
Women are also realists. They know that
jeans which aren't truly comfortable jeans are
jeans that don't get worn ever again.

■

That's a good way to sell a pair of jeans—to men or women. But what about selling women's jeans?

Figure 2-6.
How to sell a pair of
women's jeans to women.

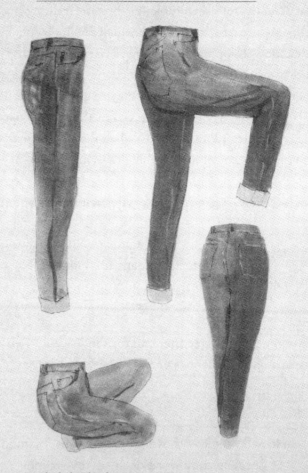

J. Peterman Jeans for Women.
Designed by Women.

Freud asked: "What do women want?"
Men, it turns out, don't even understand what women want in a pair of jeans.
Repeatedly, men sit down and design jeans that succeed only in raising women's expectations, but turn out to be torture for women to wear.
(Remember, men are the ones who, as officers at the Russian Imperial Court, put on doeskin trousers, sat in a bath, then spent the day drying them tight to the skin.)
Women, on the other hand, (unlike Freud, and unlike male designers of women's jeans) do understand what women want.

Figure 2-6 shows how it's done. The headline reads:

■

J. Peterman Jeans for Women.
Designed by Women.

■

The copy continues:

■

Freud asked: What do women want?
Men, it turns out, don't even understand what
women want in a
pair of jeans.
Repeatedly, men sit down and design jeans
that succeed only in
raising women's expectations, but turn out to
be torture for women to wear.
Women, on the other hand (unlike Freud,
and unlike male designers of women's jeans),
do understand what women want.

■

Undoubtedly, the woman who ordered and received a pair of
these jeans through the mail not only felt she was giving herself a
gift, but that someone else was, as well.

The latter-day saints of advertising, whose approaches we just
sampled, recognize the evolution of women's role in society. If
they're especially perspicacious they do not stop short at embrac-
ing the new social context; they recognize and exploit what can be
a far more effective competitive edge: the *fragmentation* of the marketplace, which opens a whole new universe of opportunities . . .
and problems.

A Look at
Opportunities . . .
and Problems . . . of
the Mid–Late 1990s

Opportunity: The marketer can target a sub-group with an appeal aimed squarely at that sub-group. How much more powerful this is than semi-targeted "This is aimed at women" advertising.

Problem: Isolating sub-groups and directing appeals to each qualifying sub-group is expensive and requires the most sophisticated database management.

A Short History, and a Short Look at Current Events

For two centuries, advertisers had no problem aiming their messages at women. Not only did they see a homogenized market, so did their targets. A woman was a homemaker. A few exceptions had so-called genteel careers—schoolteacher, secretary, receptionist, nurse. Those who violated the borders of this limited universe bore the gentle curse of the word "spinster."

Then came World War II. The dam broke. We not only had WACs and WAVEs in the armed forces, we had Rosie the Riveter. We had women reading the news on the radio, in authoritative voices. We even had women in Congress. Margaret Chase Smith was a senator. A *senator!*

With the youth revolution of the late 1960s the rebellion was complete, and fragmentation was a *fait accompli.* The problem was not so much that society didn't recognize the new role of women. Rather, the problem stemmed from the ranks of old-line advertising executives, whose image of this new splintered target was, at best, hazy. Women were women, weren't they?

During this "interregnum," only a few women had positions of power within the world of advertising, so the traditional masculine "This is male and this is female" viewpoint prevailed for 10 to 20 years longer than good marketing judgment might have allowed.

Now advance your time clock to today. Gender? Today's advertiser is lost among multiple interpretations of just who the target is. One interpretation: Divide your approach to women into two sections, homemaker and career woman. Or, if you want more dynamic terminology, passive and active (or passive and assertive).

But isn't that simplistic in today's *hyper*-fragmented society? In 1993, the magazine *Advertising Age* carried a long bylined article pointing out that magazines such as *Deneuve* and (yes, there is one!) *On Our Backs* represent an aggressive lesbian marketplace not reachable through conventional media.

Should a marketer run an identical advertisement in *Working Woman, Ladies' Home Journal, Women and Guns*, and *On our Backs?* Before reading the next paragraph, formulate your opinion.

Ready? My answer is, as it has to be, equivocal. If the advertising is for edibles, the demand is unrelated to socio/sexual positioning. For an automobile, I'd aim a hyper-targeted message foursquare at each group. For clothing? Take your best hold, depending on the type of garment. For entertainment? The person writing the advertising message can't deal in the usual platitudes and generalities. Hyper-targeting means the message-sender has to have a hyper-targeted information base.

☐ 1. If you want the busy woman of the '90s to order your product, make sure it's easy to order your product. If your product can be ordered by mail, have you installed a toll-free phone order line?

☐ 2. 1990s time constraints often result in unorthodox shopping time. If you've installed a phone-order line, have you tested keeping your lines open 24 hours against keeping them open during business hours only?

Marketing Checklist—Chapter 2

☐ 3. The 1990s woman can often be found spending most of her time working. Are you sending your sales literature to your prospect's office?

☐ 4. Conventional media don't always reach the experimental '90s woman. Are you exploring alternate media (such as on-line videotext, video mall kiosks) and using all logical sales avenues open to you (including mail, inbound and outbound telemarketing, sales representative) to reach and sell to your prospect?

☐ 5. The woman of the '90s doesn't always have the spare time or inclination to spend the extra minutes it might take to appreciate your clever advertising. Does your creative work use the power of persuasive communication, as opposed to making a work of art, designed to win awards rather than sell a product?

☐ 6. The woman of the '90s is diverse. Have you studied the database or available research on your target audience? Or have you ignored the facts based on your own personal prejudice?

☐ 7. If you're targeting many subgroups of women, have you created or modified your existing database to include an extensive information base and analysis of past advertising response?

☐ 8. If you have separate and distinct large target audiences, have you modified your sales message and designed it to appeal to each group's specific interests?

☐ 9. The '90s woman wants you to talk to her in her own language. Have you chosen your words carefully in order to connect with your target audience?

☐ 10. Even though you're trying to address many different targets, have you taken care not to hone your message down to the point where you exclude some of the people you want to reach?

C H A P T E R

"At work you think of the children you have left at home. At home you think of the work you've left unfinished."

— GOLDA MEIR

The Professional Woman: Twentieth to Twenty-first Century Transition

Thirty-five years ago, says the publication *American Demographics*, the typical American woman graduated from high school, married, had children, and stayed at home with her family. Some women worked out of economic necessity. "Career woman" was a term used for schoolteachers, secretaries trying to climb the corporate ranks, and an occasional maverick. "Career woman" as a peer of the career man was practically unheard of.

In 1960, women made up just 28 percent of the entire U.S. working population. Since then, the percentage of men in the work force has steadily decreased. By 1988—when the "explosion" was just starting—the percentage of women in the work force increased to 38 percent.

The dam broke in 1992–93. The 1992 elections were touted as "The Year of the Woman" . . . and did women make the most of it! Never did women sense such political, social, and economic strength! A woman headed a major film studio; a woman headed one of the world's biggest advertising agencies; women were in the president's cabinet. The gender differential—a vestigial structure from pre-Colonial times—returned to dust.

Some economists claim that the demands of middle-class "lifestyle" have opened the door to women in the work force; two-income families not only are no longer a novelty, they're the norm.

A recent Virginia Slims survey confirms the permanence of change. According to the survey, more than 80 percent of the college-educated women polled said they would remain working in their chosen professions even if they were financially secure.

Composition of the Labor Force: 1960-2000					
Characteristics of workers	1960	1970	1980	1988	2000
Number of Workers (in millions)	72.1	82.8	106.9	121.7	141.1
Percentage of Workers:					
White females	28%	33%	36%	38%	39%
White males	61%	56%	51%	48%	45%
Blacks	11%	11%	10%	10%	12%
Hispanics	NA	NA	6%	7%	10%
Asians/others[1]	NA	NA	NA	3%	4%

Source: "Composition of the U.S. Labor Force: 1960-2000," *America in the 21st Century: Human Resource Development*, December 1989, p. 10 (Washington, D.C.: Population Reference Bureau, 1989). Primary source: U.S. Department of Labor. Figures may not add to 100% because persons of Hispanic origin may be of any race. *Note:* 1. Includes American Indians, Alaskan Natives, and Pacific Islanders.

With the increase in income comes a parallel increase in buying power. These 1990s working women have experienced the shift from their mothers' traditional status as homemaker to their contemporary role as independent partner or major provider within a family. Their purchases are no longer limited to soap and household incidentals. Although many are still responsible for all house-

Labor Force Participation Rates for Wives, Husband Present, by Age of Own Youngest Child: 1975 to 1991

Presence and Age of Child	1975	1985	1990	1991
Wives, total	44.4	54.2	58.2	58.5
No children under 18	43.8	48.2	51.1	51.2
With children under 18	44.9	60.8	66.3	66.8
Children under 6, total	36.7	53.4	58.9	59.9
With children under 3	32.7	50.5	55.5	56.8
With children 1 year or under	30.8	49.4	53.9	55.8
With children 2 years	37.1	54.0	60.9	60.5
With children 3 to 5 years	42.2	58.4	64.1	64.7
With children 3 years	41.2	55.1	63.1	62.2
With children 4 years	41.2	59.7	65.1	65.5
With children 5 years	44.4	62.1	64.5	67.1
With children 6 to 13 years	51.8	68.2	73.0	72.8
With children 14 to 17 years	53.5	67.0	75.1	75.7

Source: U.S. Bureau of Labor Statistics, Bulletin 2340; and unpublished data.

hold purchases, still others share that responsibility with their husbands. Increasingly, women are sharing or dominating major purchase decisions as well.

Novelty? Hardly. Ask any car salesperson or a clerk in the appliance section of a department store. Women routinely buy cars,

---

How Women Feel About Their Work

The attitudes of working women toward work, according to a survey of 1,000 working women over age 18 conducted for *Ladies' Home Journal*.

1. **Fifty-seven percent**, primarily women with young children, blue-collar jobs, and salaries under $15,000 a year, said they work because they have to.

2. **Twenty-seven percent**, primarily executives, said they work "because it makes them feel productive."

3. **Seven percent** work to be around people; **5%** work to "have something to do."

4. Of the **13%** who are their own bosses, most are professionals or over sixty.

5. **Two percent** said their bosses were "incompetent." **Thirty-four percent** felt they could do the boss's job.

6. **Seventy-nine percent** said they had not been held back because of their sex. **Eighteen percent** said they have been discriminated against. Although **86%** said they had never been sexually harassed at work, **more than one woman in ten** said she had been sexually harassed at work. Those most likely to say they had been harassed were those women under 45, earning between $15,000 and $35,000, living in the South or West.

7. The question, "If you were harassed, what did you do about it?" elicited the following answers:

   Dealt with the harasser myself (**61%**)
   Complained to personnel office or other authority (**21%**)
   Complained to my boss (**15%**)
   Left the job (**14%**)
   Ignored it because I didn't want to get in trouble or lose my job (**9%**)

Source: Selected from "The Roper Poll of the American Woman, Nine to Five," *Ladies' Home Journal* 106:March, 1989: 83+.

homes, major appliances and many so-called "big-ticket items," making their own decisions—and with their own money.

So what *do* working women want?

When it comes to making a purchase, women want recognition and respect. (For some old-time salesmen, this means a reeducation.)

Recognition, Respect, and the "X" Factor

As we've already explored, 1990s women are often cash-rich but time-starved. Sometimes they just want a logical way to get from point A to point Z (and all points in between).

Let's follow busy Marcia Peters (I've changed her name, of course) as she goes through a typical Tuesday. Marcia is a media buyer at an advertising agency in Los Angeles.

Her day starts with CNN. She watches the news before and after she showers and as she gets ready to drive to the office. She's bombarded with advertising for many types of automobiles (sometimes by manufacturers competing back-to-back), orange juice and cereals, shows-to-come on other Turner networks, business publications, sweeteners, airlines, the network itself, and who knows what else.

Into her car, on goes the radio. More ads, many of which are radio versions of the television spots to which she has already been exposed, and many of which promote local businesses.

She drives. On the freeway in Los Angeles, as in most crowded cities, traffic is slow. On every freeway are billboards, some lavishly produced. They advertise cars and television's forbidden goodies, liquor and cigarettes. She notes them, sometimes subliminally.

She picks up her car phone: Why? Because she's responding to smart advertisers who now attack the mobile target, who has a car phone—and an immediate way to respond to an ad that has a toll-free order or inquiry number.

She passes a bus. "Position media," advertising signs on the side of the bus, grab her eye for a moment.

At her desk, she allows herself a fixed amount of time to read the trade magazines, because if she doesn't she'll fall behind her contemporaries in her knowledge not only of what's going on but who's offering what.

The day's office mail—some of it is business correspondence and some is unsolicited direct mail advertising. She reads both, because the mailings help keep her abreast of what's new.

On her way home she stops at the supermarket. Advertisements flank her shopping cart. A woman standing in the aisle hands her a slice of pizza, saying, "Try this," and gives her a cents-off coupon. From the ceiling hang point-of-purchase signs. Some of the shelves have "shelf talkers," immediate shelf coupons that entice shoppers to choose a particular product.

Continuing home, she stops to pick up her daughter at the day-care center. On the table in the foyer are messages to parents from parenting publications, local organizations, and companies that recognize mothers as marvelous prospects.

Back at home, the mail that comes to her house, like her business mail, contains a mixture of personal and soliciting messages.

Saturation? Possibly. More likely, though, the day begins and ends with implicit acceptance of *some* messages, implicit rejection of *some* messages, and a plastic attitude toward *some* messages.

The individual psychology determining acceptance, rejection, or plasticity — that's the "X" factor challenging marketers to women.

Let's explore some of the messages our archetype has accepted and rejected — as well as those that didn't even filter through — as she moved from ambience to ambience during her "typical" day.

Reaching the Target with Targeted Messages: The Good, the Bad, and the Totally Irrelevant

Early-morning television brings a mix of news, weather, "froth" features, and commercials. At this early point in the day, advertisers find her only half-listening, because she knows if she misses an entire news story, she can pick up the details in the newspaper, or on the radio later as she drives to work. (For most radio stations, morning drive time is the most expensive period.)

If your ad is in this early-morning slot — and if you don't have a gargantuan media budget to repeat, repeat, and repeat your ad on all media throughout the day — be sure you zero in on a "grabber" benefit to catch her attention and immediately shake her out of her early-morning passivity.

One commercial that demands attention from our half-attentive target on this morning is a spot for a local hospital. A woman looks off-camera, as though she's talking to a friend (replacing the "talking head" so many commercials use in the spokesperson format). "You didn't know she had breast cancer?" she asks her off-camera friend. We don't hear the other end of the conversation, but the on-camera woman continues, talking about the hospital where her friend has been cared for. The spot ends with the woman (still looking off-camera as though continuing her intimate conversation) saying, "That's where Joan went. She says she was treated well and that they took some of the scare out of cancer. She said she wouldn't have gone anywhere else. That's where I'd go."

What does this commercial do? It raises an issue that weighs heavy on every woman's mind right now—breast cancer. Because the subject is both timely and aimed, most advertisers would have gone for the most obvious motivator: fear. But this advertiser softens the message by letting us eavesdrop on a conversation. The "spokesperson" never addresses us, the viewers. And the advertiser turns gossip into a selling weapon as we are allowed to overhear a spokesperson endorse and recommend the service to someone else.

Good or bad?

In her book, *You Just Don't Understand,* Dr. Deborah Tannen explores the power of gossip. According to Dr. Tannen, telling secrets creates friendship. Gossip is the "grown-up" version of telling secrets. This clever television advertiser has set up a secret-telling scenario, allowing us to be willing partners in the conversation; the ad creates a friendship bond between us, the speaker, and the unheard friend off-camera. It's a subtle and persuasive way to build rapport with your audience, getting them to like and trust you. Better yet, the viewer *doesn't* regard you as a threat, which can happen when *you* try to project fear through the television screen.

Contrast that commercial with an ad for laundry detergent. A smartly dressed man comes on screen, looks directly at us, and challenges, "I'll bet you thought your socks were white with the laundry detergent you use now. But you don't know white socks, until you see them washed with [his product]." The man then shows what he calls "your socks" and throws whiter socks on top of them, calling them "your socks with [his laundry detergent]." This is the old, anti-rapport-building school of advertising, the beat-'em-over-the-head-until-they-give-up style. Sure, this advertiser shows a benefit (whiter socks) but presents it condescendingly, using a spokesman who is obviously less familiar with laundry than the woman who does it.

Much as anyone might want white socks, all the astute competition needs to do is present the same sales argument in a more persuasive way, positioning themselves against the old-school guys in a way more rapport-building to the contemporary woman. How? Someone the target regards as "like me" recounts an experience with her laundry—personal revelation. Assuming the product actually works, there goes the hard-sell guy's supermarket shelf space.

Our subject, Marcia, now turns her attention to coffee and the morning newspaper. She reads the details of the morning's headliner TV news and skims the paper looking for something that affects her or her business. While she's skimming, she chances upon a news story—actually, a public relations "plant"—telling her about a new low-cholesterol butter substitute. She's interested, and reads all.

Why does this news story motivate her far more than any advertising could? Because it appears to be a dispassionate report from a disinterested party reporting facts, not preaching sales dogma.

Point: Public relations and publicity clearly have their place in today's mass communications ambience. In fact, their value is considerably greater than it was before the typical message-target became so skeptical toward advertising messages.

Show and Tell

Outdoor signs have come into their own as a major advertising medium. This is due, in part, to the tremendous automobile flow on major traffic arteries. It's also due to technology, which has given us billboards whose images change as we look at them, billboards three or four times the size of the old and almost obsolete 24-sheet posters, billboards with dimension, and billboards so highly illuminated that they dominate the nighttime landscape.

And the cost of outdoor advertising staggers those who get estimates for the first time. A single sign can cost $50,000 a month.

The old-line argument against outdoor is that the recall factor is thin. The argument in favor of outdoor is that no other medium can approach its cost-per-exposure.

Now, what does this have to do with women?

Years ago, billboards in residential neighborhoods were the ones targeting women. Today, half the automobile commuters are women; logically, both sexes deserve equal display. So, recognizing the equality, many outdoor advertisers create unisex campaigns for the big boards.

Unisex campaigns may be economically sound, but they're psychologically weaker than a solidly targeted campaign. To many observers, solidly targeted campaigns exclude as many people as they include. Outdoor campaigns such as the one for Nike athletic shoes of a few years ago have an exclusionary "macho" overtone.

Conclusion: the technique for pinpointing women with outdoor signs is still in embryo, just as outdoor sign electronic technology is only beginning to develop.

At Her Desk I've been in the advertising business most of my professional life, and I haven't concluded that most media buyers are women.

Apparently my conclusion isn't shared by Times Mirror Magazines, who publish *Field and Stream* and *Outdoor Life*. Marcia,

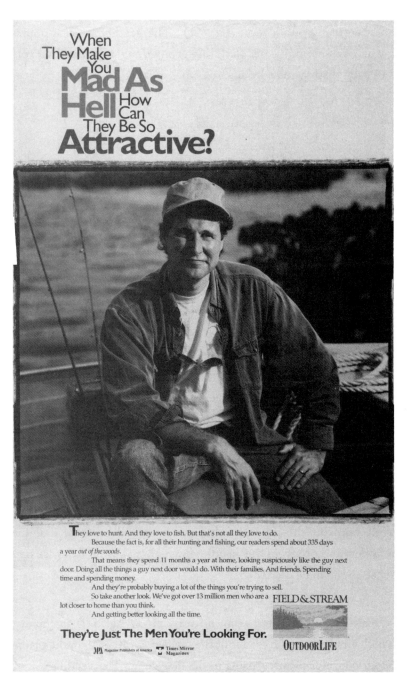

Figure 3-1.
Since when did media
buyers become an
exclusively female group?
And if they aren't, then why
is this advertising trade ad
targeted to women?

our Ms. Sample, is a full-time, career-oriented, honest-to-good-ness media buyer. She sees the ad for these outdoor magazines in an advertising publication (fig. 3-1). The heading, over a photo-graph of a smiling, jeans-clad, thirtysomething guy, wedding ring carefully displayed as he sits in a small boat:

■

When
They Make
You
Mad As
Hell How
Can
They Be So
Attractive?

■

This ad is a puzzlement. It's aimed *only* at women. After all, how can a guy in a fishing boat make another guy mad as hell? But the ad isn't aimed at women *as women;* it's aimed at women as media buyers, because the thrust of the ad is that advertising in the out-door men's magazines reaches men who are outdoorsmen 10 days a year, and loving stay-at-homes 355 days a year.

Will male media buyers rush to call Times Mirror Magazines? Well, not from this ad, which has neither an address nor a phone number; and not from this headline, which makes no heterosexual sense to the male reader.

More logically targeted is an ad for *Lear's* (fig. 3-2) magazine, which emphasizes the reader of the magazine rather than the media buyer considering advertising in the magazine. The heading:

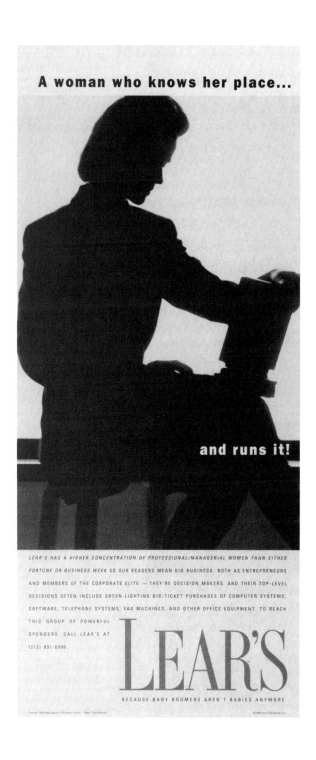

Figure 3-2.
This ad is perfectly
targeted to the media
buyer (gender unknown)
because it emphasizes
the reader of the magazine
the media buyer is trying
to reach.

■

A woman who knows her place . . .
and runs it!

■

The illustration features a silhouette of a woman with a laptop computer. The no-nonsense body copy begins:

■

LEAR'S HAS A HIGHER CONCENTRATION OF PROFESSIONAL/MANAGERIAL WOMEN THAN EITHER FORTUNE OR BUSINESS WEEK . . . .

■

See the difference? This ad pitches the executive nature of *Lear's* readership. The sex of the media buyer is, as it should be, inconsequential.

Figure 3-3.
This mailing for a
department store
contained neither a
letter nor a bold offer.

One reason for the continued existence of *Lear's* is the preexisting gap in executive-level business publications. *Why* does *Lear's* have

Discover the Difference that is Bullock's

The incomparable luxury of a cashmere sweater . . . elegant party fashions . . . distinctive accessories for the home . . . the perfect holiday gift idea. The very best of Fall is waiting to be discovered at Bullock's. Becoming a charge card customer makes preparing for the new season a very special experience.

a higher concentration of professional/managerial women than either *Fortune* or *Business Week?* Can it be because these publications, regardless of huge infiltrations of women on their own editorial staffs, still cast a masculine aura? Obviously enough women think so to give *Lear's* this demographic edge. Obviously, too, such an edge is fragile; it depends on women executives thinking of themselves as women first and executives second.

Someone once said (and it wasn't Freud), that women want the same things as men—only in prettier colors.

Safe at Home?

Figures 3-3 and 3-4 represent an advertiser who took that idea to heart, assuming women value form above function. Danger! Women who are today's best buyers resent being treated as airheads.

These are two separate mailings for a department store credit card. Figure 3-3 was addressed to a woman, while figure 3-4 was addressed to a man. Both mailings pitch the same offer: a credit

Figure 3-4.
Compare this mailing to
figure 3-3. Both have the
same offer, but the way it's
hidden in the copy, it's easy
to miss on both mailings.

BULLOCK'S

Your Personal Invitation To Discover
The Bullock's Difference

Please accept our invitation to discover the excitement of shopping at Bullock's. We want you to have a Bullock's Charge Account and experience all the personal attention that accompanies it.

As our Charge Card customer, you will enjoy many special privileges each time you shop with us. And if you open a Charge Account now, you will have this additional introductory privilege: on your first billing statement, you will receive 20% off your first purchase.

Our Charge Card comes with so many benefits, including no annual fee or transaction fee and flexible payment plans that make buying luxury items so much easier. You'll also enjoy such courtesies as our award-winning fashion and home store catalogs…advance notice of sales and special events…the ease of shopping seven days a week, 24 hours a day, by mail or by phone…more convenient purchase and return of merchandise.

Since 1907, we have been offering our customers the most current designer fashions and distinctive home accessories. And today, as always, you are assured of receiving not only the finest merchandise from such names as Baccarat, Lalique and Wedgwood, Escada, Donna Karan and St. John, but expert professional service as well. Our sales associates will assist you in wardrobe selection and in choosing the perfect gift for family and friends.

Becoming a Bullock's preferred charge customer is easy. Simply complete and return the enclosed acceptance certificate, and your Charge Card will be sent to you immediately.

I am confident we will meet your high expectations. We look forward to welcoming you to our stores.

Very truly yours,

LYNN KERN
Vice President

P.S. Send for our Charge Card now, in time for your Fall and holiday shopping, and on your first billing statement, we will credit your account for 20% off your first purchase. Our offer expires December 31, 1989.

Box 5900, Metropolitan Station, Los Angeles, California 90055

card. And the sales arguments are similar. In fact, the only real difference is in the format of the ads.

(I understand neither mailing did too well, although the one addressed to the man outpulled the one addressed to a woman by a fraction. Can we draw a conclusion from this? Yes, but it's not based on gender. It's based on a sound direct marketing principle—the addition of a letter usually bumps up response.)

Unlike figure 3-4, figure 3-3 has no letter at all and the brochure really doesn't lead us through the sales argument. The headline, "Discover the Difference that is Bullock's," could certainly be more dynamic. But even if we take it at its understated face value and search the copy for the "Difference," we're left unsatisfied.

We can search the entire brochure and never find a comparison between this store and another, or why one is better. So the reader won't understand what the "Difference" refers to. Copy *is* traditionally feminine, referring to "a cashmere sweater . . . elegant party fashions . . . distinctive accessories for the home. . . . " Does this in itself motivate the recipient to respond? The layout is softly feminine—no marketing help there.

The motivator is a 20 percent discount off the first purchase, but it bears a flaw *guaranteed* to suppress response: This offer appears on the brochure but not on the response device.

The "men's package" has no brochure. It does have a list of some of the brand names carried at the store—Baccarat, Lalique, Wedgwood, Escada, Donna Karan, and St. John. Men may recognize Baccarat and Lalique and Wedgwood; the others, tied to the statement that "Our sales associates will assist you in wardrobe selection and in choosing the perfect gift for family and friends," combine to suggest that nothing in the store is for men themselves.

The discount offer would certainly have helped increase response to both mailings, if the store had used it promotionally instead of parenthetically. But that isn't the point of *this* dissection. If the mailing was an A/B test, too many elements differed to make the test readable. If the mailing was indeed a gender test, who decided men are more interested in women's designer names than in men's designer names?

Figure 3-5.
A mail solicitation aimed at women should speak her language unequivocally. If the message is misinterpreted, the sale is lost.

Let's pick up another mailing from the stack in Marcia's hand. Here's another offer for a credit card (fig. 3-5). The sales argument is aimed directly at women; the brochure shows a woman's hand holding the credit card, with the headline, "When it's your turn to pick up the tab . . . "

The traditionalist might say "wonderful"; another woman might say it's borderline patronizing. And when she reads the first paragraph of the letter, "Take advantage of having your own credit card . . . it offers you the convenience, security, and flexibility you deserve," she might throw it into the shredder.

Here's what's wrong: She's a better target for a credit card than the traditionalist.

The marketer of this credit card asserted that targeting women in advertising—any advertising for any product—doesn't work. She based her assertion on the terrible response she got from this mailer instead of understanding that her targeting was cockeyed.

It could be that the copywriter on the credit card project just didn't know how to speak to women—or worse—was thinking in 1940s parameters. That copywriter would have done well to talk to the copywriter of figure 3-6. The headline:

■

**Most credit cards ask a woman for her qualifications.
We'd like to show you ours.**

■

The copy contains a powerfully targeted sales argument: "At Citibank, we realize that a woman's day rarely begins at 9 A.M. and ends promptly at 5 P.M. So unlike the credit card companies that only help you during business hours, we keep extended hours . . . " That's how to make your market group feel singled out and important, instead of singled out and patronized. That's how to talk to the 1990s woman who's the best prospect for a credit card. (I should note that the format of this insert in *Working Woman* magazine prevented the payoff for this headline from appearing in direct sequence; it had to appear on the back because the bottom half of the card was application/business reply.)

More Gossip = At home, reading a women's magazine, Marcia comes across yet
More Sales another message for a credit card—one arrowed directly into the

Figure 3-6.
Well-crafted copy,
such as the words chosen for
this ad, can make your
prospect feel singled out . . .
and bring her one step
closer for the sale.

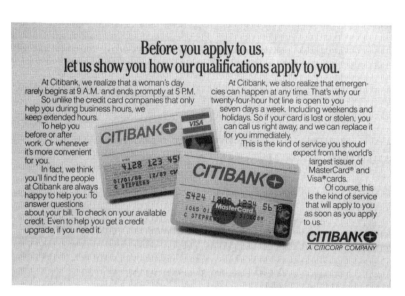

psyche of the smart woman of the 1990s (fig. 3-7).　Showing a well-dressed career woman walking toward an airplane, the ad has this heading:

■

Mother asked why I charged Jack's ticket
to my credit card.

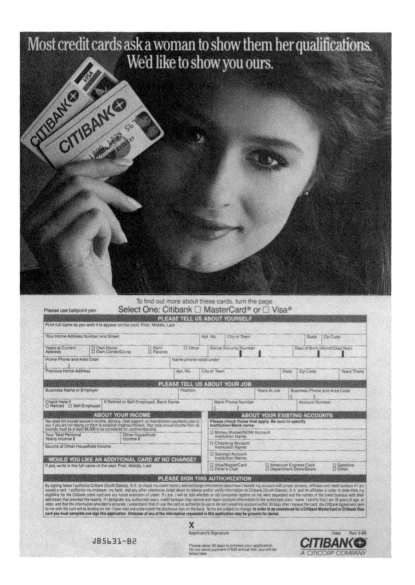

And I told her it's a Private Issue.
She said, "I understand completely, but don't
tell your father."

■

What a wonderful combination of a play on words and an under-
scoring of the difference between today's career woman and her

*Figure 3-7.
A well-done ad that brings
the reader in on a part of
the subject's life while it
underscores the difference
between today's career
woman and her mother.*

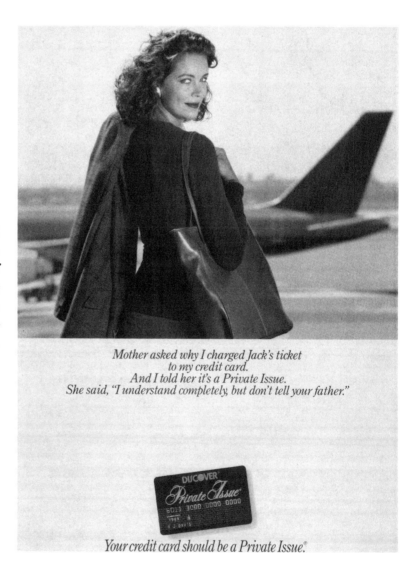

Mother asked why I charged Jack's ticket
to my credit card.
And I told her it's a Private Issue.
She said, "I understand completely, but don't tell your father."

Your credit card should be a Private Issue.®

mother! The card—in fact called a "Private Issue"—offers an automatic 5 percent rebate on travel. But beyond that, here we have a woman charging a man's ticket (her husband? her "significant other"?) to *her* card. A generation ago, the whole message would have bewildered almost anyone who read it.

See how this generation has flowered, not just into equality, but occasionally into *super*-equality?

Whose Message Is It, Anyway?

The dilemma facing so many media buyers is their inability to determine which woman buys what the advertiser is selling. A generation ago, advertisers recognized many types of men but not of women. Now, with social and political equality a *given,* the need for hyper-targeting messages has to drive the availability of hyper-targeted messages.

Which means what?

It means that during the next decade, some venerable media will perish, just as Sears' big catalog perished . . . and the big, glossy, *generalized* magazine of a generation ago, such as *Look,* and *Collier's,* and *Liberty,* began their vanishing act even as this go-getting generation of women was still in kindergarten.

New TV cable technology brings 150 channels to a home. What's on those channels? Just as Neilsen tells us the network programs most watched by men don't parallel the network programs most watched by women (Remember when almost every television-equipped home had just one set?), so can we anticipate an even greater explosion of programming aimed at hyper-specialized interests.

Fragmentation. That's it for the next decade. Women? Which women? The executive? The stay-at-home? The student? The won't-ever-be-a-student? And what's her state of mind when she sees or hears your message?

Shrewd targeting, in the early years of the twenty-first century, won't be an accident. It'll be a careful and thoughtful plan by advertisers and marketers who recognize fragmentation as a natural step in the evolution of marketing . . . and who, through the exquisitely refined scopes of their marketing rifles, will know how to aim and fire!

Marketing Checklist—Chapter 3

☐ 1. Many 1990s women have independent income sources. Have you modified your sales strategy? Are you cross-selling as often as the market will bear?

☐ 2. Have you reeducated your sales force to acknowledge the upsurge in women's disposable income? Are the words "recognition" and "respect" burned into their brains?

☐ 3. The 1990s working woman depends on widely varying media for her information. Have you pinpointed all possible ways you can get your sales message to the professional woman every day?

☐ 4. The 1990s professional is a commuter, often stuck in jammed rush-hour traffic. Have you tested toll-free phone order ads on highway outdoor media to capture car-phone users?

☐ 5. Through your language and offer, have you built rapport with your target audience in your sales appeal?

☐ 6. The 1990s woman can recognize hype from 10 paces. Have you used publicity and public relations effectively in your campaign?

☐ 7. An emotional appeal sells. If your product has no specific gender-based benefits, have you resisted forcing them and artfully positioned an emotional appeal instead?

☐ 8. Benefits appeal to self-interest. Have you romanced the benefits of what you're selling?

☐ 9. The 1990s woman responds to a sales appeal based on her frame of mind at the time she receives it during the day. Have you recognized fragmentation and aimed your marketing message accordingly?

☐ 10. The 1990s woman appreciates information, but needs persuasion to respond to your sales appeal. Is your sales message genuinely motivating your audience?

☐ 11. The 1990s woman wants to have confidence in you before she buys. Have you established your credentials with your audience?

CHAPTER

"You want the

customers to

watch the

commercial and

say, 'Yeah,

that's me'."

— STEVE MCAVORY
CHEVROLET

Building Relationships:

Selling Half the Cars

in America

What *do* women want?

Sometimes a little recognition can go a long way.

The Automobile Trade Association reports that women buy half the cars sold in the United States every year. That's an impressive number, worth about $65 billion per year. And it's estimated that by the year 2000, women will purchase more than 60 percent of the new cars sold.

Not bad, considering they purchased 35 percent in 1980 and 25 percent in 1970. Now consider this: Women buy half the cars but *influence* at least 80 percent of all car purchases.

That's more than just a buying force to be reckoned with; for automobile manufacturers and car dealers, it's a mandatory recognition of "majority rule." In fact, women under 40 comprise the *only* growing buying group in an otherwise flat market.

So who are these women and what *do* they want?

Singles, Doubles, and Multiples . . . But Universal Criteria

A truism: More women in the work force translates to more women on the road.

Fortune magazine reports that two-thirds of the population growth in the United States has occurred in the suburbs. A full 60 percent of metropolitan workers now reside in the suburbs, where 70 percent of the job growth in this country has been concentrated. So it's no surprise that in 1992, women—who represented almost half the work force—drove 50 percent more miles than they did in 1983.

Another growing number of women who are single, independent, working women either can't or won't rely on anyone else to get where they're going. They need reliable transportation.

Yet another group encompasses women in two-career couples who find they need two cars. The dual-income family often means one spouse has a long commute—and that spouse is often the woman.

Then we have the last baby-boomer and post-baby-boomer moms who need the convenience of family-sized vehicles. And we have older women who are spending an increased amount of discretionary income on luxury cars.

Everybody buys a car for different reasons, but among women, there are some universal criteria that must be met.

Reliability, for example. While virtually everyone demands reliability in a car, women absolutely depend on it. If a man's car breaks down on a dark, isolated road, it's an inconvenience. For a woman—especially a woman with children in the car—car trouble can be a nightmare that leaves her and her children vulnerable.

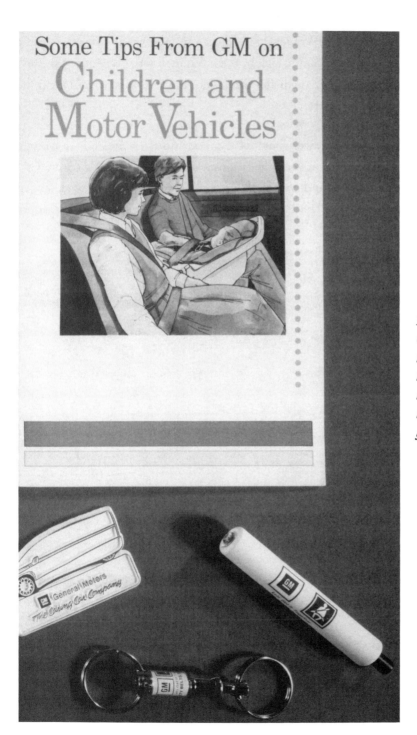

Figures 4-1, 4-2, and 4-3. GM's safety information hand-out, combined with the flashlight and refrigerator magnet work in tandem to create targeted good-will.

Safety is another factor that's more important to most women than to men. Women look for safety features such as automatic door locks and anti-lock brakes. Women who transport children, especially very small children, place the car's safety features at the top of their lists.

Figure 4-4.
Chevrolet's ad targeted
to the working woman
singles her out with the
promise of power.

Figure 4-1 shows a booklet General Motors hands out to women at auto shows around the country. Entitled, "Some Tips from GM on Children and Motor Vehicles," it's an educational piece aimed at mothers. The booklet describes the differences among safety

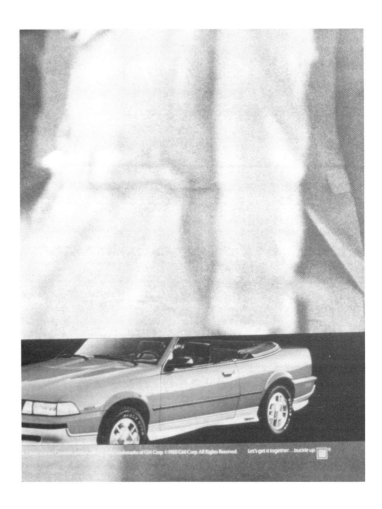

belts and shows the proper way to wear a safety belt while you're pregnant, the safest way to strap an infant into a car seat, and how to be sure you're using these devices correctly. Only incidentally does this booklet mention General Motors in a "This safety message brought to you by . . . " manner.

Along with the safety handout, GM gives away key-ring flashlights (figure 4-2) to address another safety concern among women: entering her car in dim, unlit parking lots. Another giveaway, a

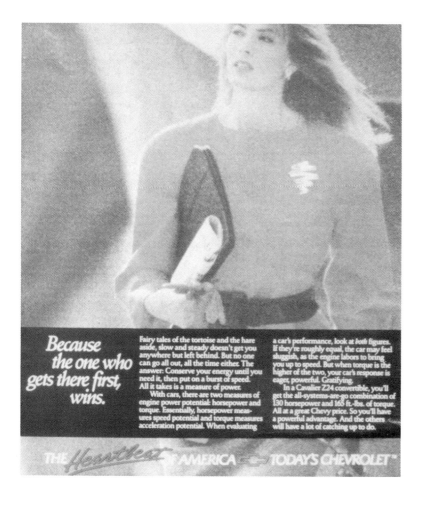

refrigerator magnet showing a minivan (figure 4-3) bears the not-so-subtle message, "General Motors. The Caring Car Company."

Does this transparent ploy actually generate goodwill? Sure it does, not because it's a brilliant marketing idea but because it's *targeted*.

A mini-rule of marketing:

More accurate targeting implies greater sincerity.

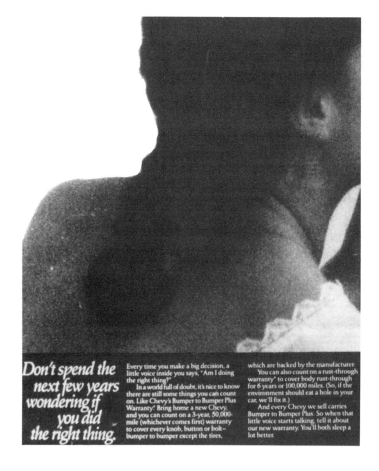

Figure 4-5.
Chevrolet's ad targeted
to the mother singles her
out with the promise of
safety and security.

Consider the difference in men's and women's perception of the same attribute:

Both women and men demand performance in a car—but for different reasons. According to an executive engineer at Chrysler Corporation, horsepower translates to "speed" in a man's mind. To a woman, horsepower means enhancing her driving ability—and being able to accelerate safely onto the freeway. Figure 4-4 is an ad that ran in *Working Woman* in the late-1980s, just as the term "women's marketing" began to dawn on the Detroit carmakers.

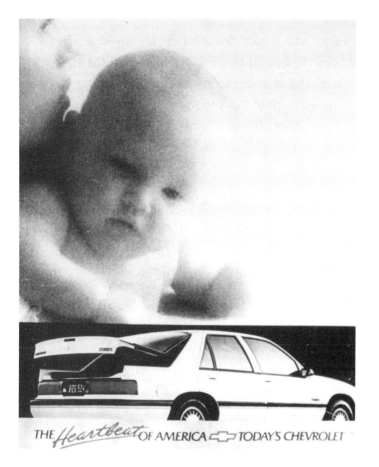

THE *Heartbeat* OF AMERICA ↭ TODAY'S CHEVROLET

(Could a magazine named *Working Woman* have attracted any mainstream advertising a generation before?) A prophetic message, this ad for Chevrolet matched not only the car but the sales appeal to the emerging economic force of the career woman.

The ad shows a racy red convertible and a striking-looking professional woman. The headline:

■

Because the one who gets there first, wins.

■

The copy platform:

■

. . . slow and steady doesn't get you anywhere but left behind. But no one can go all out, all the time, either. The answer: Conserve your energy until you need it, then put on a burst of speed. All it takes is a measure of power.

■

This message has become a classic because it's aimed like an arrow not only at the businesswoman, but at *any* woman who wants a car with power under the hood. And that's the trigger word: "power" . . . because it bleeds over into the woman's estimation of herself.

Compare Chevy's spot with a contemporaneous ad in *McCall's,* a magazine whose readership only obliquely parallels that of *Working Woman.* While *Working Woman* may reach women who have families and children, their domestic circumstance *isn't* the reason they subscribe to a career-oriented magazine.

The *McCall's* ad (figure 4-5) is targeted as well, *to the specific readership of the medium.* In no way does it have the dynamite and pace of its sister ad in *Working Woman,* and in no way does it motivate an aggressive woman to visit a showroom. The thrust is safety and stability, peripheral factors to the buying decision of an executive-minded woman *thinking like an executive,* but crucial to the buying decision of a mother *thinking like a mother.*

Price is important, too. J.D. Powers reports that in 1990, women—whose discretionary income was less than that of men—spent an average of $13,703 for a new car, while men spent an average of $15,083. For the same reason, fuel efficiency is important to a woman, as is a good warranty; in fact, the warranty can be the catalyst determining whether she might decide on a new car over a used one.

And let's not overlook style. A design reflecting personal image is just as important to the woman as it is the man who subscribes to the theory, "You are what you drive." We're seeing recognition of this motivator in automobile designs—and advertising. Automobile advertising aimed *solely* at women, unheard-of a generation ago, is not only commonplace today, it's mandatory if a manufacturer wants to sell cars and a dealer wants traffic in his/her showroom.

(Note the "his/her" in the previous sentence. As of this writing, the National Automobile Dealers Association reports that, as of December 1991 we have 350 women as car dealers. Could a car-shopper have named *one* in 1975?)

Recognizing those criteria, the list of popular cars among women shouldn't be surprising. According to the Automobile Trade Association, in 1990 60 percent of Honda Civic drivers were women. 70 percent of Tercel drivers, 62 percent of Corolla drivers, and 61 percent of Celica drivers were women. Of American cars, women bought 73 percent of the Geo Prizm sedans and hatchbacks, as well as 70 percent of the Chevrolet Berettas, 71 percent of the Geo Storm coupes, 65 percent of the Capri convertibles, 57 percent of the Dodge Shadows, and 54 percent of the Ford Probes sold in the United States.

Considering these percentages, as tempting as it might be to design and market a car as a "women's car," marketers should be

Figure 4-6.
In a radical departure
from tradition, Toyota
shows the active working
mother enjoying life with
her two sons. Dad is
nowhere to be seen.

aware of the historical potholes along that particular road. Special "feminine" models such as a limited pink edition of the Ford Mustang, the pink "Dodge La Femme," and the pink Toyota "Cutie" all became early candidates for the junkyard.

Why? Because these models resulted from primitive and prehistoric masculine role-typecasting. The designers, thinking women wanted to be segregated *as women* when driving in traffic, made a colossal mistake. The temper of the times was equality (and accompanying gender-anonymity), not emphasizing a "pink difference."

Would a man drive a pink car? For that matter, would anyone other than a Mary Kay saleswoman drive a pink car? Just knowing the obvious answer to those questions would have prevented the marketing disaster.

The fact is, women are buying almost all kinds of vehicles. They were responsible for a surprising 20 percent of the truck sales in 1990, and a not-so-surprising 28 percent of all minivan sales.

I've already mentioned the difference between approaching a working mother as a worker and as a mother. Figure 4-6 shows Toyota's brilliant breakthrough-acknowledgement of the working mother as . . . the working mother. Result: Toyota gained footing in a virtually hidden but growing women's marketplace, truck and recreational vehicle sales.

In a radical departure from the traditional "Camping trip with Dad," Toyota shows an action scene of Mom taking her two sons on a rafting trip, all three enjoying themselves immensely. How does Mom get the kids to this rugged terrain? In her rugged Toyota 4Runner.

"Whether it's up a mountain pass, or down a city boulevard," the copy tells the target-mom, " . . . it'll take on just about any terrain." The headline, "Quality Time. All the Time." taps into the working mother's cliché of the hour, recognizing the need to spend "quality time" with her children.

As a result, car manufacturers are spending a bundle on their targeted advertising.

The Moment of Truth: Where's the Payoff? So after spending all this money researching, targeting, and advertising to these women . . . somebody forgot to tell the car dealers about them. (After all, the National Automobile Dealers Association reports that even though 350 car dealers are women, about 17,000 are men.)

According to a survey conducted by CNW Marketing Research, treatment of women at the dealership level hasn't progressed much beyond the Stone Age.

The survey, covering more than 50,000 case histories, reveals episode after episode in which husbands accompanied their wives to the dealer showroom. Even though it was the woman who intended to buy the car, while the man was just along for the ride, the dealers sent the thank-you-for-the-visit notes to the husband.

Or what about the woman who makes the buying decision, writes the check, and drives the car off the showroom floor, only to receive, as the next correspondence from her dealer, a birthday card—addressed to her husband.

Too many women report they have to practically grab a salesman by the collar to get their questions answered. And considering the number of women buyers out there, the low number of saleswomen available doesn't seem to be a smart business move.

If you're ready for a break from the pages of this book, take a look at the "Help Wanted" classified ads in today's newspaper. You'll find ads placed by car dealers for "salesman," not "salesperson." Okay, no problem there . . . supersensitivity to words like "salesman" and "chairman" sometimes becomes nonsensical. But can you see *any* indication, even now that help wanted ads have to be sensitive to all the laws enforcing equal opportunity, that even one car dealer in your area specifically wants women as salespeople?

One of the fastest-growing segments of automobile marketing is leasing . . . by women. Until the 1990s, the typical leaser was a businessperson whose accountant recommended leasing for tax purposes. One traditional complaint, by both men and women who walked into a showroom intending to lease was that a salesman would pressure them to buy. That complaint has all but disappeared, *especially among women,* as luxury carmakers have become aware of a glaring sales fact: Many working women, who take a coldly analytical view of their budgets, consider whether they can afford a monthly payment, rather than the total cost of a car.

Result? A possible upsell, based on the hot area of car sales today—leasing. The car's monthly payment can be the difference between selling a basic, lowest-cost model and selling a "loaded" top-of-the-line model.

Cadillac recognizes this gigantic new marketplace in figure 4-7. This four-page "advertorial" is half educational, half image-sell. Two solid pages extol the virtues of leasing as (big editorial-type headline) "The Sensible Alternative." By using an editorial format in concert with the standard advertising format, this four-pager gains acceptance on the strongest possible level: sincerity.

(Remember the rule? More accurate targeting implies greater sincerity. This Cadillac ad ran in a women's business publication, perfect targeting for this message.)

**The Three Faces
of Eve**

Car buyers mirror the sociological patterning of women in the mid-1990s.

Since the Great Depression of the 1930s, car salesmen divided men who visited their showroom into categories:

- Tire-kickers
- Eager beavers
- I'm from Missouri
- Pipe smokers
- Love me, please
- Let's do it again.

*Figure 4-7.
Cadillac uses two pages
of "advertorial" education
and two pages of image
to get prospects to trade
up by leasing.*

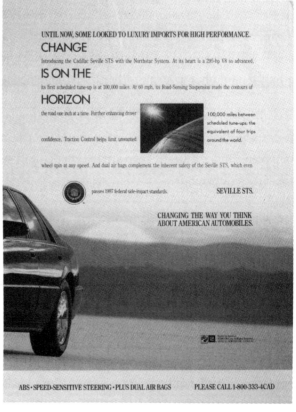

Even on a day when the salesmen spent most of their day playing pinochle together, nobody wanted to host a "pipe smoker." The term applied to a supercilious attitude in which actually buying a car would be a sign of weakness.

Career car salesmen knew how to handle all the other types. They'd mumble party-line engineering terminology at the tire kickers, who would nod as though they understood. They'd take an "I have a great deal for you!" posture with the eager beavers, who needed only verification of a prefabricated attitude. They'd be careful to extol the virtues of competing makes of cars when

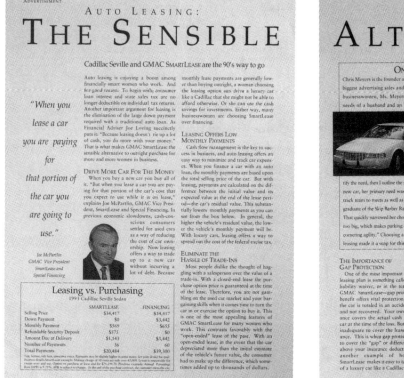

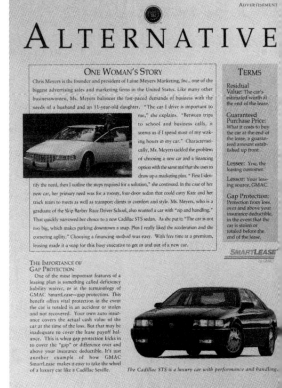

describing features to "I'm from Missouri" frowners (then easing into a comparison in which features became benefits).

They'd praise the astuteness of the timid "Love me, please" buyers whose principal fear was that the salesman would recognize their lack of sophistication. They'd fight to get at the prospect who drove up in a three-year-old model of the same car, because they'd identify that person as one ready to say, "Let's do it again."

So men weren't men. They were subdivided by type, approached by type, and sold by type.

When a couple came in, who drove the car on the test drive? The salesman always made a few complimentary remarks about the woman's taste when she would wander over to inspect a showroom model. But the hard sales pitch was invariably aimed at the man.

A woman arriving solo? Too rare to categorize.

Now switch to today.

Salespeople categorize women the same way we do, into five main prospect-groups:
- Aggressive feminist
- Aggressive non-feminist
- No-nonsense white collar
- First time buyer
- Why am I here?

For the first two categories, no question about it; the dealer who has female salespeople has a big edge. Women selling cars to women has the same advantage as Hispanics selling cars to Hispanics, Blacks selling cars to Blacks; the lingo problem is erased.

Careful, though. There must be every indication of *equality*. That female salesperson has to have her own turf. If she has to ask a salesman, "May we use your office?" the magic vanishes. The women's market is still sensitive. So the woman, selling to a woman, has to act as a man would.

(That's *now*. Advance your calendar one more generation and ignore the last paragraph.)

Women have an edge selling to "aggressives," but they also have an edge selling to some of the classic male stereotypes. No, not the tire kickers, but certainly the "Love me, please" buyers and even the dreaded "pipe smokers."

Do married women shop for cars without their husbands? Not often, but then, the typical husband no longer shops for a car without his wife. Male dominance has all but disappeared in car buying . . . so can car selling be far behind?

Marketing Checklist—Chapter 4

☐ 1. Your product can appeal to many different women for many different reasons. Have you described each different group of women to yourself and come up with different sales arguments for each of them?

☐ 2. Automobile advertising to women is fairly new, and women like to be able to identify with the person in the photograph. Have you shown women driving your cars in your advertising?

☐ 3. Five important factors motivate car buyers: reliability, safety, performance, price, and style. Do you know how women view these five car-buying factors differently from men?

☐ 4. Women change as they move on through the different phases of their lives. Have you stayed current with changing attitudes by talking to women about why they choose their cars?

☐ 5. Pink cars, like pink briefcases, work for Barbie dolls, not real women. Have you successfully avoided creating a typecast "girl's car" (anything that a man wouldn't be caught driving—and neither would a woman)?

☐ 6. The happy 1990s customer is a loyal customer. Have you laid out a plan to stay in touch with her once she's bought her first car from you?

☐ 7. A "Dark Ages" dealer can turn your women prospects into another car manufacturer's conquests. Have you made sure your dealers are educated about the changing marketplace, and are sensitive to women as independent car buyers?

CHAPTER 5

"Without the ability to establish rapport, a copywriter is just a clerk."

—HERSCHELL GORDON LEWIS,
COMMUNICOMP

One-to-One Communication —

The Big Payoff: Rapport

Sitting next to a (slightly) older female executive on an airplane, I noticed her displeasure at the ad reproduced as figure 5-1.

"Why didn't you like that ad?" I asked her.

"The same reason you didn't," she laughed. "Whoever wrote that ad points a finger at 'You women' instead of stroking us as 'We women.'"

Analyze the headline on that ad:

■

WE THINK WOMEN
SHOULD CARRY
THEIR OWN BAGS.

■

I haven't the foggiest notion whether the creative team responsible for this ad was peopled by males or females. If the team was made up of men, I resent being the subject of a play on words. If women created this ad, they were more interested in sniggering than in thinking like their targets—a basic tenet of effective communication.

Either way, the ad doesn't work as well for me as it would have if

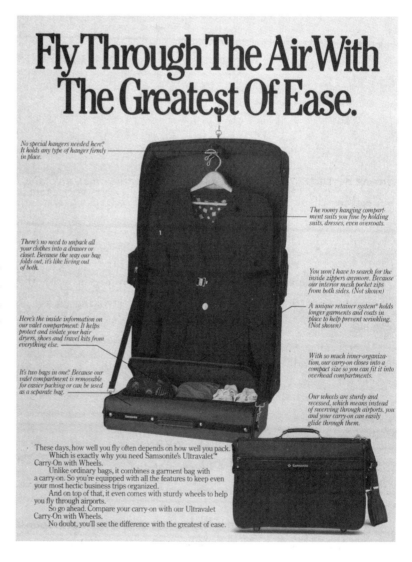

Figure 5-1.
How would you rewrite this
headline to create better
rapport (and a better
chance for a sale to your
target market)?

the illustration had shown a businesswoman with a load of luggage and this headline:

■

I THINK WOMEN
SHOULD CARRY
THEIR OWN BAGS.

■

See the difference between "We think" and "I think," with an accompanying change of illustration? In one word:

Rapport.

Figure 5-2.
Cleverness for its own sake
may destroy rapport instead
of bringing the reader into
your arms as "one of us."

Figure 5-2 falls into the same psychological slough:

■

It's time for women to put on
their aprons and start doing some
housework.

■

Who wrote that? A disgruntled Archie Bunker? Once again, women wouldn't resent this approach if the words came from another woman. In limbo, the message is a complaint . . . no, worse—an unjustified complaint.

Beware of cleverness not tied to *rapport*. Imagine, instead, a picture of a woman wearing a carpenter's apron, with a headline such as:

■

Let's put on our aprons and do some
housework.

■

The difference between their headline and ours: Theirs relies solely on cleverness. Ours uses cleverness to build rapport.

No one key unlocks the door to rapport. But even half-aware creative teams recognize at least two keys:

1. The declarative, "You're one," must be accompanied by "I'm one [or we're one] too"; and

2. suggestion for improvement must be accomplished without denigrating the existing posture of the target.

One advantage of first-person advertising copy is its *implicit* opening of the rapport door. While "I-to-you" advertising is arm-around-the-shoulder; "you" without "I" ads can be preachy.

Recognition not only of the value of rapport but of the techniques by which it becomes available could be the reason behind catalog copy written in the first person. The dear departed Sears catalog never used this device; that may have contributed to its departure.

Endorsers and spokespeople are keys to *some* rapport doors, but not all. Celebrities are by no means universally accepted with

Endorsers and Endorphins

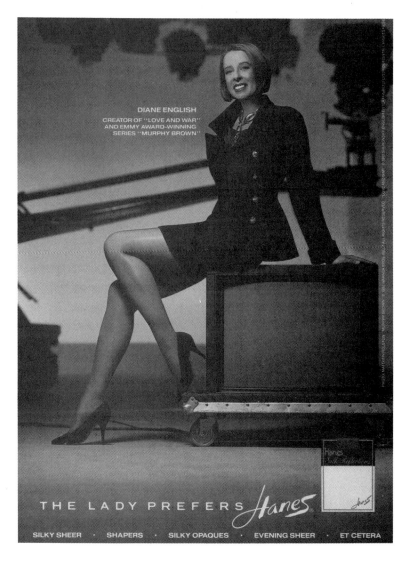

Figure 5-3.
Finally, the advertiser takes the lady's preference into account . . . but can she be comfortable in that pose?

warmth, and many women are resentful of others whose successes make *them* feel less successful.

An endorser is even less likely to open the door to rapport than a spokesperson, because an endorser represents the product rather than the typical user. (Chapter 7 discusses this point further.)

A full-color "bleed" two-page ad for Hanes Hosiery (figure 5-3) shows a carefully posed Diane English, sitting atop a television with lots of leg showing.

So who's Diane English? The ad tells us she's "Creator of 'Love and War' and Emmy award-winning series 'Murphy Brown'." Nothing explains why Ms. English is the model for this Hanes advertisement. And the new Hanes tagline: "The lady prefers Hanes" replaced the venerable "Gentlemen prefer Hanes," not with a bang but with a whimper.

Did Hanes omit masculine approval from its tagline because women complained that they, not men, were the ones hosiery should be pleasing? By using Diane English, the very model of the successful and independent 1990s woman, Hanes underscores its change in advertising philosophy.

Now: Does this endorser generate *rapport?* The ad has style but lacks warmth—deliberately, it seems. Rapport is the destination of the words but not of the photograph; the pictorial aspect would have better enhanced rapport had Ms. English not been so carefully and artificially posed, and had the photographer told her to look at the camera (ergo, at the reader).

Although the "I" endorsement in figure 5-4 conforms with the first-person requirement, it isn't a rapport-builder because it's aimed inward instead of outward:

■

"I can candidly tell you that Pitney Bowes
transportation software has saved Dannon
millions of dollars."

■

You've noticed that the business card is the only Pitney Bowes
item shown in this ad. Placed in *Working Woman,* the ad's

Figure 5-4.
Is this endorsement,
"It worked for me"
strong enough to lead
others to believe it'll
work for them, too?

spokesperson quite rightly was a female executive, the director of distribution for the Dannon Company. But credibility is tempered by lack of specifics concerning what's being offered. Curiosity (if piqued) and greed (in the form of career enhancement) are as likely as rapport to induce readers to call a toll-free number.

Figure 5-5.
Confiding an insecurity
creates a carefully indirect
product endorsement.

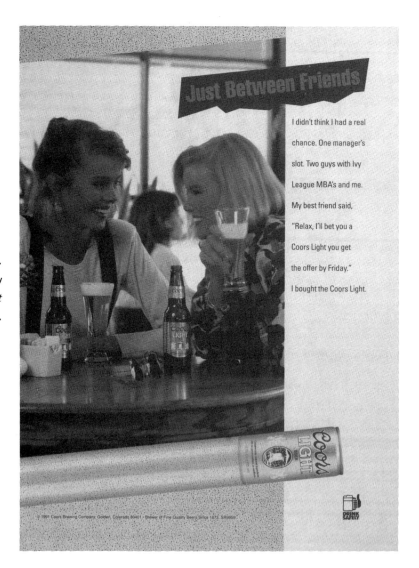

But that doesn't seem to be what's behind this ad. "If it works for her it'll work for me" is the apparent intended selling-hook.

A carefully indirect "I" endorsement sells Coors Light beer to the "young sophisticate" woman. Headed "Just Between Friends," this ad delivers a targeted if unsubtle message (figure 5-5):

■

I didn't think I had a real chance.
Two guys with Ivy League MBA's and me.
My best friend said, "Relax, I'll bet you a
Coors Light you get the offer by Friday."
I bought the Coors Light.

■

Notice the ambience, the hairstyles, the upbeat setting. Coors appeals to women by suggesting its beer parallels wine as an upscale refreshment.

Nike's first-person baby ad (figure 5-6), aimed at parents, is in a stream-of-consciousness style that many parents will think is cute. Here again the "I" is product-oriented rather than "I-to-you." Using an infant whose demeanor and setting are atypical is a disarming ploy.

Nike often boldly goes where no . . . er . . . man has gone before. The company bought four consecutive pages in *Working Woman* (figures 5-7 and 5-8) with an ad whose *ostensible* message encourages rebellion. The key text:

■

All your life you are told the things you
cannot do. All your life they will say
you're not good enough or strong

I'm far from graceful.
I want to be right up front about that.

I'M JUST A BABY.

But I do have dreams. Fast, blurry,

ZIPPY

dreams.

I WANT TO RUN.

I want to run the Boston Marathon backwards.
I want to challenge a cheetah.

I WANT TO GET UP AT SUNRISE,

run all day, eat spaghetti,
and then run some more, running west,

CHASING

the sunset. I want a poseable action figure

MADE IN MY LIKENESS.

I want to organize
a celebrity ping-pong tournament. And

I WANT TO LAUGH EVERYDAY.

But before I can do any of that, what I really

NEED

now is a pair of Baby Huarache shoes with
flexible soles and extra-wide toe-boxes.

For more information on Nike products call 1-800-462-7363.

Figure 5-6.
A lot more than baby-talk
at work in this product
endorsement.

enough or talented enough, they'll
say you're the wrong height or the
wrong weight or the wrong type to
play this or be this or achieve this.
THEY WILL TELL YOU NO,
a thousand times no until all the no's
become meaningless. All your life they
will tell you no, quite firmly and very
quickly. They will tell you no. And
YOU WILL TELL THEM YES.

■

(text continues on the fourth page of the ad, closing with . . .)

■

. . . Say you want
the Air Pegasus because it never says
no and it never says perhaps it says
YES YES YES. There is a road. And
you are just the woman to run it. Say yes.

■

Four pages. Will women go out to buy a pair of Nikes because they feel "reinforced" by this message? Will, in fact, all readers of the magazine react favorably to the suggestion that they've been pushed around until now?

Some will. Some won't.

As this book discusses in Chapter 8, even a homogeneous group doesn't react uniformly. The benefit of ads such as this Nike insert is that they solidify a relationship with *some* readers, who are convinced "Nike tells it the way it is." The other readers? The ad won't damage what hasn't been established.

Figure 5-7, 5-8.
An inspirational message to
the woman who needs a new
pair of running shoes.

ALL YOUR LIFE YOU ARE TOLD THE THINGS YOU
CANNOT DO. ALL YOUR LIFE THEY WILL SAY
YOU'RE NOT GOOD ENOUGH OR STRONG
ENOUGH OR TALENTED ENOUGH, THEY'LL
SAY YOU'RE THE WRONG HEIGHT OR THE
WRONG WEIGHT OR THE WRONG TYPE TO
PLAY THIS OR BE THIS OR ACHIEVE THIS.
THEY WILL TELL YOU NO,
A THOUSAND TIMES NO UNTIL ALL THE NO'S
BECOME MEANINGLESS. ALL YOUR LIFE THEY
WILL TELL YOU NO, QUITE FIRMLY AND VERY
QUICKLY. THEY WILL TELL YOU NO. AND
YOU WILL TELL THEM YES.

YOUR LIFE IS A SERIES OF WHAT EVERYONE SAYS
ABOUT YOU AND WHAT YOU SAY ABOUT YOUR-
SELF. SO SAY YES. IF YOU WANT TO RUN, SAY YES.
IF YOU WANT A ROAD OR A HILL OR A NEIGH-
BORHOOD STREET SAY YES. SAY YOU WANT
SHOES THAT ARE LIGHTWEIGHT AND DURABLE
AND CUSHIONED BY
NIKE-AIR. YES, YOU SAY.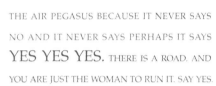
YES. SAY YOU WANT
THE AIR PEGASUS BECAUSE IT NEVER SAYS
NO AND IT NEVER SAYS PERHAPS IT SAYS
YES YES YES. THERE IS A ROAD. AND
YOU ARE JUST THE WOMAN TO RUN IT. SAY YES.

Genuine "I" to "You" Direct marketing has an edge over conventional advertising in its rapport-building potential. Most solo mailings include a letter. The letter is addressed to an individual — *you.* Someone signs the letter — I.

Because direct marketing can target absolutely, the creative team can pinpoint message-tailoring to a degree impossible in mass media. The relationship between vendor and prospect *is* I-to-you.

Many letter openings exploit this automatic rapport-builder. A few examples:

- I have something good for you.
- If you're like I am, you . . .
- I invite you to . . .
- Will you help us/me?

Catalogs, too, have this capability. The "President's letter" has become a staple component of the inside cover of many catalogs. An example is figure 5-9. Pictured are a man and a woman; but the text is signed by the woman:

■

Hello, I'm Nina Balducci. My husband, Andy, and I welcome you to Balducci's Catalogo Del Buongustaio, the Shop-From-Home Catalog for the Gourmet.

■

Does It Grab You, and If So, Do You Want to Shake Loose? Now consider a hosiery ad (figure 5-10) that has this headline:

■

What makes you feel most FEMALE? Silk.

■

Every woman to whom I've shown this ad without telling her where it ran reacted . . . negatively. The typical comment: "Everything about the visuals, from the raised leg to the deep decolletage are at odds with the word 'female.' The wording to go with this image would be 'most feminine' or 'sensual'; 'silk' is luxurious and sexy; while 'female' is a gender-description."

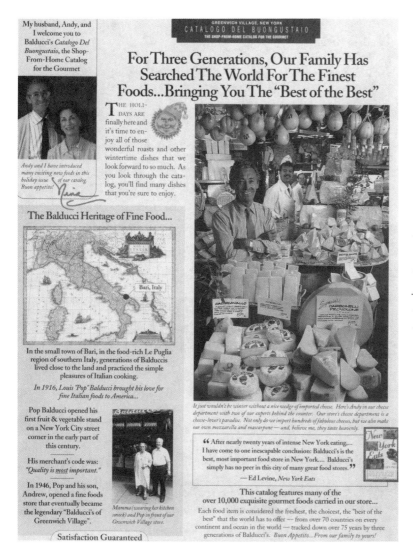

Figure 5-9.
The use of "I" in this catalog letter creates a feeling of intimacy, as though she's inviting the reader into her kitchen.

Then I explain the ads ran in *Cosmopolitan*. "Oh, in that case it's all right," is the usual rejoinder.

The point: *Where* an ad appears affects its rapport-building potential. The sub-point: A woman adjusts her attitude to match the medium, provided she is a *willing* reader, viewer, or listener.

Figure 5-10.
This ad was perfectly matched to the reader in Cosmopolitan *magazine. But what kind of reaction do you think it would have generated if it ran in* Family Circle?

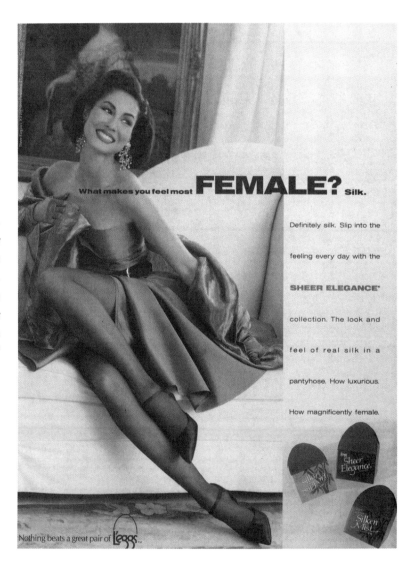

Advertisers can exercise this advantage over subscribers. The same advertiser, however, may not have this advantage over the woman who picks up a copy of a magazine on an airplane.

It's the same advantage the advertiser has over the week-to-week viewer of a "salty" or "daring" television show, which the same sponsor may not have over the casual tuner-in.

The Coors Beer ad raises no hackles in *Working Woman;* in the pages of *Good Housekeeping,* however it could elicit some angry "cancel my subscription" correspondence.

Not that publishers or networks need be unduly alarmed. Religious and parental "watchdog" groups regularly threaten boycotts of advertisers whose space ads or broadcast commercials appear in media of which they disapprove. The repeated failure of such boycotts is ongoing proof of market segmentation which is, after all, a principal subject of this book.

We've come a long way, baby, since the actress Ingrid Bergman was driven temporarily into Coventry because of a publicized extra-marital affair. Rapport is considerably harder to establish today than it was a generation ago, but the "flip side" is that once established, rapport survives negative information unconnected to the relationship between advertiser and target. That's true of life as well as advertising in the 1990s.

A pure 1990s development: aggressive copy.

Aggressive Copy and Rapport-Building

This seems to be more than a trend; it's a movement. An ad shows a woman who obviously doesn't give a damn. The words the ad puts in her mouth would outrage her grandmother.

The growing cadre of women who seem to have graduated *cum laude* from assertiveness school reacts to these messages as if they were gospel. And to this hyper-liberated segment, the words *are* gospel, declarations of independence.

An ad (figure 5-11) that appeared in *Vanity Fair* would be a game of Russian roulette in a less "hip" publication. A Lilyette ad shows a woman clad in jeans and bra, with this hard-to-read text:

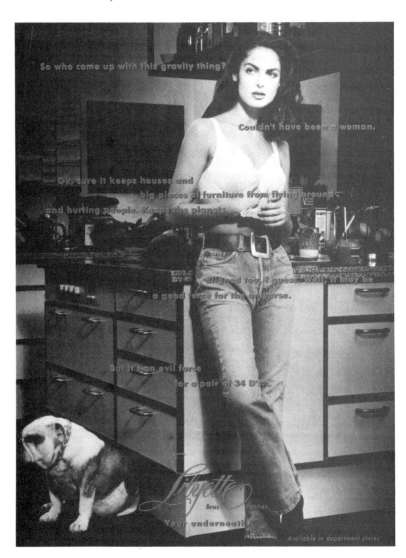

Figure 5-11. Humor and an attitude punctuate this message.

■

So who came up with this gravity thing?
Couldn't have been a woman. Ok, sure it
keeps houses and big pieces of furniture from
flying around and hurting people. Keeps the
planets aligned too, I guess. Well, it may be a
good force for the universe. But it's an evil
force for a pair of 34 D's.

■

Total 1990s. Total vernacular. Aggressive, but it sells the product.

Compare it with figure 5-12, for a competing line of lingerie. This
one is headed:

■

A HELPFUL GUIDE FOR THOSE WHO STILL
CONFUSE WOMEN WITH VARIOUS
UNRELATED OBJECTS.

■

The four "unrelated objects" shown in the ad are a chick, a Barbie
doll, a tomato, and a fox.

Aggressive? What else? But does it sell the unshown lingerie? In
keeping with one approach to advertising—that is neither universally endorsed nor embraced—its defenders will claim that the
image it builds will result in sales. Detractors will claim that
Maidenform is belatedly hopping on the feminist bandwagon,
foregoing immediate sales in favor of long-range applause from a
specific group of women (whose baby-boomer forebears may have
burned a few of the brassieres they bought).

**Elusive but
Attainable**

You can't please all the people all the time. Not in the marketing jungle of the 1990s.

Smart advertisers try to please one group at a time by establishing rapport with them on *their* level, even at the expense of an immediate sale.

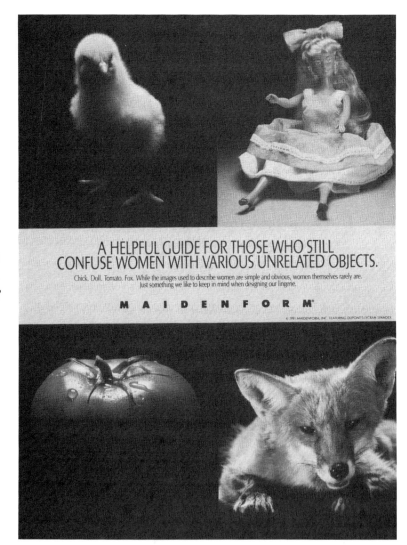

Figure 5-12.
The ad gets attention.
Does it sell the product?

Many, many old-timers think such pinpointed targeting, which eliminates more prospective readers than it attracts, is wasteful. You know what? They could be right. Let's wait a decade or two and judge this again.

Marketing Checklist—Chapter 5

- [ ] 1. When your message is on-target, it places your arm around your audience's shoulder to create rapport. Is your copy rapport-building or "arm's-length" copy?

- [ ] 2. Your customer needs to identify with you. Does your sales copy deliver the message, "We're the same. I'm like you"?

- [ ] 3. Ads that reach too far to be clever can kill rapport. Have you avoided cleverness for its own sake as an anti-rapport builder?

- [ ] 4. A good salesperson is a warm salesperson. Does your advertising exude warmth?

- [ ] 5. The 1990s woman likes to be singled out. Have you included the personalized letter approach of direct marketing in your rapport-building campaign?

- [ ] 6. Ads written for a particular publication or group of publications are automatically better aimed at the audience, so they increase rapport. Have you considered the placement of your ad to enhance rapport?

- [ ] 7. The 1990s woman will respond to different benefits depending on her personal situation, or her frame of mind when she receives an advertising message. When economically possible, have you systematically separated every target and set out to establish rapport for each individual group to maximize sales?

- [ ] 8. Get the woman of the 1990s involved in your message, and she'll be in a better frame of mind to respond to it. Is your message involving to your target audience?

- [ ] 9. Clarity is imperative in the fast-paced 1990s. Is your message instantly clear? Or are you making your prospect work too hard to figure out what you're trying to say?

☐ 10. The woman of the 1990s is interested in what you can do for her. Is your message "we"-driven, or is it pompously "me"-driven?

C H A P T E R 6

"I think housework

is the reason

most women

go to

the office."

— HELOISE

The New Traditionalist:

If a "Tradition" Is "New,"

Is It a Tradition?

The year: 1988.

The product: Puritan Oil.

The advertising strategy: Capitalize on the health and fitness trend by positioning Puritan Oil as *the* oil the health-conscious person uses every day.

The tagline (figure 6-1):

■

Make it Your Oil for Life.

■

Not terribly catchy, but the company made its point. And they sold a lot of Puritan Oil.

Enter the magazine: *Good Housekeeping.*

Back in 1988, just as what we might call the "Women's Movement" was beginning to fragment the marketplace, *Good Housekeeping*'s ad pages, like all magazines' ad pages, had fallen off. The magazine launched its new *positioning* ad campaign directed at ad agencies. *Good Housekeeping* introduced a new character: the New Traditionalist.

Figure 6-1. Puritan Oil's tagline invites the reader to consider it "your oil for life."

The New Traditionalist: If a "Tradition" Is "New," Is It a Tradition?   CHAPTER SIX

107

Here are the ad's first words of text (figure 6-2):

■

The New Traditionalist.
She started a revolution—
with some not-so revolutionary ideals.
She was searching for something to believe in—

Figure 6-2.
The newly discovered
"New Traditionalist"
got Good Housekeeping's
seal of approval.

and look what she found:
Her husband, her children, her home, herself.
She's the contemporary woman who has made a
new commitment to the traditional values that
some people thought were old-fashioned.
She wasn't following a trend. She made her own
choices. But when she looked over the fence she
found she wasn't alone.
In fact, the market researchers are calling it the
biggest social movement since the sixties . . . .

■

The tagline:

■

America is coming home to
Good Housekeeping.

■

What's the point of analyzing this ad and discovering its significance in the ongoing battle to sell products to women?

Look at the way this ad is written. It acknowledges a woman's
desire for autonomy and plays on it by pointing up this "New
Traditionalist" as an independent thinker who made her own
choices and started a "revolution." She's not following a trend.
She is the trend . . . "the biggest one since the sixties."

This ad campaign was very influential—not to the woman who
reads *Good Housekeeping* but to its *intended* target. It hit advertisers
who decide—based on the psycho-demographic makeup of the
publication's primary readership—what (if anything) they'll promote within the pages of that magazine.

The New Traditionalist: If a "Tradition" Is "New," Is It a Tradition?   CHAPTER SIX

109

Women in Labor Force, by Marital Status and Presence and Age of Children: 1960 to 1991

In Labor Force	Single	Married[1] (millions)	Other[2]
1960	5.4	12.3	4.9
1970	7.0	18.4	5.9
1980	11.2	24.9	8.8
1985	12.9	27.7	10.3
1986	13.1	28.2	10.4
1987	13.5	29.2	10.4
1988	13.8	29.7	10.6
1989	14.0	30.5	10.7
1990	14.0	31.0	11.2
1991	14.1	31.1	11.1
With Children Under 6			
1960	N/A	2.5	0.4
1970	N/A	3.9	0.6
1980	0.3	5.2	1.0
1985	0.7	6.4	1.1
1986	0.8	6.6	1.2
1987	0.9	7.0	1.1
1988	0.8	7.0	1.1
1989	1.0	7.0	1.1
1990	0.9	7.2	1.2
1991	1.1	7.4	1.2
Children 6 to 17 Only			
1960	N/A	4.1	1.0
1970	N/A	6.3	1.3
1980	0.2	8.4	2.6
1985	0.4	8.5	2.9
1986	0.4	8.8	2.9
1987	0.5	9.0	2.9
1988	0.5	9.3	2.9
1989	0.6	9.4	2.8
1990	0.6	9.3	3.0
1991	0.6	9.1	3.0

N/A Not available. [1]Husband present. [2]Widowed, divorced, or separated.

Source: U.S. Bureau of Labor Statistics, Bulletin 2307; and unpublished data.

After *Good Housekeeping* began this positioning campaign, Puritan Oil ran this ad (figure 6-3) in its pages—a direct appeal to the "New Traditionalist" subscriber.

Compare the copy in the first Puritan ad (figure 6-1) with the copy in figure 6-3, which says:

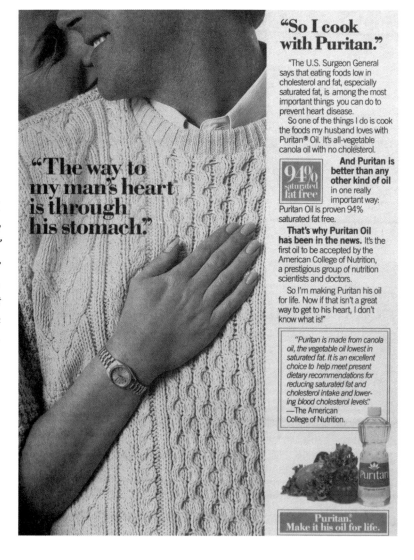

Figure 6-3. Puritan's new appeal to make it "his oil for life" didn't sit well with new traditionalist women, or old traditionalist women, or even the men they wanted to feed it to.

"The way to my man's heart is through his stomach."

"So I cook with Puritan."

"The U.S. Surgeon General says that eating foods low in cholesterol and fat, especially saturated fat, is among the most important things you can do to prevent heart disease.

So one of the things I do is cook the foods my husband loves with Puritan® Oil. It's all-vegetable canola oil with no cholesterol.

94% saturated fat free

And Puritan is better than any other kind of oil in one really important way: Puritan Oil is proven 94% saturated fat free.

That's why Puritan Oil has been in the news. It's the first oil to be accepted by the American College of Nutrition, a prestigious group of nutrition scientists and doctors.

So I'm making Puritan his oil for life. Now if that isn't a great way to get to his heart, I don't know what is!"

"Puritan is made from canola oil, the vegetable oil lowest in saturated fat. It is an excellent choice to help meet present dietary recommendations for reducing saturated fat and cholesterol intake and lowering blood cholesterol levels." —The American College of Nutrition.

Puritan
Puritan® Make it his oil for life.

The New Traditionalist: If a "Tradition" Is "New," Is It a Tradition?   CHAPTER SIX

111

■

"The way to my man's heart is through his
stomach. So I cook with Puritan."

■

Puritan changed its tagline to appeal to the woman it perceived as *Good Housekeeping's* New Traditionalist. Instead of

■

"Your Oil for Life,"

■

the revised tagline read:

■

Make it his oil for life.

■

Remember, please: This was the late 1980s. What do you think the public's reaction was?

It's my guess your answer to that question depends on how old you are. (None of us can totally eradicate the impressions and prejudices superimposed on us by our parents and by our early learning environments.)

Our job as advertisers is not only to transcend our own parental and environmental impressions and prejudices, but—if we're professionally adept—to project ourselves into the attitudinal core of our targets. Did Puritan do this?

The Information Gap and How to Close It

The brand managers, the public relations people, the advertising people, the grocery stores, and especially the correspondents at the convenient write-in address published in the ad—all were deluged with phone calls from outraged women.

What women? The newly outraged New Traditionalists . . . New Traditionalists who clearly resented being relegated back to their retro-traditional status. These women even looked up Puritan's toll-free phone numbers and yelled at the company's telephone operators. They yelled at the magazine. Even men called to complain. Callers seemed to band together with a single, simple request: a large vat of Puritan Oil in which to boil the advertisers. "What do you mean, '*his* oil for life'? Isn't my life just as worthwhile? What century is your company living in, anyway?"

What went wrong?

By late-twentieth-century yardsticks, nothing extraordinary. The medium and the message matched, but the target wasn't standing still.

Even the giants stumble. But any astute marketer of any size, selling any product or service, *can* hit the center of this huge but ever-moving target by recognizing the one facet of organized society that hasn't changed: Women have always been the driving force behind household product sales . . . and they still are. Today's husband isn't embarrassed and doesn't feel demeaned when he accompanies his wife on a shopping trip to the supermarket, but he's the one who asks, "Should we buy Puritan or Wesson?"

According to a recent Grey advertising study, women manage five out of six of today's U.S. households. Two full decades of rapid change have only increased their buying power. In fact, with more than 60 percent of women now working, women's influence over all consumer *and business* purchases is not simply increasing—it's skyrocketing.

The New Traditionalist: If a "Tradition" Is "New," Is It a Tradition?   CHAPTER SIX

113

Inability to recognize evolution, devolution, and revolution has cost advertisers millions of dollars, an unmeasurable loss of market share, and an unrecoverable loss of goodwill. The cream of the jest: As often as not, committees and creative groups making these lethal miscalculations were (and are) largely composed of women.

Does the "traditional" housewife still exist? Ask the housekeeping expert, Martha Stewart. Her magazine, *Martha Stewart Living* is as much a homemaker's reference as the late *Women's Home Companion* ever was.

With articles entitled "Making Pillows," "Redoing Bathrooms," and "Step-by-Step Soufflés," we can find a well-thumbed *Martha Stewart Living* in many an upscale homemaker's magazine basket. We find well-targeted ads such as figures 6-4 and 6-5 nestled in between recipes for hazelnut biscotti and beauty shots of a pork chop dinner served on Wedgwood china. We also find figure 6-6, an ad that reads:

Potato Talk With
Elizabeth
Saco, ME

At first glance, "Potato Talk" seems to be well-targeted to the *Martha Stewart* homemaker. Then we read the first line of copy:

Elizabeth gave up trying to be the perfect wife
around the third week of her marriage and
hasn't looked back since.

By the second line ("She does some cooking, but only when she feels like it"), we sense immediately that Elizabeth is not the prototypical *Martha Stewart Living* reader.

The recipe included in the ad:

Figures 6-4 and 6-5 Logical ads created and placed to appeal to the reader of a homemaker's magazine.

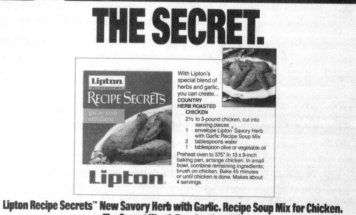

The New Traditionalist: If a "Tradition" Is "New," Is It a Tradition?   CHAPTER SIX

115

■

Elizabeth's Spontaneous Mashed Potatoes—
Slice two large potatoes and place in
microwave dish.
Microcook for 7-10 minutes.
Mash with butter and Parmesan cheese
or whatever you feel like.

■

How will the reader react? Will she identify with this ad? I don't think so.

But picture our reader trying to assemble one of Martha Stewart's soufflés. As she struggles arduously to follow each complicated

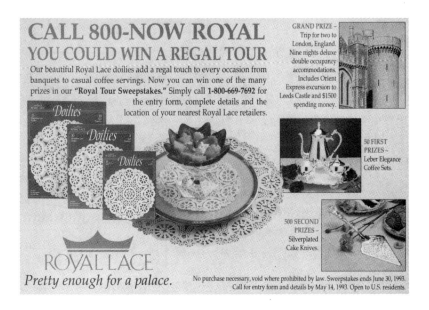

Figure 6-6
"Potato talk with
Elizabeth." An irreverent
look at a simpler
way to cook.

step in the recipe, she turns the magazine page and sees this ad. I'm betting we'll never find her more receptive to trying Elizabeth's Spontaneous Mashed Potatoes.

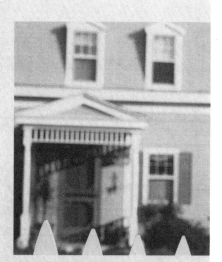

Elizabeth gave up trying to be the perfect wife around the third week of her marriage and hasn't looked back since.

She does some cooking,

Potato Talk With
ELIZABETH
SACO, ME

but only when she feels like it.

Elizabeth likes to keep a nice ten pound bag of potatoes around the kitchen, just for inspiration.

Potatoes are a fresh vegetable.

The New Traditionalist: If a "Tradition" Is "New," Is It a Tradition?   CHAPTER SIX

117

Symbolic of the new role in which so many women perceive themselves is this quarter-page newspaper ad placed by a hospital (figure 6-7).

Evolution? Devolution? Or Revolution?

Potatoes are spontaneous, like Elizabeth. She can walk away from them and make a phone call to her mother, and they won't be ruined.

Potatoes don't pressure Elizabeth to be perfect, the way rice does. Because when Elizabeth feels pressured, she can't enjoy herself. And neither can anyone else. *Potatoes*

THE POTATO BOARD

Elizabeth's Spontaneous Mashed Potatoes—Slice two large potatoes and place in microwave dish. Microcook for 7-10 minutes. Mash with butter and Parmesan cheese or whatever you feel like.

Figure 6-7
How "celebrity" sometimes
translates to "expert."

FOR WOMEN
about women

A *free* WEEKLY WOMEN'S LECTURE SERIES SPONSORED BY
MEMORIAL HOSPITAL DESIGNED *for women of all ages.*
REGISTRATION BEGINS AT 7 P.M. ALL PROGRAMS WILL BE HELD

FROM 7:30-9 P.M. IN THE HOSPITAL'S MAIN AUDITORIUM.

REFRESHMENTS WILL BE SERVED.

Call 985-3455 for reservations.

march

1 HAVING IT ALL
DIANA GONZALEZ-DURRUTHY
Healthbeat Reporter, WPLG CH. 10

8 HOW TO GET FINANCIALLY FIT
MEG GREEN, *Certified Financial Planner*
FORMERLY OF WIOD RADIO
TALK SHOW HOST, WTVJ CH 4
AUTHOR OF "MEG GREEN'S FINANCIAL WORKOUT" VIDEO

15 UNDERSTANDING PMS
DR. BURTON CAHN, *Memorial Hospital Chief of Staff*
DR. YVETTE ANS, *Memorial Hospital Chief of OB/GYN*

22 THE IMPORTANCE OF BREAST CANCER SCREENINGS
DR. MARY HAYES, *Memorial Hospital Radiologist*

Especially for WOMEN

**Memorial
Hospital**

3501 JOHNSON ST. / HOLLYWOOD, FL 33021
CALL 985-3455 FOR RESERVATIONS

The New Traditionalist: If a "Tradition" Is "New," Is It a Tradition?   CHAPTER SIX

119

What are they advertising? A free lecture series, "Especially for Women."

Two of the subjects are indeed medical—"Understanding PMS" and "The Importance of Breast Cancer Screenings." But note, please: These are the *last* two subjects. The first two are "Having It All" and "How to Get Financially Fit."

This hospital concedes that medical lectures are old-hat. PMS and breast cancer? Sure, they're safe topics, but nobody is going to get excited about them. What will bring women through the door are discussions of more aggressive, traditionally masculine subjects.

The trend toward the slightly pugnacious isn't at all subtle, and women who would have blushed at the thought in the 1950s not only shop for cars and houses without their husbands (that is, if they're even married), they discuss openly, in mixed company, nights out at Chippendale's where they enjoy ogling "beefcake" men, and which brand of condoms they buy at the supermarket.

The ad in question supplies a big part of the rationale. Who's the speaker at the "kickoff" (a once-masculine word, in case you didn't notice) session? A woman television reporter.

This woman, despite her "Healthbeat Reporter" title, is certainly no expert on health. The station appointed her as healthbeat reporter, just as it might appoint another staffer to cover City Hall.

The hospital's strategy reflects the attitude so many 1990s women have toward other 1990s women: They view celebrities and authorities *interchangeably*. Advertisers must make sure the celebrity appears to be an authority, to avoid the negative reaction against celebrity endorsers.

Pure "Televiewer Syndrome" in action! Authorities are too authoritarian for the woman emerging from centuries in a chrysalis; celebrities are the authorities of our decade.

Why? Because they're not condescending. Do television viewers expect female reporters and anchorwomen to adopt a condescending tone? No, but it's the traditional relationship authoritarian figures superimpose on a relationship.

Warranties: Yes. Celebrities: Yes, But . . . In 1991, Good Housekeeping, now aware of the dynamite implicit in the word "Traditionalist," explored the ongoing cultural evolution/devolution by polling women. The result no longer surprised anyone in advertising or public relations; women react to ads based on factors unrelated to the ads but directly related to their own upbringing and beliefs.

Only 20 percent of the women polled admitted that celebrity endorsements mean anything to them. Question: Are they telling the truth? Question: If they *are* telling the truth, can they distinguish between a genuine authority and a celebrity-authority?

One of advertising's great successes in the 1970–1990 period has been the ability to obfuscate. An early ad for a beauty aid had its spokeswoman explain, "I'm not a doctor, but I play one on TV." The line between the voice of authority and those who, in the words of historian Daniel J. Boorstin, are "well-known for their well-knownness," blurs. Celebrities *become* authorities by simple declaration. Automobile dealers qualify for the "Andy Warhol Syndrome" ("Everyone will be famous for 15 minutes")—people ask them for autographs because they appear on television in commercials that they themselves have paid for.

The New Traditionalist: If a "Tradition" Is "New," Is It a Tradition?   CHAPTER SIX

121

The president of the United States has become more a celebrity than a father figure. Young people would rather have his autograph than his words on the economy.

So the hospital using a television reporter to speak on "Having It All" might have had Ivana Trump, or Hillary Rodham Clinton, or

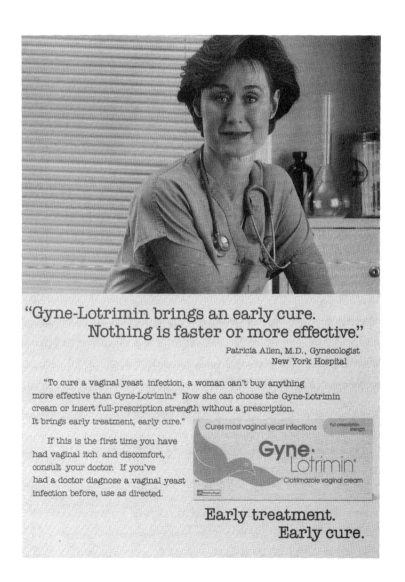

Figure 6-8
Here the advertiser uses a real doctor, not a celebrity (not yet, anyway) to endorse the over-the-counter medical treatment.

Mr. or Mrs. H. Ross Perot. The rationale is undeniable: These are celebrities, and many consider their words, wise or not, inviolate.

The *Good Housekeeping* study also finds some 89 percent of respondents said warranties and guarantees are important to them. (Why not 100 percent? Can you think of a safer assumption, especially from a publication whose "Seal of Approval" has been the benchmark of guarantees for generations?)

But assuming almost all women *do* think a guarantee is important, is this a factor in which women differ at all from the other gender?

Brand Sensitivity

Sensitivity to warranties and guarantees doesn't mean that all women want is "just the facts, ma'am." Of the survey's respondents, 23 percent said an entertaining presentation in an ad is very important, while 42 percent said it's somewhat important. But ask yourself this: Would the pre-television generation have delivered a 65 percent endorsement of entertainment as part of the marketing mix?

Another section of the survey uncovered deep skepticism about ad claims. For example: When asked about food brands that promise to reduce the risk of a serious health problem, 20 percent of the women said they believe "almost none" of the claims, while another 44 percent said they believe "only some" of them.

This may help to explain why *brand sensitivity*, relative to a past history of satisfaction, exerts less influence in the marketplace than *price sensitivity*. Today, even brand loyalties—which a generation ago would have been unassailable—are vulnerable to two mighty forces: 1) comparative advertising by competitors, which exposes the Achilles heel of brand after brand; and 2) television-

The New Traditionalist: If a "Tradition" Is "New," Is It a Tradition?   CHAPTER SIX

123

induced skepticism, fueled by "investigative reporting," a multitude of parallel claims by competitors, and almost uncontrollable introduction of "new and improved" products with little evidence of superiority over existing products.

In late 1992, *The Wall Street Journal* reported that private label sales accounted for an incredible 18.3 percent of grocery store units sold. Only three years earlier, the number was 16.4 percent. (We aren't talking about 1.9 percent; the increase over the earlier figure was 11.5 percent.)

"What is really rattling industry executives," said *The Journal,* "is that private-label products are rapidly gaining share in product categories that once were considered bastions of brand loyalty."

So major manufacturers, according to *The Wall Street Journal,* respond to the superiority of price sensitivity over brand sensitivity in the only logical way they can: They get into a price war, *brand against brand.*

Does this mean that in the twenty-first century brand loyalty will no longer be a viable marketing weapon? As iconoclastic as this concept might once have been, many indicators have validators supporting it:

Validation: Automobile brand loyalty has already largely vanished.

Validation: The trend toward myriad cable television channels means greater fragmentation of the marketplace, isolating some brands from their traditional customers.

Validation: Rampant—and often well-founded—skepticism toward all advertising claims has made brand loyalty a dinosaur, with the manufacturers of brands contributing to that skepticism by constantly fiddling with brand image.

Validation: Brands fragment themselves. Cases in point: Coca-Cola and Pepsi-Cola invite cross-experimentation by ongoing product introduction under their existing brand names. Brands are no longer singular but belong to a "family."

Frequency Marketing: One Way of Combating Brand Abandonment

When American Airlines invented the frequent flyer program in the early '80s, the move was more historic than even those who first applauded it might have imagined.

The airlines' frequent flyer programs exercise a classic marketing strategy for the skeptical 1990s; they *enforce* brand loyalty. Travelers willingly accept peculiar routing, delayed flights, and uncomfortable schedules to build frequent flyer miles on a particular airline. Airlines that have toyed with the suicidal notion of dropping their frequent flyer programs quickly come back into the fold as their bookings drop.

What a perfect marriage of what's left of brand loyalty and buyer "Me"-ism! But most frequency marketing is more reactive than proactive. Rick Barlow of Frequency Marketing, Inc., says this is a major blunder many marketers make. "When discounts and hard benefits represent a brand's genuine investment in an ongoing dialogue with the customer," he says, "the customer will gladly reciprocate with ever-increasing brand loyalty. In effective frequency marketing programs, the benefits are the lure, but the dialogue is the glue." When executed correctly, frequency marketing works, and in today's brutally competitive marketplace—where vendors can no longer retreat safely within the cocoon of brand loyalty—what works is light-years ahead of what marketers wish would work.

The New Traditionalist: If a "Tradition" Is "New," Is It a Tradition?   CHAPTER SIX

125

A frequency program called "Air Miles" gives airline mileage credit. For what?

Not for flying. "Air Miles" is aimed foursquare at people who *don't* fly enough to accumulate free travel. The program awards customers with frequent flyer miles on participating airlines for buying products such as Kingsford Charcoal Briquets, Clorox Pre-Wash Stain Remover, ScotTissue, Finesse Shampoo, and Saran Wrap. What's the connection between these and free flights? Exactly.

Frequency marketing is an idea in perfect sync with the realization that *any* successful incentive to buy a specific rather than a generic brand is worth money. For example, Kimberly-Clark, manufacturer of the Huggies diaper, calculated that the typical new mother spends $1800 per baby on disposable diapers. This justifies a considerable expenditure to recruit that mother.

So Huggies has a Huggies Toyland Catalog. Parents can buy toys from this catalog using "points" they accumulate for buying Huggies.

These programs are all the natural descendants of the S&H Green Stamps which forced customer loyalty at participating stores a generation ago. Green Stamps became unwieldy, but the concept still exists, in an electronic form.

And electronic entries may be the future of frequency marketing. Almost every credit card offers a spectrum of incentives. Why use a "General Motors" Visa card instead of an AT&T Visa Card? Because you're building points good for partial payment on your next GM car. Why use the AT&T Visa card instead of the GM card? Because you save 10 percent on the phone call you make with this card. Why use the American Express card instead of the others? Because you build frequent flyer mileage on your choice of airlines.

Are any of these "brand loyalties?"

Of course not . . . at least not in the classic sense. They're adaptations of the *concept* of brand loyalty, grafted onto the increasingly toughened hide of the post-traditionalist woman.

Do venerable concepts such as Betty Crocker still influence buying? Are Betty Crocker, the Pillsbury Doughboy, and the Maytag Repairman tributes to a bygone era and icons of latter-day brand loyalties? We'll explore the rationale of these marketing personae in the next chapter.

Marketing Checklist—Chapter 6

1. The 1990s woman you want to reach may not be the woman a media salesperson describes. Have you backed up media kit demographic claims with market research of your own to prevent misjudging your target audience?

2. The woman of the 1990s may not, in fact, be exactly what you'd like her to be. Does your advertising message transcend your own personal prejudices?

3. Have you recognized change in the marketplace (women's increased buying power) without ignoring what hasn't changed (most of today's households are still run by women)?

4. Are your endorsers credible authorities? Or have you chosen a celebrity endorser solely for her "celebritydom?"

5. In certain sales situations and family-targeted media, showing a joint decision can be more influential than showing an independent decision. Do you picture women equally with men in advertising for family major-purchase items?

The New Traditionalist: If a "Tradition" Is "New," Is It a Tradition?   CHAPTER SIX

127

☐ 6. The woman of the 1990s responds to guarantees. Have you emphasized your guarantee?

☐ 7. Have you tested brand sensitivity against price sensitivity?

☐ 8. Shopping often demands comparing one brand to another. Recognizing the time constraints of the 1990s woman, if your product is superior to your competition, do you do comparative advertising?

☐ 9. Even if she's happy with your product, the 1990s are a decade of ever-increasing lines of new products to try. Customer loyalty flags. To prevent your customer from succumbing to the competition's offers, have you tried a frequency marketing program?

☐ 10. The woman of the 1990s is influenced when she feels special. Does your message make her feel singled out?

CHAPTER

"Everyone knows and likes Betty. Women write to her for advice, men write proposing marriage. Even in the 1990s, she's still the most popular homemaker in the country."

— MARCIE HOERNER,
ADVERTISING COPYWRITER

Religious Icons of Advertising — Crocker, Doughboy, and the Lonesome Repairman

Who is Betty Crocker?

The simple answer is: She isn't.

Betty Crocker has received requests for recipes, letters and calls asking for baking advice, even marriage proposals (so the way to a man's heart is still through his stomach!).

Not bad for a woman who—had she begun her career when she first reached majority—would be more than 90 years old. But there is no—and never has been a—real General Mills woman named Betty Crocker. You know that. I know that. An astonishing number of women *don't* know that.

Does the Betty Crocker imprimatur affect a customer's decision to purchase a particular brand of potato buds? Obviously, the General Mills market research team thinks it does. Obviously, too, in an era in which the gulf between producer and consumer is ever widening—and in which brand sensitivity has crumbled under the inexorable onslaught of price sensitivity (see Chapter 6)—*any* loyalty-enhancing image is pure gold.

So the Betty Crockers and Aunt Jemimas and Elsie the Borden Cows of our day may be on their way to that great who's who of anachronisms in the sky. But until aging brand-conscious consumers are entirely replaced by television-driven, price-conscious, "me"-centered consumers, they do serve as brand identifiers and confidence-builders. They are nameplates, icons, a familiar marker in a land without street-names.

Whither Betty Crocker? The Betty Crocker name was invented in 1921. Betty was the ultimate homemaker. She could whip up a cake, cook a meal, and answer any baking question you could dream up. Her origin stemmed from a Gold Medal Flour promotion that offered a pincushion premium to anyone who could solve a jigsaw puzzle depicting a milling scene.

To General Mills' surprise, readers who wrote in didn't much care about the pincushion. They wanted answers to their Gold Medal Flour baking problems. So the advertising department created the name Betty Crocker to answer letters and oversee the test kitchen. From a marketing perspective, a proprietary name made sense: It wasn't subject to an employee leaving the company, retiring, or going to work for a competitor.

(For that matter, until well after World War II, many radio stations used proprietary names for their newscasters. The station "owned" the newscaster's name, and continued to deliver the news under that name. The fact that different voices delivered the news under the same name might have puzzled some listeners for a day or two, but stations maintained the image of news department stability.)

For the historically minded, a bit of trivia: The name Betty Crocker wasn't chosen at random, nor was it—as some of the strange corporate names of our time (such as Unisys and Nynex)—chosen by computer. Crocker was the name of the first flour mill in Minneapolis, the home city of the forerunner of General Mills and of the food giant today.

In 1924, with the popularity of radio gaining speed, Betty Crocker began her reign as mistress of ceremonies for the "Cooking School of the Air," which offered listeners a chance to "graduate." (Over the years in which the show remained on the air, more than 1 million listeners graduated.)

By 1940, nine out of 10 American homemakers knew Betty Crocker's name. In some areas she was better known than presidential nominees.

Fashion and hairstyles change. As a bellwether of cooking fashion, Betty Crocker's appearance has kept pace with mainstream fashion—never "far out," always conservative, and never stuffy.

And here's proof of Betty's influence: According to a recent Donnelley Marketing study, more people would buy a product endorsed by Betty Crocker than by Ann Landers, Bill Cosby, James Garner, or Oprah Winfrey.

Why? The answer is obvious. Ann Landers? She's highly opinionated. Bill Cosby? He's openly for sale to the highest bidder, regardless of the comparative worth of the product. James Garner? He had a heart attack while endorsing the Beef Council. Oprah Winfrey? A sensationalist, a female Geraldo Rivera. But

*Figure 7-1
Betty Crocker has
managed to update her
image and keep up
with the times, even
though she's more
than 90 years old.*

THE STORY OF BETTY CROCKER

1936

1986

Since 1921, the Betty Crocker name has symbolized the General Mills continuing tradition of service to consumers. Although Betty was never a
real person, her name and identity have become
synonymous with helpfulness, trustworthiness and
quality.

Betty Crocker has survived the decades by
providing consumers with food information and
food products that are contemporary without being
faddish.

Betty Crocker:
The Helpful Home Economist

In 1921, a promotion for Gold Medal® flour offered
consumers a pincushion resembling a flour sack if
they correctly completed a jigsaw puzzle of a
milling scene. The Washburn Crosby Company, a
flour milling concern and forerunner of General
Mills, Inc., received thousands of responses and a
flood of questions about baking. Advertising
Manager Sam Gale believed a woman would be
an appropriate spokesperson, so he created Betty
Crocker as a signature for responses to inquiries.

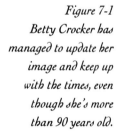

1955

1965

1968

1972

1980

Betty Crocker? Fictional, but always credible. Her brand loyalty is unswerving. She's informative but noncontroversial, ergo unassailable.

This may be a clue to the endurance of Betty Crocker, *beyond* the Cosbys and John Maddens and semiliterate basketball stars whose agents issue news releases when they sign an endorsement contract for a product to which, hours before, they were totally indifferent . . . and the public knows it.

Racial sensitivity has entered the marketing mix with the charac- **Aunt Jemima et al**
ter of Aunt Jemima. At one time, a Hattie McDaniel character was the broadcast version of this hawker of pancake mixes. In the mid-1990s, *using* a racial stereotype as a selling tool (compared, even subliminally, with the race-ignoring Bill Cosby approach to endorsement) would have activists picketing the supermarkets.

Want proof? Look what happened to the Frito Bandito. The character did a passable job of selling Fritos, until Mexican-Americans' complaints forced the company to drop the campaign. Imagine the outcry if a foolhardy broadcast producer announced a resuscitation of Amos & Andy.

A given: Women will accept the word of people—or semi-peo- **Why Pay for Icon-**
ple—they a) trust, b) admire, c) want to emulate, d) know.   **Building Advertising?**

Betty Crocker's ongoing success is congruent with this set of standards.

The application of these standards to *live* contemporary presenters is more to the point. Their fame, image, and effectiveness is implicitly transitory. Today's basketball star will be as distant as Millard Fillmore to new consumers 10 years hence. Today's leading man has endorsement opportunities that will give way to a different grouping as his facial skin requires tightening and his hair requires enhancement.

Women who go to self-beautification lengths their mothers—and certainly grandmothers—would have regarded as outlandish will respond to a celebrity spokesperson who seems genuine, not "plastic." Thus actress Candice Bergen's success as spokesperson for Sprint.

Ms. Bergen has dimension. She *is* a person, and she generates a reaction closer to Betty Crocker than to Zsa Zsa Gabor. From a marketing point of view, her immediate predecessor was Dinah Shore, who sold Chevrolets for years. Both Shore and Bergen share a visual impression: sincerity.

So in the 1990s, pure celebrities such as Cher, Kathy Lee Gifford, and Victoria Principal pick up endorsement contracts just as basketball, football, and, to a lesser extent, baseball players do—with mixed success. And usually, the time clock's ticking away even as their artificially created words of praise hit the airwaves.

If by some lucky stroke you read these words ten years after publication, proof will be the number of endorsements still offered to *this* in-and-out group of celebrities. They'll have been replaced by the next layer, the way loaves of bread come out of the oven, are dated, go to the shelves, and are consumed.

No, this is not an editorial. Rather, it's an analysis of the celebrity syndrome that induces advertisers, in desperation, to favor touchstone recognition instead of product benefit.

Thus Candice Bergen becomes an icon—a viable individual whose credibility *adds* stature to whatever she sells. The typical celebrity, on the other hand, *absorbs* stature from whatever he/she sells. The advertiser should consider this type of evaluation when selecting a spokesperson.

What about *building* a spokesperson—taking an unknown and, by force of advertising power, building an identity solely tied to a specific product?

Depending on the creative psychology underlying the concept, this is sound marketing. It includes both a mnemonic device—a unique image—and a proprietary persona unavailable to other advertisers.

In such a category, an advertiser is safer with a character such as the Ajax Laundry Detergent White Knight or the Man from Glad or the Maytag Repairman than with an unknown actor or actress who *becomes* a celebrity through artificial exposure. The key: The character transcends the individual.

Thus, Maytag replaced its repairman without losing the image it had so expensively built up. Again, the character transcends the individual.

Similarly, non-characters such as the Pillsbury Doughboy or Elsie the Borden Cow function entirely as mnemonic devices, or identity-markers.

The Eveready Energizer Bunny, which began as an appendage to an idea, switched roles over time. Even as the Bunny became a celebrity, its identity with Eveready became secondary. What, ultimately, can be the effect on market share?

The Cloudy Future of Endorsements

The twenty-first century will differ from the twentieth century in myriad ways. One such difference, relative to this chapter, is the public's *split* reaction to endorsers.

For a century following the first advertising aimed directly at women—possibly in the pages of Godey's *Ladies' Book* before the Civil War—through the two decades subsequent to World War II—advertisers could regard women as women. Subclassification and any segmentation were fragmentary.

As previous chapters of this book (and, for that matter, every woman's life experiences) have pointed out, today's woman responds from a framework of personal experiences that have formed and hardened prejudices—pro and con—that affect her buying decisions.

So the *image* of a presenter alienates some even as it attracts others. Even God in advertising (used by marketers ranging from the Disney organization to Memorex) has detractors.

So what?

So this: Creating a single spokesperson, whether live, puppet, or animated, is no longer the universal solution to a generic marketing problem. Gigantic gaps between generations . . . between economic levels . . . between racial/ethnic groups . . . and even between geographic areas dictate *fragmentation of marketing appeals*.

Should we spend as much on celebrities as we do on buying the media? And are they worth those dollars? Assuming the validity of the previous paragraph, only in a singular circumstance: Selling vertical-interest concepts to women who share that vertical interest, i.e., Cher selling membership in fitness salons.

If Nostradamus were reincarnated as head of an advertising agency's market research department (And many such departments wish that were possible!) he might recommend a "pool" of endorsers for the twenty-first century, each conveying a specific image that generates a specific following.

Endorsements demand *singularity* for credibility. Remember how actor Alan Alda's credibility disappeared overnight when his endorsement commercials for one brand of computer were replaced by endorsements for a competing brand? Two problems would kick this concept in the head. Problem 1: The amount of money a recognizable endorser would demand for product exclusivity would make multiple endorsers for multiple submarkets prohibitively expensive. Problem 2: The number of *credible* endorsers continues to shrink, not expand.

Aunt Jemima is a pleasant anachronism today. But in the year 2001, will enough consumers still regard her as "pleasant" to warrant ongoing marketing support?

The challenge, then, is the ability to give birth to another Betty Crocker without encountering the displeasure of those who look for trouble rather than for a reason to buy.

A company mascot identity can be a friendly beacon of familiarity if it's positioned correctly.

☐ 1. If you've created a "character" for your company image, is the character emotionally accessible to your customer?

☐ 2. Does your character inspire confidence?

☐ 3. Is your character able to change with the times without losing brand identity?

**Marketing
Checklist—Chapter 7**

☐ 4. Does your character have a friendly name?

☐ 5. Have you created a character of principle? Is your character credible?

☐ 6. Does your character cross racial boundaries easily?

☐ 7. Does your character inspire:

    a. trust

    b. admiration

    c. emulation

    d. recognition

☐ 8. Does your character reflect your target audience's framework of personal experiences?

☐ 9. Have you tested several related characters to appeal to each segment of your target audience?

CHAPTER 8

"A woman does not

become interesting

until she

reaches forty."

— COCO CHANEL

Are the "Over 40s" a Different Market? You Better Believe It!

About 13 million American women are between the ages of 45 and 54.

By the next decade that number will grow to more than 19 million. And the curve is straight upward in keeping with the highly publicized "graying of society."

Makers of soft drinks to the contrary, the mature marketplace is where the greatest amount of *discretionary* buying power lies. And the marketer who wants to crack that marketplace can find no more logical nor approachable target than the over-40s.

Smart Marketing: Match the Message to the Target

Smart marketers stopped bombarding every woman with ads featuring fresh-faced 17-year-old models long ago. They know women 45 and older are the ones buying more than a lipstick now and again at supermarkets.

Certainly this age group mirrors all of society in its composition. Some live at the edge of poverty; some are comfortable but nervous; some are still upwardly mobile. But, this group has by far the greatest percentage of those who have "arrived" and who can, without bending the family budget, stop at a department store cosmetic or jewelry counter and buy without guilt.

This affluent group is buying cosmetics by the bagful (not just lipstick but a fully orchestrated set, including facial creams, hair care products, and makeup). And they often buy different packets for morning and evening regimens. Even those with borderline discretionary income might acquire yet another full set of makeup for travel, and perhaps a fourth full set for the gym locker.

Lear's magazine, the periodical "for the woman who wasn't born yesterday," hits this group where they live with a subscription mailer from founder Frances Lear, who originally positioned herself as the archetypical *Lear's* reader. The key to this subscription letter is also the key to the affluent mature woman:

■

The women's magazines were urging me to travel, but every resort showed pictures of slim young women in bikinis sipping tropical drinks with slim young men in bikinis. There was no room on those beach chairs for me— even if I had been married.
The magazines I had been reading all my life seemed to have stood still filled with ads for rejuvenating creams on 17-year-old faces— while I had gone on, the way all of us have . . .
That's why I decided to publish *Lear's,* a magazine for "the woman who wasn't born yesterday."

■

Are the "Over 40s" a Different Market? You Better Believe It!   CHAPTER EIGHT

145

As of this writing, *Lear's* is the only mass-circulation publication aimed directly at the affluent over-40s woman. (While the "Seven Sisters"—*Woman's Day, Family Circle, Redbook, McCall's, Ladies' Home Journal, Good Housekeeping,* and *Better Homes and Gardens*— *include* affluent over-40s, they in no way regard them as their primary readership.)

Within the pages of *Lear's* we find ads for Mercedes and BMW as well as Pontiac and Buick. We find Chanel as well as Avon, and Gucci along with Lands' End. We find cosmetics, estrogen tablets, investment products, luggage, coffee, and vodka. *Lear's* is to the women's marketplace what *Esquire* is to the men's marketplace.

And just as *Esquire* readers dip below the age-40 boundary, so do readers of *Lear's*. Note the curious psychology: These aren't women who want to seem older than they really are. Rather, they are women who *want* to identify with the powerful combination of maturity and success. For a woman of 35 *Lear's* on the coffee table represents the next step *up*.

Buying power is buying power. The reader encounters almost as much diversity in the product-mix displayed in *Lear's* as she does in a general interest magazine such as *Time* or *Newsweek*. Why? Because advertisers know that the editorial thrust of this magazine appeals to active women with the means to build, change, and improve their personal image. This applies to women over 40 as well as to younger, active, image-conscious women who aspire to the sophistication of the woman over 40.

If you think sophistication isn't a more pivotal motivator than age, consider this: As an advertiser, would you run the same ad for beauty aids, cars, ready-to-wear, and self-improvement products in both *Lear's* and *Grit*?

If your answer is yes, and you would place your ad based on age alone, you aren't a marketer. You aren't tailoring your sales message to the recipient. You're thinking of what you're selling, not who's buying. *Grit* has a primarily rural circulation. The *Grit* reader views with suspicion an ad pitching the Nike "Women's Source Book," a two-page spread in *Lear's*. The *Lear's* reader, on the other hand, regards as laughable some of the home remedy mail order ads in *Grit*.

Lear's Reader's Service Guide (or "bingo card") bound into its pages often includes an inquiry for Rolex watches, obviously tied to a Rolex ad. We don't need a media expert to tell us that such an invitation to obtain information about Rolexes in *Grit* would produce a higher percentage of lookers than buyers. The editorial thrust of *Grit* aims itself at women with a different lifestyle, with different buying abilities, ergo different buying patterns.

(A disclaimer, please: All generalizations are inherently false. The concept behind this mini-analysis isn't to glorify *Lear's* nor to denigrate *Grit*. Rather I want to highlight demographic differences among *all* publications whose circulations have *some* common elements.)

Do *Grit* and *Lear's* have overlapping readership? After all, the women who read *Lear's* — *and*, more significantly, the women who respond to advertising messages in its pages — are a diverse group and they vary dramatically in age and income. The common denominator of any publication — and, for that matter, of any successful advertising medium — is *attitude*. Appealing and catering to this attitude is the key to marketing within the pages of this magazine.

HYPER-Fragmentation: Reaching an Ever More Elusive Target The marketers who place ads in a well-targeted magazine with smart space salespeople sometimes ignore this diversity, concluding that it is far down the totem pole in a compendium of the typical reader's buying motivators. Attitude dictates the impulse to buy.

Are the "Over 40s" a Different Market? You Better Believe It!   CHAPTER EIGHT

147

Are those who create the multitargeted ads right in bypassing the reality of reader fragmentation? In most cases, probably. Even the "selective binding" techniques, which have come into prominence in the 1990s, can't isolate individuals on a plane dynamic enough to justify the horrendous increase in advertising budget. Imagine the cost of individually tailored ads for a dozen or more subgroups of readers; imagine the ensuing marketing catastrophe if the advertiser were to misread who is in what group.

In *Lear's* case much of the market fragmentation is accomplished at the moment of subscription. The careful advertiser recognizes that despite the "vertical" nature of readership, subscribers are not a homogenous group.

The careful advertiser may opt to manipulate attitude not by showing an older woman using the product—far from it—but in presenting a "limbo" *circumstance,* or generic situation, into which the individual reader can project herself without encountering an element that would lead her to conclude, "Oh, this doesn't match me."

So many advertisers in this magazine play it safe by going out of their way *not* to show anyone with the product. In figure 8-1 BMW shows the car, and nothing but the car. Despite the headline saying:

■

Introducing the BMW 740i.
A car built around a philosophy
built around a driver.

■

No driver appears. The car—black, not usually thought of as a female-owned automobile—is shown in a "muscle" pose. Typography is masculine. Every detail, every word of copy is not

Figure 8-1
The advertiser here
chose not to show anyone
in the ad, and risk
having the reader say,
"That's not me."

about the driver, but about the car. So if our target audience can identify with a large hunk of metal which, as the copy says, "must be the ultimate driver's engine . . . that showed no signs of stress . . .

INTRODUCING THE BMW 740i.
A CAR BUILT AROUND A PHILOSOPHY
BUILT AROUND A DRIVER.

Some companies build their cars around a price tag. Some build their cars around a gas tank. And some, well, they just build their cars around mere cosmetics.

At the Bavarian Motor Works, however, we've always believed that a vehicle should satisfy all the needs of its driver. Not just one or two of them. So it's not surprising that we chose

to build the new BMW 740i around you.
AN EIGHT-CYLINDER TESTAMENT
TO THE DRIVER.

If our engineers build the ultimate "driver's car," then this must be the ultimate "driver's engine."

Five years in the making, our 4.0-liter, V-8 power plant was tested to run — at redline — for over 70,000 miles straight. And showed no signs of stress.

It had sand blasted into its intake. And didn't falter.

It even had ice blasted through its radiator. And didn't miss a beat.

All so that you, the driver, would not only have a powerful engine capable of transporting you from 0-60 mph in a scant 7.1 seconds.

And a fuel-efficient engine* due to its featherweight engine block cast in

*EPA estimated [16] mpg, 22 mpg highway estimate. Use estimated mpg for comparison to other cars. Your mileage may vary with speed, trip length and weather, actual highway mileage will probably be less. ** See your BMW dealer for details

Are the "Over 40s" a Different Market? You Better Believe It!   CHAPTER EIGHT

149

that didn't falter . . . and didn't miss a beat. . . '' then this car surely
is for her.

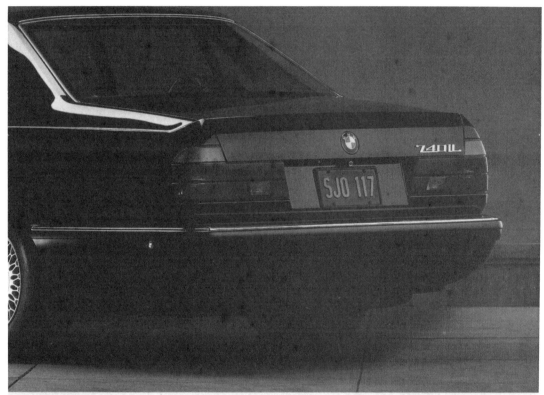

Is she masculinizing her desires? Is she supposed to "think like a man?" Maybe the ad's creators intended her to, maybe not.

Another product doesn't play it so safe. A Chanel ad, also in Lear's (figure 8-2), has this headline:

■

Is your skin aging faster than you are?

■

The illustration: a carefully posed young fashion model who can't be out of her 20s and, as posed, appears to be about 18. Yes, the woman over 40 may want young-looking skin, but using this model stretches the bounds of credibility beyond the reader's own mirror. Without credibility we have no rapport; without rapport, chances of a sale are minimal.

Why use as a model a girl the typical subscriber regards as a baby? While "agency think" generates an ad, the media depart-ment—which may never see the ad's content—determines where the ad goes.

Some logic does apply in depicting an idealized image. This is a sounder strategy in upscale selling than in the mass market . . . and Chanel Lift Serum isn't for the masses. For this cadre of prospec-tive buyers, reality is best disguised with a gauzy veil of romance.

The woman who squeezes her size-9 foot into a size-7 shoe has this romanticized vision of herself. If the ad shows a woman of her own age, she may reject the whole concept: "That isn't for me."

On the other hand, the woman whose psyche is anchored in real-ity needs to see a woman of her age in the photo to identify with. So the marketer faces another set of problems. This fragment of

Are the "Over 40s" a Different Market? You Better Believe It!   CHAPTER EIGHT

151

the target has *pre*-decided to settle for products specifically formulated for the "older woman," and that very decision makes her a less likely prospect for a youth cream than her hang-on-to-youth sister. She has told her mirror, "I'm getting old, and that's it."

The woman who says, "I'm getting old, and that's it," is a poorer prospect (in terms of response, not in terms of buying power)

Figure 8-2
Having so young a model in a magazine like Lear's risks destroying the credibility of the ad claims.

than her more youth-determined counterpart, and this applies to most advertising appeals. The exceptions are those selling concepts related to retirement (euphemistically, "golden age"). This "calm acceptance" attitude isn't uncommon; in fact, the majority of ads in *Modern Maturity* cater to it.

But mass marketing embraces the youth-conscious mature woman. "You don't have to look older" is a mighty weapon in the hands of a smart marketer.

Figure 8-3
The problem this
advertiser attacks
isn't vision-related,
it's age-related.

Advertisers can make this type of product particularly viable by using psychological recognition: This group of women can value

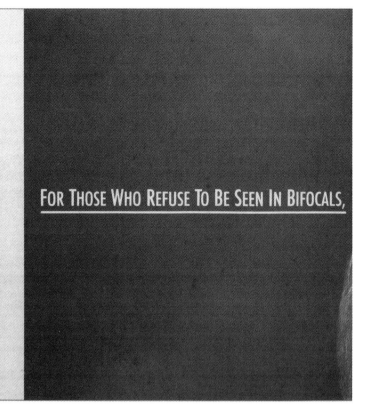

You'll like the way you look and the way you see in our no-line bi-focals. No lines. So you won't have to refocus between near and far. In fact, with Varilux® lenses you'll see clearly—near, far and all the distances in between.

Make an appointment for your yearly eye exam and insist on genuine Varilux lenses. Go ahead. Because your biggest excuse for avoiding bifocals has just been eliminated.

VARILUX®
NO-LINE BIFOCALS

CALL FOR A FREE DEMONSTRATION
COUPON 1-800-VARILUX, EXTENSION 1131

FOR THOSE WHO REFUSE TO BE SEEN IN BIFOCALS,

Are the "Over 40s" a Different Market? You Better Believe It!   CHAPTER EIGHT

153

form as much as substance . . . and they have the means to implement such values.

An example of how this market-responsive set of values attracts advertising is figure 8-3, an unusually shaped ad—two horizontal half-pages, separated by a bind-in card.

The headline is pure form-as-much-as-substance appeal:

■

For Those Who Refuse To Be Seen In Bifocals,
We Offer The Perfect Disguise.

■

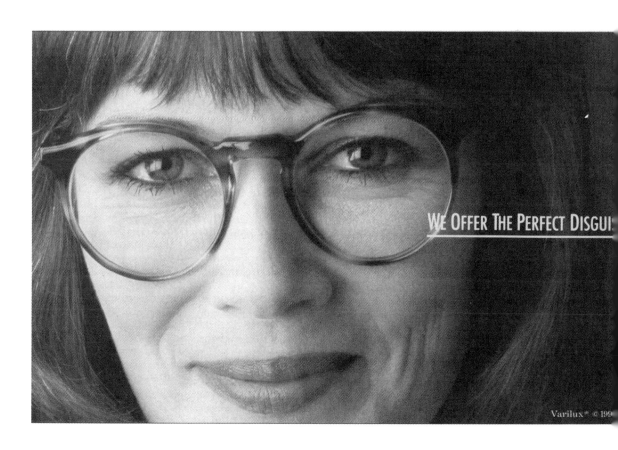

The model in the photo is wearing an ordinary pair of glasses. These aren't "high fashion" glasses; such a prop would muck up the pitch. They're everyday glasses. What underscores the headline is that the usually apparent dividing line one expects in bifocals isn't there.

Conclusion: Wearing glasses isn't associated with aging; wearing bifocals is. The problem the ad attacks isn't the concept of vision-assistance; it's apparent aging-assistance.

"Yes, That's for Me" Suppose you market an estrogen replacement product. Your market is absolute: post-menopausal women or women who have begun to anticipate menopause. Question: What would you use as an illustration?

Your answer obviously depends on the motivator you're building into your ad. Fear? Reassurance? Whatever your thrust, let's assume you want the mature woman to conclude that her lifestyle, her appearance, and her sense of well-being don't have to change.

Let's look at what two advertisers did use—widely diverse approaches. Which would have caused you to lift the phone and call an 800 number? Figure 8-4 is an ad for an estrogen-replacement tablet. The headline begins:

One out of four women over 50 will get osteoporosis.

With this headline is the only logical illustration—four women who appear to be about age 50. (Of course it would be ridiculous to show young women in the photo.)

Are the "Over 40s" a Different Market? You Better Believe It!   CHAPTER EIGHT

155

None of the women seems particularly happy, nor should they be, with fear as the motivator. Fear is a *negative* motivator. Can we sell the same concept using a positive motivator?

In a master stroke of positioning, a competing product's campaign *debunks* the negative approach.

One out of four women over 50 will get osteoporosis.

To help avoid being one of them, call
1 800 388-5880.

After 50, a woman begins losing her natural defense against osteoporosis...estrogen.
Estrogen, together with calcium, can play an important role in keeping your bones strong. As you reach menopause, your estrogen levels begin to drop, and you become increasingly at risk of developing weakened bones and potentially crippling fractures.
Taking low dose PREMARIN® (conjugated estrogens tablets) is the single most effective way to prevent osteoporosis after menopause.
Premarin® is estrogen obtained exclusively from natural sources, and has been used and trusted by women and physicians for nearly 50 years.
See the following page for more information

Call today for free information.
We'll send you a brochure that tells you what you should know about estrogen, menopause, and osteoporosis. Then, we strongly suggest you visit your doctor, since taking any drug may involve some chance of side effects, and only a doctor can tell you whether Premarin is right for you. In fact, we'll even send you a certificate you can redeem for a free exercise videotape after you make that important visit. Just call the toll-free number above or write: Premarin Osteoporosis Information Center, Box 5201, Miami, FL 33102

WYETH-AYERST | WORLDWIDE LEADERSHIP
LABORATORIES | IN FEMALE HEALTHCARE

Figure 8-4
Using fear as a motivator to sell is tricky because fear is a negative.

One headline for this transdermal patch (figure 8-5) says:

◼

Menopause Myth No. 1
"No Man In His Right Mind Would Be
Interested In A Menopausal Woman."

◼

Figures 8-5 and figure 8-6
These ads sell the same type
of product as figure 8-4 by
focusing on the positive.

Are the "Over 40s" a Different Market? You Better Believe It!   CHAPTER EIGHT

157

Illustration: a white-haired, sexy-looking, vibrant woman.

The campaign takes form with a second ad (figure 8-6):

■

Menopause Myth No. 2
"You'd better leave sports to the Youngsters."

■

MENOPAUSE MYTH NO. 1

"NO MAN IN HIS RIGHT MIND WOULD BE INTERESTED IN A MENOPAUSAL WOMAN."

Hot flashes and night sweats certainly don't make women feel very attractive. And while no one should expect to stay young forever, you owe it to yourself to learn as much as you can about menopause, and the symptoms that could affect not only how you feel, but how you feel about yourself.

THE ENLIGHTENED APPROACH TO MENOPAUSE.

Menopause remains a subject often clouded by myth, misinformation, and fear. But its symptoms are very real. They may be mild, or quite severe, and they're different for every woman. But the hot flashes, vaginal dryness, and night sweats that can cause insomnia are not "all in your head." They are the result of your body's loss of estrogen. Estraderm® "puts back" some of this estrogen in a very unique way.

ESTRADERM WORKS THE WAY YOUR BODY DOES.

"THE PATCH"
A NON-MEDICATED SAMPLE IS INCLUDED IN THE FREE INFORMATION PACK.

Estraderm is a clear, round patch that you apply directly to your skin. The Estraderm Patch relieves your symptoms by delivering small, steady doses of estradiol into your bloodstream, similar to the way your ovaries did before menopause. Estraderm is the only estrogen replacement therapy that works this way. It is identical to the estrogen your body produced and, because you don't ingest it, Estraderm bypasses your liver and stomach. Plus, The Estraderm Patch is easy to apply and stays in place during bathing or swimming.

WHAT TO ASK YOUR DOCTOR ABOUT THE ESTRADERM PATCH.

Q: What are the benefits and risks of Estraderm versus other treatments?

Q: How can I tell if The Estraderm Patch is right for me?

Q: Can Estraderm help relieve vaginal dryness?

Q: How long will I need to wear The Estraderm Patch?

A FREE MENOPAUSE INFORMATION PACK.

The researchers, pharmacists, and physicians at CIBA have compiled the latest information about menopause, its symptoms, and The Estraderm Patch. To receive it free, call 1-800-521-CIBA, or send this coupon.

TO RECEIVE YOUR FREE MENOPAUSE INFORMATION PACK, MAIL TO CIBA, PMSI STA., P.O. BOX 13217, BRIDGEPORT, CT 06673-3217

1-800-521-CIBA, EXT. HB031

NAME

ADDRESS

CITY   STATE   ZIP
                                          HB-03

ESTRADERM® ESTRADIOL TRANSDERMAL SYSTEM AVAILABLE IN 0.05 MG AND 0.1 MG STRENGTHS.

FOR BRIEF SUMMARY OF PRESCRIBING INFORMATION, SEE NEXT PAGE.

Estraderm
ESTRADIOL TRANSDERMAL SYSTEM

NOW THE CHANGE OF LIFE DOESN'T HAVE TO CHANGE YOURS.

Figure 8-7
Using a 40-year-old
model for fashion was an
iconoclastic idea in the
1980s, but it's a logical
move in the 1990s.

Illustration: a vivacious woman in tennis garb. Is she over 40? The mature reader *assumes* she is, and assumes she's the very image of youth after menopause.

The tagline of each ad in this campaign ties up the sales argument nicely: "Now the change of life doesn't have to change yours."

Can both approaches coexist? Obviously they do. The most typical reader of *Lear's*, who counts herself, as the tagline goes, "the woman who wasn't born yesterday," might well respond better to the second upbeat approach, because it matches the attitude of the magazine itself—mature women who compete on equal terms in glamour, lifestyle, and sexiness with their younger competitors.

The takeaway from these examples: Even in the most targeted of publications, subgroups exist.

An Advantage to the Advertiser: Buying Power

In 1991, the trade publication *ADWEEK* described a marketing move by astute designer Calvin Klein. He used 40-year-old Lisa Taylor (his model of the 1970s) as the focus of an ad campaign, not aimed solely at mature women but at all women (figure 8-7). "Women get more beautiful as they get older, but we hadn't shown that until now" Klein said of his decision to use an older model.

He knew what he was talking about. In fact, what he may have meant was, "Women's ability to buy what I'm selling gets more beautiful as they get older."

A new generation of working women is approaching retirement age. They're more affluent, and they're gaining more economic power every year. Mature women of the '90s are not only healthier than their counterparts were 10 years ago; they're more affluent, and they don't worry about showing off their affluence.

Are the "Over 40s" a Different Market? You Better Believe It!   CHAPTER EIGHT

159

Beyond that, another aspect of sociological change helps this group throw its weight around. They no longer have to answer to *anybody* for their purchases—not their parents, not their spouses, and not their rapidly vanishing sense of guilt.

Reader's Digest carried a textbook-worthy example of the dichotomy of its readership in two facing pages, both of which were placed by the hair coloring agent Clairol.

Who Are These People, Anyway?

The left-hand page showed a mature woman with striking auburn hair. The headline:

■

Gray hair lies.

■

The thrust of the ad—"Keep your hair young-looking and vibrant. (Like the rest of you!)"—obviously strokes, but our interest lies in its excluding all women but those whose hair is turning gray. So an advertiser in a magazine whose circulation is polyglot chose to single out one reader-group.

The same advertiser singled out a second reader-group on the facing page, which features a "reader" ad, headed "Woman to Woman with Carolyn Carter." Carolyn Carter, whose picture is the ad's only illustration, is an advertising executive.

This ad, designed as so many effective *Reader's Digest* ads are, to look like editorial matter, is aimed at women just beginning their careers. It offers prizes to "aspiring women" for describing "the value of a good mentor." Qualifications to enter: "You must be a female U.S. citizen at least 22 years old," working within a specific group of businesses.

The very terminology "at least 22 years old" eliminates those over age 25, who would perceive this as a pitch to the less sophisticated. Are these women, whose discretionary income has to be minimal (in fact, they're chosen that way), good prospects for Clairol? The next chapter answers this question.

The magazine *Folio,* published for the magazine industry, lists these as publications whose readership has a high percentage of over-50 readers:

■

Reader's Digest, Prevention, Organic Gardening, Travel Holiday, Kiplinger's Personal Finance, and---the giant---Modern Maturity.

■

Is the *Modern Maturity* reader parallel to the *Lear's* reader? In age, partly; in fact, undoubtedly some overlap in circulation exists. But many advertisers regard the *typical Lear's* reader as super-sophisticated and the *typical Modern Maturity* reader as a financially naive retiree.

There's the rub—the word "typical." For most advertisers, being able to find the most common denominator is an edge far sharper than might be available in mounting an appeal to the general marketplace.

As fragmented as the "mature woman" marketplace may be, it still is far more cohesive than other segments.

After being assaulted with advertising for years, the over-40s woman is accustomed to dismissing your ad with barely a blink. How can you make her sit up and take notice of yours?

Are the "Over 40s" a Different Market? You Better Believe It!   CHAPTER EIGHT

161

☐ 1. She responds to ads aimed at her lifestyle. Have you created your marketing message to appeal to your reader? Or have you mistakenly created it to appeal to your own interests?

☐ 2. She's more tradition-oriented than her younger sisters. Have you tested a traditional approach when addressing her?

☐ 3. The ads she notices likely reflect how she perceives herself. Have you mirrored your audience in your advertising?

☐ 4. She's in a different frame of mind each time she picks up a different magazine, or watches a different television show. Have you matched your message to the medium you're advertising in?

☐ 5. She's acutely aware that a product right for her younger sisters will probably not be right for her. Have you emphasized the benefits of what you're selling? And are those benefits specifically targeted to the older woman?

☐ 6. She often dismisses a model in a photograph as having nothing to do with her. Have you tested a product shot alone against showing a photo of an older woman using your product?

☐ 7. She often resents the unrealistic look of nubile models chosen to sell a product to her. Are you making the mistake of showing a younger woman in your advertising to the over-40 woman?

☐ 8. If she decides she likes something, she isn't always willing to wait for it from you if she can get it from your competition more quickly. Have you tested a response-device (a postcard or telephone number for responding) in your space advertising? Does your response device make it easy for your prospect to order?

☐ 9. She resents advertisers who don't recognize the differences between her and her grandmother or mother. Have you updated your marketing approach to mature women (increased buying power, better health) to strengthen your sales message?

Marketing Checklist—Chapter 8

CHAPTER

"I'm tough, ambitious, and I know exactly what I want. If that makes me a bitch, okay."

—MADONNA

"Twentysomethings" —

Tough, Aware, and

Waiting for the Payoff

They've been tagged "Generation X": that 18–29-year-old generation of young women wedged in between the baby-boomers and
the baby-boomers' kids. Marketers also call them "Busters,"
"Twentysomethings," "X-ers," "the Repair Generation," "the
Shadow Generation," "Slackers," and "Post-Boomers."

They're young, they're angry, and as of this writing, they number
about 24 million. *U.S. News and World Report* (perhaps in an
attempt to recruit them as subscribers) calls them pragmatic, non-
ideological, high-tech, entrepreneurial, and action-oriented.

Why are they angry? Sociologists and advertisers use different
criteria. The sociologist might attribute twentysomething anger
to AIDS-enforced sexual caution, heavily documented lying by
political leaders, and observation of parental dereliction. The
advertising analyst might attribute their anger to the multiplicity
of identical claims in advertising for automobiles, beer, detergents,
beauty aids, running shoes, and even "help wanted."

Add to this a fragmentation far beyond that in any other age group (for example, within this same group we have those who blast heavy metal music out of the windows on a jacked-up truck, those who frequent coffeehouses and listen to alternative music, and those who don formalwear for a symphony concert).

Figure 9-1
Mazda uses the "you're only young once" appeal to sell its sports car.

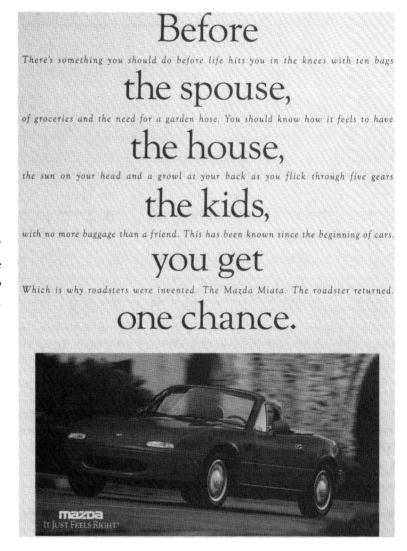

Advertisers understandably have to chain themselves to a wall to avoid running after a less-murky target.

What a tough market!

Typical of marketing arrowed at this segment is a billboard on whose panels a twentysomething blond "with an attitude" glares at passing drivers. The legend:

Breaking and Entering the Tough Twenty-something Market

■

Totally Kool.

■

Cigarettes are in disrepute. How to sell them? Who, in fact, responds to a message *ostensibly* aimed at the twentysomethings?

With marketing to this group comes a serendipitous trickle-down benefit: The next group of twentysomethings may react more favorably to such a message than the professed target. In fact, studies show that few smokers begin their lung damage after age 18. Twentysomethings are role models.

And what powerful role models they are! The thirtysomethings have little sway over *them*, and the forty-and-fiftysomethings exist within their own insulated spheres. But, ah, the twentysome-things! One of them, as a celebrity endorser, is worth five or six from other age groups because this group—as splintered as it is— still trusts itself and distrusts outsiders.

The archetypes of this group are the cast of the television show "Beverly Hills 90210." When a member of this show's cast makes a personal appearance at a department store, mobs—unseen since

Figure 9-2
Maybelline pokes fun at its traditional sales copy with a dash of '90s realism. The page tears off and the copy underneath says, "Get real." The revised, down-to-earth, anti-hype copy then simply describes what the product does.

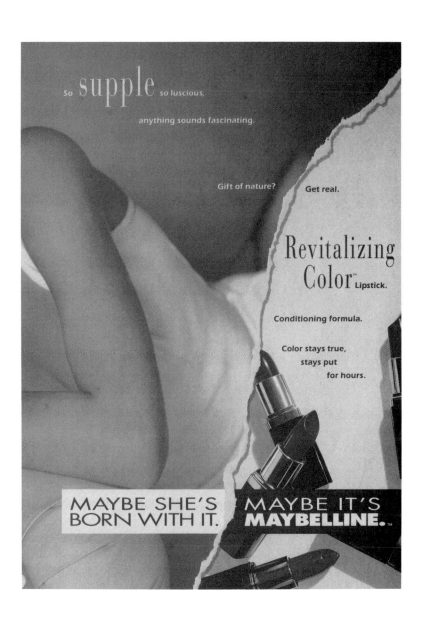

the halcyon days of the Beatles—rip clothing, paw for autographs, and clamor for whatever that cast member is hawking.

The Fox Network signed sixtysomething licensing deals tied to this one program! And the licenses aren't exclusively directed at twentysomethings or their teen camp-followers. Licenses are out for lunchboxes . . . trading cards . . . vanity license plates . . . Noxzema . . . Oxy acne medication . . . Bold Hold hair styling products . . . clothing, of course . . . and for the subteens, "Beverly Hills 90210" action figures.

Any question this group has the advertising community squeezed in its fists?

	Boomers under 30 then (1978)	Twenty-somethings now (1992)	Boomers now (1992)
Home of your own	82%	87%	89%
Yard & lawn	53%	54%	61%
Vacation home	21%	36%	35%
Happy marriage	85%	74%	82%
Interesting job	69%	68%	68%
Job that pays more than average	51%	67%	62%
College education for self	38%	59%	53%
Job that contributes to society	35%	43%	43%
Nice clothes	48%	56%	45%

What Constitutes the Good Life: Then & Now

Source: Marketing to Women, October, 1992 (Boston, MA: About Women, Inc., 1993).

A counter-thrust movement within advertising anticipates the next move up. Just as immediate product sales can come from a "You need this now" message, so can immediate *and future* sales result from a "You need this now so you'll be ready for tomorrow" message.

The difficulty lies in creating a message these people believe. Their innate suspicion of those outside their own orbit sometimes borders on paranoia.

So we sell them without apparently selling. We make our messages non-generational. This is the third television generation, and they shoot "hype" dead in its tracks. They demand—and are simultaneously suspicious of—sincerity.

But we know where they live. And we know they want to:
- feel good about themselves;
- feel superior to their failed predecessors;
- know answers to questions they haven't yet been asked;
- have a good time and worry about their personal futures later, if ever;
- be involved in "save our planet" movements;
- be recognized as individuals even as they run on tracks;
- have every cell in their superfit bodies in perfect shape;
- travel to offbeat destinations;
- own or lease a jazzy car (VW Beetle, *ja! BMW, nein!*).

We know where they live. Pick something they want and hammer away. The only restraint is to avoid being obvious.

Do these parameters apply to the twentysomething woman? You bet they do. This group is the most gender-rejecting target that advertisers of products unrelated to gender have ever faced. The

Sex and the Twentysomething Girl

Figure 9-3
Value-added advertising
gives away something of
value such as this bound-in
shampoo sample . . .

TAKE IT.

(If you never thought a two-in-one could work on dry or damaged hair.)

THE PERT PLUS HEAD TO HEAD CHALLENGE

NEW EXTRA CONDITIONING

PERT PLUS

Shampoo Plus Conditioner in One

15 FL OZ

We're going head to head with whatever you use, no matter how many steps you're taking. And no matter how demanding your hair type, you'll be convinced new Pert Plus Extra Conditioning can leave it soft and manageable. Because after it cleans, this new formula conditions two ways. One conditioner targets the damaged parts while the other conditions all over. So, take the Challenge. Your hair will convince you.

NEW PERT PLUS EXTRA CONDITIONING.
GREAT HAIR. NO FUSS.

same automobile ad, properly structured, will appeal to both men and women . . . a phenomenon not usually true of other age groups.

Why is this? It's probably the natural result of greater sexual equality, from childhood. Kindergarten teachers of the 1980s were careful, careful, careful not to suggest that Janey could not engage in the same activities as Johnny. The sociological vaccination took.

If we believe the data from two recent surveys, marketers who assume they can sell their products to baby-busters in the same

"Money? We Have More Important Considerations."

way they've sold them to the baby-boomers had better reconsider their approach.

A *Fortune* magazine survey reports that 64 percent of 18–29-year-olds say a full personal life is more important than money. And a survey of *Mademoiselle* readers conducted by the Roper Organization (an advertising research company specializing in ongoing attitudinal studies) validates this attitude: 44 percent say no job is worth sacrificing your personal life; 78 percent said they spend their leisure time watching movies; 75 percent spend it at the beach; and 64 percent said they dance in their leisure time.

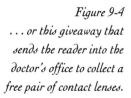

Figure 9-4
... or this giveaway that sends the reader into the doctor's office to collect a free pair of contact lenses.

According to this same survey, just 54 percent of them have credit cards. Fewer than half are currently married. Here's the one group of women whose interests center inward as well as outward. When they buy, they look for brands. To this age group, brands reflect product quality as well as personal image. Fifty-five percent believe brands say a lot about themselves. While the baby boomers go on shopping sprees for organic groceries, the X-ers pamper themselves by splurging on the extras such as high-priced shampoos, toiletries, and liquor. The survey indicates value-added advertising and free gifts are important to 82 percent of this age group.

Even though these young women spend about two hours reading two magazines every week, they're not easy to find in mainstream media. Many marketers are turning to interactive direct marketing (electronic networks), cable TV, computers, and video games. Some advertisers feel uncomfortable with the media that do seem to penetrate this group. For example, in 1993, *Advertising Age* named Conde Nast's *Details* "Magazine of the Year." This publication, with 300,000-plus circulation, hardly qualifies as a "major medium."

**How Do
We Reach Them?**

Although the editorial thrust seems to be primarily masculine, one media director is quoted as saying *Details* "is the only publication geared to that younger, 'grunge' type of individual." An advertiser explains the magazine's appeal: "serious issues are treated in an MTV style that makes it very accessible and entertaining for the reader."

The magazine's editor, commenting on the magazine's considerable female readership, refuses to categorize the magazine. And why should he? Ask any young, hip, woman what magazines she reads and *Details* will probably be right up there with *Rolling Stone.*

(Interestingly, *Details* started out, during the mid-1980s, not as a men's magazine, but as a magazine for both sexes. After a few years, it was reintroduced as a men's magazine.)

Now, if you're an advertiser, how can you feel secure in your targeting as you generate a campaign? The twentysomethings are not only fragmented intramurally; many individuals are fragmented in themselves.

"In Your Face"   Advertising executives in their 40s and 50s are nonplussed. Many don't understand what "MTV style" means, but they know the "in-your-face" advertising this group admires has two very sharp edges that have cut deeply into the egos and pocketbooks of advertisers whose transparent messages have been created by "outsiders."

Can the conventional advertiser reach this group at all? And having reached them, can we sell them dresses, cereal, beauty aids, jewelry, and automobiles?

The influence of "Beverly Hills 90210"—which far outweighs the program's ratings—may seem to be preposterous. To attribute this segment's "in-your-face" cynicism and belligerence to this single factor confuses the mirror with the original image. The program succeeds because it *reflects* an attitude, not because it generates an attitude.

If you're reading this book eight or ten years after publication, you may wonder what the fuss is all about. "Beverly Hills" will long since have been succeeded by more timely sociological reflections. And so it has been since television became the dominant medium of communicative influence: "The Ed Sullivan Show," "Leave it to Beaver," or "You Bet Your Life" wouldn't make it today. They're bits of history housed in those protective walls of nostalgia, that museum of television, "Nick at Night."

In a 1993 *Advertising Age* interview, the actress Shannon Doherty, star of "Beverly Hills 90210," was asked about her reputation as the archetype of the twentysomething woman. The interviewer referred to her as being "among a growing list of outspoken actresses, like Sean Young, who provide fuel for the tabloids." Doherty's reply: "I'm not saying I don't have my moments. I've always been a pushy kid."

Is that the key adjective? Pushy?

Advance your calendar a decade. The "Home Alone" group advances into the twentysomething ranks. This subgeneration worships the concept that youth can outwit age (a direct repeat of the Haley-Mills-movie-influenced baby boomers).

Is This the "Degeneration" Generation? And If So, So What?

The advertiser who wants to sell dresses, cereal, beauty aids, jewelry, and automobiles to this segment, seems to have two choices. They can hire creative teams representative of this group to create messages within their own societal framework—or they can stick with a mainline approach, using appeals to apparent logic, sincerity, glamour, and greed, which have the ability to overcome antagonism and will penetrate the less-bellicose segments of this age group.

Peer-group creative teams have seldom worked in the past. Their ability to communicate is too vertical, and the rule seems to be: The more they represent an in-group, the less value they tend to have communicating with any other groups.

Mainline advertising always attracts some and repels some. The Cola Wars have repeatedly proved this point. High-budget cola advertising, attempting to construct a "with it" image to establish a buying pattern among the younger element, has those outside this group wondering whether this drink fits their mold.

There lies the paradox. Pre-twentysomething young people are less and less tractable. They're television-skeptical. Their icons change monthly, and their brand loyalty depends on a) peer pressure and b) which brand gives them free gifts with purchase.

Their grandparents were shocked by the actress Ingrid Bergman's peccadilloes. Their parents were shocked, then amused by Archie Bunker's rednecked racism in "All in the Family." They think nothing of it when their current role model has a baby out of wedlock or is arrested for drunk driving or drug possession.

How to reach them?

The advertiser who thinks in terms of marketing rather than social analysis does have at least a partial solution . . . one that safeguards the budget and doesn't require a separate hit-or-miss campaign.

Using media they regard as contemporary, advertisers can transmit messages that neither patronize nor recognize a cultural difference. One tradition crosses all boundaries of communication: Targets respond to apparent benefits.

What Happens Next? Advertising pundits are famous for after-the-fact guesswork. When the rebels of the late 1960s cut and washed their hair, hit Wall Street, accepted affluence, and became parents, they claimed to have predicted it.

The question isn't *whether,* but *when.* Are twentysomething women like a college class that will graduate and lose their brashness, their rejection of "traditional" values, their determined funkiness, their MTV simplistic attitudes?

To some extent this has to happen. But we can expect to find a residue, not only within the psyches of this group of determinedly independent-minded consumers, but in their worshippers, who will emerge from their teens to assume their mantle.

☐ 1. Twentysomethings shoot hype in its tracks. Have you analyzed and purged "hard sell" from your advertising to them?

☐ 2. Twentysomethings respond to sincerity. Is your message sincere without sounding "adver-sincere?"

☐ 3. Twentysomethings shun the generation before them. Have you scrupulously avoided all identification with the baby boomers in your advertising?

☐ 4. Twentysomethings look for added value. Do you incorporate free gifts and added value into your advertising?

☐ 5. Twentysomethings are technologically sophisticated. Have you explored and taken advantage of alternate media?

☐ 6. Twentysomethings recognize and reject advertising that doesn't ring true to them. Have you "tried out" your advertising on several of them before launching to see if it rings true?

☐ 7. Twentysomethings expect your advertising to answer one question: "What's in it for me?" Does your advertising emphasize the benefits of buying your product?

Marketing Checklist—Chapter 9

CHAPTER 10

"I'm going to clean

this dump—just as

soon as the kids

are grown."

—ERMA BOMBECK

"The New Mother:" How New?

How Maternal?

And How Receptive?

Count the baby buggies on the streets these days and then calcu-
late the average age of the new mothers you see pushing them.

The 1990s mother parallels every other category of 1990s womanhood. Finding a common denominator, other than the biological
fact of motherhood, isn't easy.

According to a recent survey by Simmons Market Research
Bureau of New York, most of today's mothers (60.5 percent) are
(not surprisingly) under age 30. At the same time, however, more
new mothers than ever are over age 35 (13.4 percent).

One sees television anchorwomen well into their forties making
on-the-air pronouncements of their intention to become pregnant.
"The biological clock is ticking" has become a professional cliché.
Late-in-life first-time pregnancies no longer are a phenomenon;
for many 1990s career-oriented women they're the pregnancy of

choice, the result of a cold economic decision rather than a hotly passionate one.

Complicating these statistics is the economically staggering reality that a gigantic proportion — one out of four — of the very youngest mothers is unmarried and has no buying power at all according to *The New York Times* (Dec. 1991).(Don't confuse that group with the deliberate single parent who decides to have a baby without the encumbrance of a husband.)

"New mother" doesn't necessarily mean *brand-new* mother. Nearly half of women who give birth — 42 percent — already have children aged 2–5 years old. One in four already has school-aged children.

Additional evidence from the *Simmons Report* that the "New Mother" market is actually a multiplicity of markets:

Among those who already have other children, 42 percent have either graduated or attended college; 39 percent are high-school graduates; and 20 percent never completed high school.

One more statistic influences what we can sell them and how we can tailor our advertising messages to them:

Almost half — 46 percent — of these new mothers work full-or part-time and will continue to work within about three months after their child is born.

The Hot Buzzword: PARENTING   The Baby Boomer generation added a word to the lexicon. Being a parent no longer could be considered a passive, untended activity. Parents had to tackle their roles aggressively. The new word: *parenting*.

"The New Mother:" How New? How Maternal? And How Receptive?　CHAPTER TEN

185

So the high-circulation *Parents Magazine* suddenly faced an upscale competitor, Time Inc.'s *Parenting*, whose publisher's self-declared editorial profile stated: *"Parenting* focuses specifically on a parent's needs as they relate to living with children through their first ten years."

Figure 10-1
Acknowledging the time
constraints of this target
audience, and the need to
be in several places at one
time, Motorola created
this logical appeal to the
working mother for a
pocket pager.

Yes, the names of both magazines imply the inclusion of the father, but both include themselves in category 49 of *Standard Rate* & Data *Service;* that is, they place themselves in the "women's" category.

The difference between *Parents* and *Parenting*—simplistically, of course—is the difference between the parent and the New Age mother. Both are marvelous marketing targets. Technically, both publications are directed at the same age group (*Parents* says it's edited "for young women 18–34 with growing children"), but neither the editorial stance nor the consistent advertisers parallel those of *Parenting*.

Who's the best buyer? Consider a little rule of marketing:

An appeal to an intense attitude has a better chance of success than an appeal to a tractable attitude.

So for product introduction *as an improvement over an existing product*, the traditional approach within the traditional media seems to be a safe course. For product introduction *as a departure from existing products*, the apparently innovative medium seems to be a safe course.

In between the two extremes, we have products everyone can use. But how do we sell them?

The Disposable Parents reacted according to their circumstances when con-
Diaper Menace fronted with the intelligence that disposable diapers are the biggest single source of pollution.

While some "aware" parents reacted with statesmanship and called the nearest diaper service, others were aware but undaunted.

"The New Mother:" How New? How Maternal? And How Receptive?   CHAPTER TEN

187

Within the traditional ranks of parenthood, an astounding number of parents either never saw nor heard this information, or disowned it as competitive name-calling. Far fewer, within this group, put the statesmanship of flushing before the convenience of tossing.

Now, let's look at this circumstance from the smart marketer's perspective. To the "parenting" parent we broadcast reassurance. To the "parent" parent, we broadcast . . . yes, the same message, reassurance. Let's not let hyper-awareness of fragmentation get in the way of a universal message.

To cover both groups, we place cents-off coupons in freestanding newspaper inserts, and we regain lost momentum.

An inside-out look: Suppose our job is to create a public service "awareness" campaign opposing disposable diapers. For the "parenting" parent, we structure what seems to be an intellectualized appeal to reason. For the "parent" parent we structure an emotionalized appeal about the way this planet will look when mounds of disposable diapers stink to high heaven . . . just when babykins is giving birth to her own children.

Some advertisers have an advantage when recruiting customers from the ranks of new mothers. Assuming the mother has at least minimal buying power, appealing to a mother *as a mother* requires only the proper ambiance for the message to get through.

Should an advertiser try to isolate the more mature mother? Certainly, but this may be an impossible task outside the realm of direct marketing.

The mature new mother almost certainly has greater buying power than the twentysomething new mother. But another little rule of marketing spoils the fun:

Your best buyers are the ones most likely to be the targets of parallel appeals by your competitors.

That's the curse of the database: Information based on hard fact can't be kept a secret for very long. Others know what you know. This leaves comparative marketing success in the hands of your own talent for persuasion.

Point of Purchase   In the cuddly world of disposable diapers, baby soaps, baby foods, and squeezable toys, the classic marketing method has been standard media advertising.

What a waste! And what a necessity!

For every new mother media advertising reaches, that same ad or commercial reaches dozens of women who *don't* qualify for your message. But how else can you reach them?

A handful of astute marketers have discovered a powerful secret: direct sampling.

Direct sampling differs from direct marketing through the circumstances in which the sample is delivered. A woman appears at the supermarket. Her baby is safely strapped into the shopping cart (or, more and more frequently, onto her back or her husband's back).

A cheerful demonstrator, who last week passed out pizza samples, recognizes her target and homes in. "Here," she says. "Baby will love this." "This" is a baby food sample, or an inexpensive giveaway toy, or a demonstrator-size sample of baby soap or shampoo. If the marketers acted with forethought, a cents-off coupon accompanies the sample.

"The New Mother:" How New? How Maternal? And How Receptive?   CHAPTER TEN

189

The success of this type of sampling is unquestioned. But it's a mixed bag. A demonstrator can stand in a store for hours and pass out only a half-dozen samples. So the laws of economics dictate that this device be used only in neighborhoods that have a high percentage of new mothers.

"Where did they get my name?" sounds the chorus of direct mail-stricken new mothers.

The Old-Line Powerhouse: Direct Marketing

They got it from the hospital, of course. Mailing list companies salivate at the prospect of getting today's load of new-mother names. The list companies' clients are so ready to jump they often mail first class instead of risking third class mail—which might mean an earlier bird would get the jump on a buying decision that could last for two or three years.

The new mother, home from the hospital, is flooded with "Welcome, New Mother" offers. They come in the mail; they come by delivery services; they're hung on the front doorknob. They come by telephone—too often just when the baby or the new mother is falling asleep.

But they come. They're free. And Mom uses them and may decide to continue using them.

We're in the fourth generation of sampling-by-mail and offers-by-mail. Here the diaper services go toe-to-toe with manufacturers of disposable diapers. Here, the various magazines aimed at new parents take their best shot. Here is the most logical of all battle-grounds—the exact place where whatever we're selling *can* be used.

Every marketer who targets the new mother is aware of a) this medium; b) the response-depressing effect of getting dozens of offers at a time when leisure reading moments are few; and c) the reality of competition within the medium.

Why, then, doesn't awareness lead to innovation?

One semi-solution: Send to the male parent. It's a weak semi because—even in an age of parenting in which each parent duti-

Figure 10-2
Information is important
to a new mother. She reads
everything she has time for
if she perceives that it could
have an impact on her
baby's health.

"The New Mother:" How New? How Maternal? And How Receptive? CHAPTER TEN

191

fully takes a turn at "quality time"—the father is less likely the decision-maker for buying baby goods. But mailing to the father does offer the advantage of targeting, which improves the possibility that the message will be read.

(Addressing the mail to the parents as a team *isn't* targeting the father. "Mr. John Brown" differs dramatically from "Mr. and Mrs. John Brown" or "To the parents of Jimmy Brown.")

Another solution: Use sequential mailings. One mailing may not crack the clutter. A series has a better chance.

A third solution: a brightly colorful "Welcome!" package mailed to the baby. Perhaps our package boasts a clever rubber stamp with wording such as "We want to be the first to salute a proper candidate for President of the United States in the year 2040."

A fourth solution: A handwritten note—yes, handwritten, not computer-generated—that has a personal signature and an aura of sincerity bleeding over to whatever enclosures the handwritten message touts. Any number of lettershops (mailing services) offer this option. The technique is exactly as it appears to be: People sit at a table for two to three hours at a time, writing the message. It's a wonderful part-time job for students.

Breaking through the direct mail clutter isn't a problem unique to the new-mother marketer. Nor is it an insurmountable problem, as this medium's steady growth proves year after year. Color works. Provocative envelope treatment works. Manila envelopes work.

Above all, sincerity works. The new mother quickly becomes disenchanted with the plethora of offers that don't even bother to mask the naked greed of their vendors. A money-making admonition to marketers: Place yourself in the position of the harried new mother. What will get through? What seems to ease her burden?

**How Far Does
Parenting Go?** A "new mother" isn't new very long. She quickly becomes a veteran. The golden glow a woman enjoys in the spotlight of recent delivery gives way to whoever on the block has the next baby.

The turnover among new parents is worse than the turnover of players on a girls' college soccer team. The marketer resting on his/her laurels won't be wearing laurels very long.

*Figure 10-3
A new mother isn't only
interested in a product's
effect on her baby now — but
also what impact it can
have on her baby's future.*

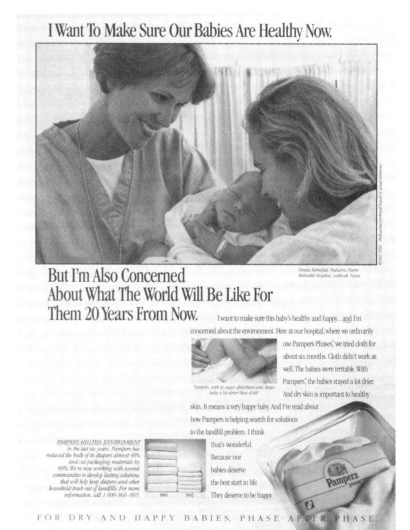

"The New Mother:" How New? How Maternal? And How Receptive?   CHAPTER TEN

193

Marketers to the new mother seldom observe all five practices that tend to maximize response. How many of them did your last campaign include?

☐ 1. New mothers are very aware of the significance of their choices. Have you used strong and specific competitive/comparative claims? Have you named the competition?

☐ 2. New mothers don't have ample free time to analyze advertising messages. Are your messages pointed and benefit-laden?

☐ 3. New mothers see too many identical appeals. Have you distinguished yours from your competition's in both appearance and apparent offer?

☐ 4. New mothers deal in both the present and the future. Have you offered benefits that make sense to them right now as well as carrying over into the future?

☐ 5. New parents are proud but fearful. "What did we get into? How can we pay for all this? What happens if we have an economic reverse?" Does your campaign feed both the pride and the fear?

Marketing Checklist— Chapter 10

CHAPTER 17

"Behind every

great man,

there is a

surprised woman."

— MARYON PEARSON

NOW Who's a Dumb Blond?

Male-Bashing in

1990s Advertising

I have (to the delight of some and the exasperation of others) hard proof of ongoing *male-bashing*. In fact, it's the *hardest* proof of all: Men are used as goats in advertising.

Donald brings the boss home for dinner. The boss compliments Joan on the tasty homemade dinner. Joan accepts the compliment; then, *to the camera*, she points out what a jerk the boss and her husband both are, because she served a prepared main course.

Who's Sorry Now?

Harmless? Yes, if Joan weren't smugly superior. Pointing out that the prepared dish is as tasty and fresh as a homemade dinner is good advertising, if emphasis is on the *dinner* and not on the *diner*. In fact, Ragu built a massive comparative campaign using this theme. But we have to ask: Does making the men in this mini-episode the butt of a joke add to the salesworthiness of the product?

If it does, we've learned much about the attitudes of many 1990s women. And it does.

Let's turn this latter-day phenomenon inside out.

First, we have to recognize that Joan herself may have spent a full day at the office, so *any* dinner is a culinary miracle. Second, we can easily assume that Donald was with her at the supermarket; in fact, they went as a team, with Donald as full shopping partner. So the joke both expands and collapses when we add a dollop of logic.

Logic doesn't always prevail. Attitude will always triumph over logic, just as emotion triumphs over intellect.

Example: Figures 11-1 and 11-2 are ads for what's called Cool Down, an "After Exercise Refresher For Women." It's a soft drink, and the ads target women with "in" jokes about men. Here's what the first frame of cartoon dialog in 11-1 says:

■

What men hope women are saying when they
go to the washroom together:

"Bill is the world's best lover."
"Ken is even better."

■

Second frame:

■

What they're really saying:

"Do you think cake is better than sex?"
"What kind of cake?"

■

NOW Who's a Dumb Blond? Male-Bashing in 1990s Advertising

CHAPTER ELEVEN

199

Figures 11-1 and 11-2
Two examples of "attitude"
reigning supreme over logic
or selling arguments. Most
women will chuckle
knowingly at the copy . . .
will it give them a good
reason to buy the soft drink?

Figure 11-2 is a "pop quiz":

■

How well do you know your gender?
two people have colds.
one of them is lying in bed moaning,
"Call a priest."
the other one is walking through the door
carrying a tray with hot tea,
english muffins, and a cold compress.

■

The tagline for both ads:

■

Cool down. Guys just don't get it.

■

An advertising executive named Leonard Pearlstein pinpointed this attitudinal differential a few years ago, when the male-bashing movement was gaining steam: "Advertisers are trying to make women look smart because they know women do most of the shopping. If that has to happen at the expense of men, well, they figure that's okay."

See the cynicism so typical of the 1990s? Anything goes if it sells. This goes because it sells. Advertising is a reflection of society, not its creator. So many women regard the 1990s man as a bumbling Dagwood that the image is a sales weapon.

What power! Put women in that same bumpkin-position today and the phone rings off the wall—as witness the Stroh Brewery "Swedish Bikini Team," mentioned in Chapter One. Men don't object as vehemently either because they don't (yet) feel as threat-

NOW Who's a Dumb Blond? Male-Bashing in 1990s Advertising

CHAPTER ELEVEN

201

ened by the ads or because they're more apt to be oblivious to ads not aimed at them.

Who objects the loudest and the most frequently? Yep—male advertising executives. And—my opinion—they aren't objecting to the content of the ads as much as they are to what's behind them. They're objecting to the replacement and replenishment of their ranks by women. The situation presents a double threat—as men, they're threatened on an ego basis, and as advertising communicators, they're threatened on a professional basis.

Does their position have merit? Will it expand to a war between the sexes? If this were the 1960s and the sex roles were reversed, you know it would. But this is the 1990s, and open warfare is less likely than archetypical sniping.

A family sits outside what appears to be a doctor's inner office. The door opens. Who's dispensing the medicine? "Dr. Mom." She's in charge. She decides which variation of a cough medicine goes to whom, *including her truckling husband.*

Dr. Mom and Her Patient Patients

The superior female hasn't been considered a novelty since *Lysistrata.* What's strictly twentieth century is the use of female dominance to sell. Nobody regards female wrestlers (not the "mud" type, but the muscular type) as a novelty any more; they're wrestlers. Women file lawsuits to join football, basketball, and hockey teams . . . and they win the lawsuits. Chances are they won't go up against a 300-pound linebacker (not in a football game, anyway), but the law says they're equal. Female tennis players threaten to quit unless they're paid as much as the men . . . and the tournaments say, "Yes, Ma'am."

Mom has traditionally been in charge of the kids, so when a sly youngster brings home a more-expensive toothpaste dispenser, suspense hangs heavy until *Mom* approves. This isn't male-bashing, and as an advertising ploy it's neither novel nor clever.

Don't equate that harmless commercial with the cereal ad that builds its point around a pair of tennis partners. The man is so hopelessly inferior that when he finally gets the ball over the net — when it bounces off his head — his distaff counterpart says, "Nice shot, honey."

Remember that ice cream commercial in which the woman decides her bulldog is better-looking than her ex-boyfriend? How about the ad for Radio Band of America (figure 11-3) that appeared in advertising trade magazines whose text was, "As her date removed his pants, Sheila suddenly recalled a hilarious radio spot she'd heard that morning. Later, when pressed, she'd admit the timing was unfortunate." The picture showed a laughing woman and a befuddled, semi-pantsless male.

Analyze the "joke" here. Sheila is, first of all, totally in charge. She's either unaware or unconcerned (or both) that her date is left, literally, hanging in midair. His discomfiture — caused entirely by her laughter, which he assumes is aimed at him — *is* the ad.

Think back. In the 1950s Springmaid showed an Indian lass and her disheveled boyfriend with the tagline, "A Buck Well-Spent." The response included editorials, picketing, and who knows what else! Womanhood was insulted!

Oh, sure, we've come a long way, baby. But is it reasonable to assume that our own desensitization extends to the newer male target?

As far back as the antediluvian year 1989, Bruce Horovitz wrote in *The Los Angeles Times* — without quoting anyone — "In almost all

NOW Who's a Dumb Blond? Male-Bashing in 1990s Advertising

CHAPTER ELEVEN

203

advertising, someone has to be the foil." Mr. Horovitz went on to quote Renee Fraser, then general manager of the Los Angeles office of the Bozell advertising agency, as saying these days it's virtually impossible to cast a woman in that role. Ms. Fraser's justification was, "Now, so many women's advocacy groups will come after you, you don't dare take that chance."

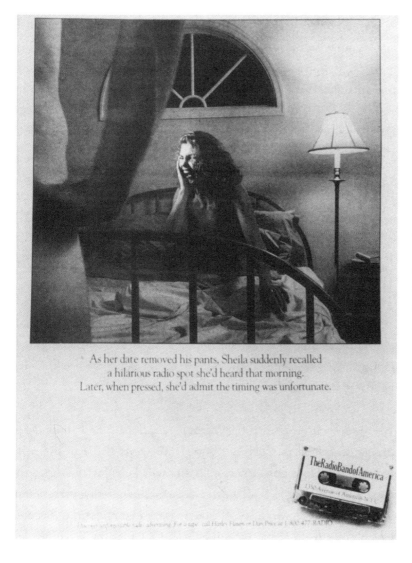

Figure 11-3
The woman leaves her date hanging in mid-air, and leaves the target audience laughing. A safe sales ploy in the male-bashing 1990s.

That was 1989. This is now. Women's advocacy groups are more hair-trigger militant than ever, but their rationale is history. Advertisers willingly walk on eggs to avoid offending women. That's a given. What's becoming another "given" is the realization that this ban doesn't apply to men. Make women the butt of jokes, and people will ask if you're crazy. Make men the butt of jokes, and they'll ask, "What's the angle?"

Incompetence and Incontinence

A man fumbles with a diaper. The television viewer laughs. A man fumbles with a dinner menu. The television viewer laughs. A man mispronounces Nina Ricci's "L'Air du Temps" and his Significant Other corrects him; the television viewer laughs again.

Okay, just *who* is that television viewer? We can draw two conclusions:

1. Television is the principal teacher/offender/perpetrator in these little dramas.

2. If the viewer doesn't laugh, the product doesn't sell. Ergo, the viewer is either female or female-dominated.

We cannot overstate the role of television in granting super-equality to our sisters. Television is real, it's in motion, and it's a glitzy-glossy larger-than-life production. It adopts a newsy mask, which validates its authenticity.

We're well into the third television generation. The twentysomethings described in Chapter 9 are embryonic proof of the positive and negative power this colossus wields. Now we have the most impressionable of all viewer groups, the fourth generation of TV-influenced children. Will they mature just enough to become psychological mutants, viewing Dear Old Dad as a hapless in-

NOW Who's a Dumb Blond? Male-Bashing in 1990s Advertising

CHAPTER ELEVEN

205

Figure 11-4
Jackie Gleason was the butt
of "The Honeymooners"
jokes. Häagen Dazs pokes
fun of him as a 1990s
everyman to emphasize
their 98% fat-free dessert.

competent and Stern Old Mom as the family savior? Will they regard bachelorhood as the just dessert of a man who can't compete within society and bachelorette-hood as the just triumph of the woman who supercompetes?

Probably.

I say "probably" because, as of this writing, we have no evidence of any movement other than intensification of the trend. No, no, this isn't going to throw our social order up for grabs. After all, we have the increasing counter-trend—the down-the-nose view of television, not necessarily as the corrupter of public taste but as a separate universe, a coexisting "twin-earth" of science fiction.

So television spawns weeds as well as seeds, helping demean itself even as it has become far and away the dominant means of communication. Women are pleased that advertising agencies mirror their newfound dominance, and men aren't yet so displeased that they're rising up in wrath.

The point? Men may *never* be so displeased they'll rise up in wrath because upcoming generations of television-spoon-fed viewers may simply learn that this is the way things are.

Men As Sex Objects

Some years ago, the football player Joe Namath modeled panty hose. So what? He-men don't wear panty hose, but the consummate playboy does? Was that the base of a then-startling message?

The standard perfume ad of the 1990s places the woman in a position to accept or reject a perfectly formed man who seeks her favor. The scantily clad man, popularized by Calvin Klein, no longer startles.

NOW Who's a Dumb Blond? Male-Bashing in 1990s Advertising   CHAPTER ELEVEN

207

Who, in the 1960s, would have predicted a product such as Jockey Shorts for women? Can you envision the derision the concept would have generated then? Now, we see both sexes in their Jockey Shorts, and we don't wonder which reader is paying the most attention to the other sex in the ad.

The Chippendale concept exemplifies what some commentators call "the new freedom" and others call the evolution of box-office attraction. Wives say to husbands, "I'm going to see some male strippers tonight," and the husbands don't snort in derision or say, "No, you can't go." The shirt-shedding, crotch-grabbing male entertainers attract more women than men.

Women are even more likely than men to shout, "Take it off!" while watching some form of entertainment, because men have been educated to think of this as sneaky and not-quite-nice when *anyone* they know is also present in the audience. Women don't have this restriction.

What age groups regard men as "beefcake?" Judging by the advertising we've seen, the typical emancipated woman—that is, a woman who was brought up to believe that nice girls don't ogle—is in the 30- to 45-year-old age group. The twentysome-things don't qualify because they were never taught that ogling isn't nice, and the over-45s are more social-stratum conscious than their younger sisters.

What's It All Mean?

Let's start with a cold-blooded point of view: To a fast-growing group of female targets, the dumb male is a potent sales weapon. If that dumb male also happens to have not-too-hairy a chest, a trim waistline, neatly firmed buttocks, and not-too-threatening a demeanor, so much the better.

Certainly this is cold-blooded assessment, just as all bald facts are cold-blooded. If we want to heat this up, we'll have to add some cautious 1990s qualifiers.

First, under no circumstances would anyone but the most doggedly determined gender-booster claim this is the advertiser's road to nirvana. Sexual connotations aside, the absolute rule of the road is:

■

Novelty wears thin faster than any other form of advertising.

■

The easiest proof is your own set of experiences. You see a "clever" commercial. Gee, wasn't that clever! Second time: Here it is again. Ninth time: It's worn out. This isn't true with a more conventional type of sales message.

So the novelty of male bashing must be continually replenished from a new spring. It *has to* wear itself out from overuse unless, like fine wine, it's sipped sparingly.

Novelty aside, the sociological teeter-totter swings until the two sides are balanced. Certainly, in our lifetimes, we won't see a total role reversal with "Mr. Mom" typifying the male's role. Biology will prevent that regardless of what women want to have happen.

The result of all this awareness—which so often translates into sexual antagonism—might not, in Elizabethan or Victorian times, have resulted in equality. Today it does. We've seen too many research reports damning inequality in the workplace to think the ancient rules still apply today. And we've seen too many dumb blond men humiliated on the screen to think this bottoming of the

NOW Who's a Dumb Blond? Male-Bashing in 1990s Advertising   CHAPTER ELEVEN

209

seesaw won't reverse itself . . . at least to the point where the teeter-totter is balanced.

Want a guess? The year 2001.

☐ 1. The woman is generally the decision-maker in many 1990s buying situations. If your target is the 1990s woman, has your advertising put her in charge of the situation you've set up?

☐ 2. The decisions the 1990s woman makes extend beyond buying decisions into a wider array of life's choices than her mother enjoyed. Are you mirroring that "new freedom" in your message?

☐ 3. Attitude often prevails over logic in advertising. Have you incorporated the attitude of the 1990s woman into your message?

☐ 4. Novelty wears thin quickly. Unless you have an unlimited advertising budget and can change your television commercials every few weeks, have you substituted sound selling arguments for a novelty situation?

☐ 5. The pendulum's swing is influenced by reactions to current events and male-bashing will inevitably be replaced by something different. Are you keeping your finger on the pulse of reactions to your advertising, instead of resting on past laurels?

Marketing Checklist— Chapter 11

CHAPTER 12

"I am sure we all agree that as we approach the next century the media are too important to leave to men alone."

— JUDY WOODRUFF
CO-CHAIR OF THE
INTERNATIONAL WOMEN'S
MEDIA FOUNDATION

Targeted Media:

To Reach Them, We Have to Know Where to Find Them

Thirty years ago, every daily newspaper and most weekly newspapers had a "Women's" section.

Editorial focus was narrow: A "Woman" was a homemaker who bought items for the home, raised children, cooked, and provided a pleasant environment for the family.

Only in 1992 did we begin to see a resurgence of "Women's" sections, no, not *resurgence*, but more accurately an addition to "Lifestyle" sections. One group of women—with family buying power—insists on being treated as women. Homemakers? Some of them are, but they aren't the apron-clad Donna Reeds of the 1950s and 1960s.

The "Lifestyle" section itself is unisex. Yes, it has recipes and advice columns, but both women and men read them, just as they read other inclusions in this section such as the bridge column, comics, horoscopes, and crossword puzzles.

Many newspapers have created sections aimed directly at women: the *Arizona Republic*, the *Plain Dealer* in Cleveland, and the *Herald-Leader* in Lexington.

A section aimed directly at women seems targeted at the upscale woman. In the *Chicago Tribune*, the "Womanews" (figure 12-1) section is labeled, "for and about Women on the Move" and it includes a classified ad section aimed at women.

Why are papers rededicating a group of pages to women, a reader segment once thought to be scrambled into a larger mix? Focus groups (which are always suspect but better than no evidence) said the paper had nothing expressly for them — "them" being, according to *Chicago Tribune* assistant managing editor Brenda Butler, quoted in the *Wall Street Journal*, women interested not only in child-rearing but in "health and fitness, entrepreneurship, and balance of family and career."

How many major newspapers, in 1960, had a woman as assistant managing editor? A guess: none.

But that's not the point. The point is that newspapers, more than any other medium, address cross-sections of society because their circulation is within a specific geographic area and has no reading-time specifics. So the appeal can't be vertical, or written for an exclusive target group. Broadcast stations also penetrate a specific geographic area, but these demand time-specificity. Magazines, on the other hand, are interest-specific and, except for metropolitan journals, geographically nonspecific.

The War Against Women

It may seem strange to see the war between the sexes still raging (quietly) during this decade. But evidence abounds.

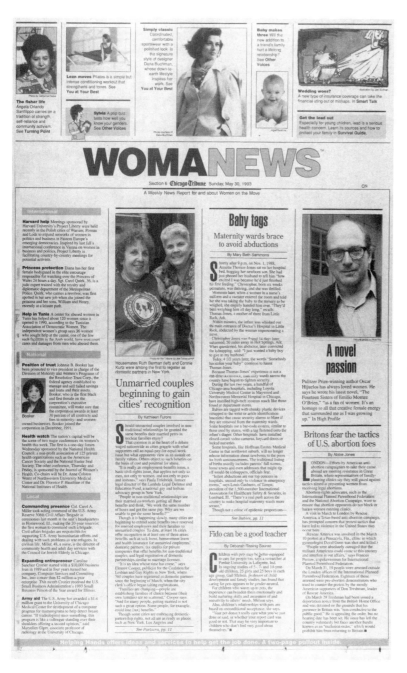

Figure 12-1
The "Womanews" section
of the Chicago Tribune
calls itself "A Weekly
News Report for and about
Women on the Move."

For example, Supreme Court Justice Clarence Thomas was a member of a panel that ruled a Connecticut woman could not get an FCC license for a radio station whose programming was declared to be aimed exclusively at women. The judicial argument: The station's focus was too narrow and would not serve the public interest.

Ver-r-r-y interesting . . . especially since so many radio stations are regularly licensed and renewed, targeting ethnic groups, foreign language listeners, and for that matter, music lovers—any group of which is numerically inferior to women.

Advertising in Women's Magazines

Shares, by publication, of advertising in leading women's magazines. Shares represent percentages of group total ad pages (6,266) for the first half of 1990.

Title	Shares
Vogue	21.6%
Cosmopolitan	17.5%
Glamour	14.3%
Good Housekeeping	13.3%
Woman's Day	12.0%
McCall's	7.8%
Working Woman	7.6%
Soap Opera Digest	3.3%
Woman	2.4%

Source: *Wall Street Journal*, July 26, 1990, p. B1, from Publishers Information Bureau.

The Angry Woman is a contemporary icon. A group called Fairness & Accuracy In Reporting (FAIR) has on its advisory board such individuals as Susan Faludi, Gloria Steinem, Eleanor Smeal, Susan Sarandon, and Callie Khouri—all of whom are well-known as super-active feminists.

FAIR's key mailing (figure 12-2) asks recipients, "Does media coverage of women make you mad?" The photo shows Anita Hill sitting at the Senate floor microphone. "The 'living room war' is back," the letter declares. "The 'backlash' against feminism is fueled by the media's own gender bias." The mailing asks for funds to help support FAIR's Women's Desk which "will corre-

Radio Format Preferences

Number of persons, in thousands, who listen to a station with a specified format any time during an average week.

Radio Format	All Adults	Women	Men
Adult Contemporary	31,401	16,774	14,657
All News	9,408	4,069	5,339
Album-Oriented Radio/Progressive Rock	19,401	7,737	11,664
Black	1,569	855	714
CHR/Rock	26,445	14,053	12,392
Classic Rock	6,780	2,447	4,333
Classical	3,573	2,025	1,548
Country	28,743	14,219	14,524
Easy Listening	9,602	5,589	4,013
Golden Oldies	11,240	5,182	6,058
Jazz	2,246	1,007	1,239
MOR/Nostalgia	6,208	2,936	3,271
News/Talk	16,348	6,929	9,419
Religious/Gospel	5,425	3,380	2,045
Soft Contemporary	5,141	2,793	2,348
Urban Contemporary	9,995	5,247	4,748

Source: Selected from *Mediamark Research Multimedia Audiences Report, Spring 1990*, p. 3 (New York: Mediamark Research Inc., 1990). Reprinted by permission.

spond regularly with journalists to make them aware of inaccuracies, imbalance and underreported or missed stories."

From another point of view, the *Los Angeles Times*, reporting right after the Clarence Thomas hearings, quoted Nancy DeStefanis, cochairperson of Women Are Good News as saying, "This is a terrific year for all-woman [television] programs." She cites the PBS news analysis series, "To the Contrary" and CNN's "Crier and Company," both of which are moderated by women. Nina Totenburg, the journalist who reported Anita Hill's sexual harassment allegations against Clarence Thomas, hosts "To the Contrary." According to the same *Los Angeles Times* article, Totenburg maintains that the predominantly male perspective in journalism sometimes reveals only half the story.

Figure 12-2
Direct Mail fund raising
piece targeted to angry
women shortly after the
Clarence Thomas hearings.

Cathrine Crier of "Crier and Company," a news interview show, features women as guests, but not to the exclusion of men. "We tend to showcase women," she says, "but if the debate requires a male guest, then by all means."

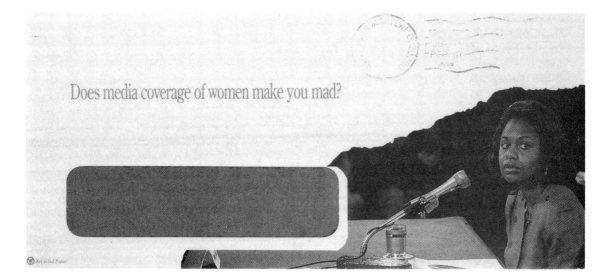

Does media coverage of women make you mad?

Recycled Paper

So as women ponder which camp to join, history will judge this period not on the basis of who gets the most airtime, but on the basis of total awareness of women's issues.

News Inc., a newspaper trade publication, commented in late 1992, "The bottom line for publishers is that women have been abandoning newspapers just when their demographics and buying power are most commanding." As evidence, *News Inc.* claimed that between 1970 and 1990, newspaper readership among women fell 18 percent, as opposed to 12.5 percent among men.

Which Newspaper Reports it Right?

Some papers believed the answer was to create Women's sections. Feminist Susan Faludi calls the restoration of Women's sections "a step backward."

Are either of these opinions valid?

In my opinion, only partly. Newspapers print what they think will sell papers. If they're losing women, the knee-jerk reaction is to print what women want to read. A Women's section is no more a step backward than a circulation-building contest.

As for the original loss of readership, any number of possible causes exist, including a downshifting of women's interests as they enter the work force and depend on other media. Does the 18 percent drop in readership mean fewer women than men read newspapers? Or was the original balance predominantly female, which would mean the new statistics reflect a more unisex society?

If a newspaper had no Sports section, some men would buy another paper. So would *some* women. If the Financial section were removed, *some* men and *some* women would drop their subscriptions. If adding a Women's section attracts more readers without repelling others, why not keep the circulation level as high as possible? Much of a newspaper's appeal lies in its inner-section division into special-interest segments, as long as it holds total community appeal within the main news sections.

You Mean the Lifetime Channel Is Aimed at Women?

Men who don't see the Lifetime Cable Channel's advertising in trade media are often blissfully unaware that this channel regards itself as a women's channel.

But *Advertising Age* quoted Doug McCormick, CEO of Hearst/ABC-Viacom Entertainment Services—parent company of

Newspaper Readership			
Daily and Sunday newspaper readership, in thousands, 1990.			
	All Adults	Females	Males
Total	180,974	94,667	86,307
Daily newspapers: read any	104,220	53,600	50,621
Read one daily	82,253	44,183	38,070
Read two or more dailies	21,968	9,417	12,551
Sunday newspapers: read any	117,846	61,402	56,444
Read one Sunday	104,283	54,668	49,615
Read two or more Sundays	13,563	6,734	6,830

Source: Selected from *Mediamark Research Multimedia Audiences Report, Spring 1990,* p. 2 (New York: Mediamark Research Inc., 1990).

Lifetime—as calling it "the first network for women." McCormick said he wants to increase awareness of Lifetime among female TV viewers. Male viewers? Not mentioned.

Here's how targeting is formulated: A study for *TV Guide* indicated that 47 percent of the women polled think television has "too much violence." Only 24 percent of the men share that view. So Lifetime shows reruns of "L.A. Law" but not "Miami Vice."

(A curiosity tied to the fallacy of such studies: The second strongest objection attributed to women (37 percent, as opposed to 15 percent of men) is "too much sex." Yet from its inception, the

Circulation of Women's Publications	
Women's periodicals with paid circulation over 500,000.	
Title	Circulation
Canadian Living Magazine	515,756
Chatelaine	1,089,496
Cosmopolitan	2,778,497
Country Woman	650,000
Family Circle	5,212,555
First	2,000,000
Glamour	2,273,039
Good Housekeeping	5,114,774
Health	800,000
Ladies' Home Journal	5,117,712
Mademoiselle	1,141,271
McCall's	5,088,686
New Woman	1,390,830
Playgirl	600,000
SELF Magazine	1,173,440
Shape	794,675
True Story	1,240,252
Woman's Day	4,705,288
Working Woman Magazine	903,704

Source: Selected from *Gale Directory of Publications and Broadcast Media 1991*, p. 2691+ (Detroit: Gale Research Inc., 1991).

Lifetime channel has been loaded with sex, including Dr. Ruth
Westheimer's more-than-candid comments . . . and for that matter,
reruns of "L.A. Law.")

Get this: In 1993 *Telenation Reports*, a service of Market Facts,
reported that violence *in advertising* bothers an astounding 76 percent of women polled. Quick, now: Think of a commercial that
includes violence. Reebok once committed a colossal gaffe by
showing a boy bungee-jumping off a bridge; the athletic shoes
stayed hooked to the bungee cord while the boy disappeared into
the depths. This is as close to "violence" as most memories can
recall.

	Television Viewing Time Hours and minutes per week spent watching television, by age.				
Age	Hours and minutes of viewing time				
	Mon-Fri 10am-4:30pm	Mon-Fri 4:30pm-7:30pm	Mon-Sun 8-11 pm	Sat 7am-1pm	Mon-Fri 11:30pm-1am
Total women age 18+	5:55	4:44	9:49	:38	1:18
18-24	4:55	3:18	6:43	:32	:57
25-54	5:06	3:52	9:18	:39	1:20
55+	7:52	6:55	12:06	:38	1:22
Female Teens 12-17	2:40	3:30	6:27	:46	:36
Total men age 18+	3:31	3:46	9:05	:40	1:20
18-24	2:56	2:35	5:55	:33	1:14
25-54	2:56	3:05	8:46	:41	1:20
55+	5:37	6:07	11:46	:41	1:23
Male Teens 12-17	2:20	3:35	7:16	:55	:49

Source: "Average Television Viewing Time," *World Almanac and Book of Facts 1991*, p. 317 (New York: Pharos Books, 1991). Primary source: Nielsen Media Research. Also in source: data for men and children. As of February 1990.

So why would 76 percent of women say violence in television commercials turns them off? Are researchers setting up straw men as artificial targets?

Another questionable statistic: The same report showed 63 percent of women objecting to sexual activity in commercials, against 34 percent of men. But where does the suggestion of sexual activity appear most often? It's in television advertising targeting women—perfumes and designer jeans.

Fewer women than men eat dinner while watching television, many more women than men change channels to prevent their children from watching a show, and an equal number of men and women watch the home shopping channels.

Multi-set homes are the norm these days, especially among families with the buying power television advertisers seek. So a woman can watch Show "A" while the man watches Show "B"; in fact, this is exactly what happens about 20 percent of the time.

We have to remember: Respondents to surveys tend to philosophize on a level far higher than they actually observe. For example, 27 percent of women reportedly object to *all* television advertising. Now there's a great statistic.

Does sex sell? This report says no, not to women. The report also claims one of four women objects to ads for feminine hygiene products (only half the men do!). Question: Are the women who object to ads for feminine hygiene products the same women who *buy* feminine hygiene products? That's the key question, because sophisticated advertisers learned, long ago, a primitive rule of salesmanship:

■

Alienating determined nonbuyers has little
effect on the advertiser's bottom line.

■

Note the word "determined." Sophisticated advertisers also know
they have only two major sources of increased business: 1) inten-
sified use among existing buyers, and 2) recruitment of "plastic
attitude" nonbuyers.

Magazines Are
ALWAYS Targeted
Which woman's magazine group, month after month, carries the
most advertising?

You guessed it: bridal magazines. In a recent count of magazine
advertising linage, *Advertising Age* reported that the current
month's *Bridal Guide* carried 202 pages of advertising. Compare
that with 83 for *Family Circle*, 26.6 for *Mirabella*, 63 for *Vogue*, 60
for *Working Woman*, and 68 for *McCall's*.

One reason advertisers have to stay with bridal magazines is the
quick turnover of readership. The trade term is "lifetime value."
Except for some movie stars, women aren't brides more than two
or three times, and they don't regard themselves as the "something borrowed, something blue" type of bride more than once a
lifetime. So advertisers have to appear in every issue if they don't
want to miss the bridal train.

A "hot" new magazine is Condé Nast's *Allure*, which published its
first issue in 1991 and carried more than 183 pages of advertising
in the first quarter of 1993, up more than 70 percent from the previous year. Circulation is above 600,000 and climbing. What
makes it hot?

The cover doesn't give much of a clue. Featured articles have bland titles such as "Eight Ways to Save Your Skin" and "Beauty Sleep — New Cures for Insomnia." This type of article is old-hat among the Seven Sisters — *McCall's*, *Ladies' Home Journal*, *Redbook*, *Family Circle*, *Women's Day*, *Better Homes and Gardens*, and *Good Housekeeping*.

Advertising Age's editor's explanation may be at variance with what many women *think* is the reason for a magazine's success in the mid-1990s. The editor's analysis is that the magazine was too avant-garde in the beginning, and gained reader loyalty only after moving back toward a more traditional content — as witness the type of articles in its pages.

Along with its traditional approach to reader-appeal, *Allure* moved its graphics and visual appeal far ahead. The security reflected by articles founded in absolute reality combined with stunning visuals founded in a "tomorrow" type of layout, was the successful formula.

Note, please, that *Allure's* covers and graphics aren't "far out." This approach was what gave the magazine an uncertain start. Rather, the magazine's visual appeal reflects the image of its target: trendy, "with it," reader-friendly and still "hip."

This is the niche other magazines haven't filled. Any magazine, to survive, has to pick its spot and hammer away. Each of the "Seven Sisters" parallels the others while maintaining its own identity, without which it would have no *raison d'être*.

To appeal to the 1990s woman, the Seven Sisters have modernized both their image and their editorial content. For example, *McCall's* has moved toward *Cosmopolitan* with articles that would have been too daring for this magazine a decade ago, such as:

"What Other Couples Do In Bed" and "The New Secret to a Sexier Marriage." *Redbook* joined the heat-up trend with "Sex and the Single Mom" and "Menopause in Your 30s." *Adweek* credited the editor of *Family Circle* with a telling quote: "The days when we could get a woman's attention simply by putting a chocolate cake on the cover are over."

Valerie Muller, media director at DeWitt Media, describes the Seven Sisters as giving readers "a little bit of everything, a taste of all parts of life. It's escape for women that doesn't cost much."

A magazine such as *Working Woman* might reach the same reader as *Allure* or the Seven Sisters, by addressing a different plane of their existence. *Working Woman* carries automobile ads for the woman who buys a car for herself, not for her family. An appeal to independent thinking underlies both the editorial content and the advertising in this magazine, and some advertisers create ads especially for this niche. *Working Woman* regularly carries about 60 percent more advertising than *Working Mother.* Why? The independence factor is only part of the reason. Right or wrong, advertisers are responding to a perceived difference in discretionary buying power.

What about *Vogue* and its lesser competitor *Harper's Bazaar?* Again, these are niche publications, neither with the editorial power it had in the 1960s . . . because these magazines no longer reflect "fashion" as a genre; they reflect *one facet* of fashion, albeit the highest facet.

Publications aimed at health-conscious women represent a huge growth area. Most women's magazines have always carried articles concerning health and fitness, but the 1990s have spawned a niche devoted to this area, including *Self, Shape,* and *Weight*

Watchers. Of this group, *Shape* is (at press time) the champion, averaging about 70 pages of ads.

Magazines such as *Prevention, Longevity,* and *American Health* parallel these fitness magazines, with one difference: *Prevention, Longevity,* and *American Health* are unisex; *Self, Shape,* and *Weight Watchers* are women's magazines. In this era of hyper-specialization, not all will survive. The most targeted publication has the best chance, provided the target is big enough.

(A curiosity: *Weight Watchers* is a self-declared women's magazine, although many men belong to Weight Watchers.)

Gee! Yellow Pages Just for Us!

If you don't live in an area in which somebody is publishing and circulating *Women's Yellow Pages* (figure 12-3), don't worry: This book will soon be in your area, but it isn't free.

How can anyone get away with charging money for a specialty Yellow Pages book? Answer: Hyper-targeting, plus the implicit edge the Yellow Pages have over all other media.

Yellow pages are the most targeted of all media, even more so than direct mail. Want proof?

If I send you a piece of mail, knowing you have a three-year-old car, I've reached someone who should logically be a new car buyer.

If, on the other hand, I advertise new cars in the Yellow Pages, and you see my ad, I've reached someone who *is* a new car buyer. You don't look in the Yellow Pages until and unless you have a buying impulse.

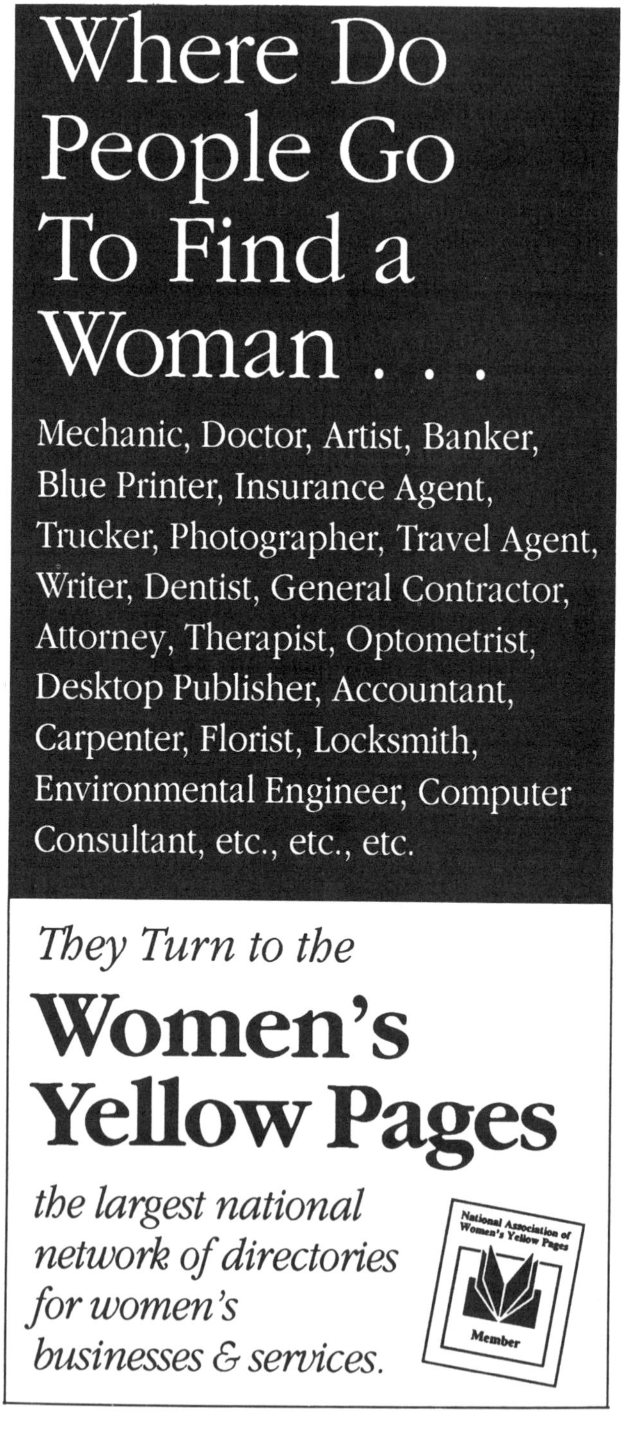

Figure 12-3
Yellow Pages just for
women? Yes. And they're
so popular, women pay
$10 and more for a new
copy every year.

Where Do People Go To Find a Woman . . .

Mechanic, Doctor, Artist, Banker, Blue Printer, Insurance Agent, Trucker, Photographer, Travel Agent, Writer, Dentist, General Contractor, Attorney, Therapist, Optometrist, Desktop Publisher, Accountant, Carpenter, Florist, Locksmith, Environmental Engineer, Computer Consultant, etc., etc., etc.

They Turn to the

Women's Yellow Pages

the largest national network of directories for women's businesses & services.

National Association of
Women's Yellow Pages
Member

Accepting that, what's the rationale behind a *Women's Yellow Pages*, especially since it is neither an "official" phone company directory nor free?

Three components: First, some of the listings don't exist in the conventional *Yellow Pages* directory—battered wives' help groups and shelters, lesbian groups and clubs.

Second, the very existence of the word "Women's" on the cover is a reassurance that the listed vendors are soliciting women's business. A plumber listed in this directory is less apt to give us one of those "Now, little lady" down-the-nose comments. In fact, the plumber might be a woman.

Third, hyper-targeting itself is "in." A *Women's Yellow Pages* is implicitly more selective than Yellow Pages aimed at everyone.

Is the concept valid? As recently as 1990, almost no one had even heard of this type of publication. As of this writing, *Women's Yellow Pages* are available in most metropolitan areas.

(How about *Men's Yellow Pages?* Are you kidding?)

The Expanding Media Universe

Women's media are expanding, even as general media are contracting. Increased attention by advertisers within both traditional and new media is a fact, not a speculation.

As the twenty-first century dawns, women are more than an advertising segment. As targets, we have divided and subdivided again, offering advertisers many ways to reach us. Advertisers, in turn, have begun to tailor their messages not only to women, but to women based on the individual appeal of a particular advertising medium.

That's progress—for the advertiser as well as for the advertiser's target.

Marketing Checklist—
Chapter 12

☐ 1. Media focus changes and expands every day. Are you keeping abreast of your changing media options?

☐ 2. Are you monitoring your media choices not only for changes in reader-content appeal, but changes in graphics-visual appeal as well?

☐ 3. Some media choices represent unique reader niches. Are you testing ads created specifically for these niches?

☐ 4. The woman of the 1990s is in the marketing spotlight, and new media are being created to solicit business exclusively from her. Does your media plan include future tests of these new media to reach her?

CHAPTER 13

"I won't

settle for

skimpy towels.

Why should you?"

— LEONA HELMSLEY

The Traveling Woman:

Packing a Wallop in the

Business Travel Industry

According to the U.S. Travel Data Center, of the 35.1 million Americans who travel on business every year, nearly 40 percent are women.

That's about a 15 percent hike since 1980. And both the ratio and the total numbers of women are rising at a strong pace.

What do these women want when they travel?

According to a recent study by Wyndham Hotels in Dallas, asking women what they *don't* want gives marketers a better understanding of what they do want. (How true this is of so much "attitudinal" research!)

For example, topping the list of pet peeves was "Unfriendly and Inefficient Front Desk Personnel." Just under three-quarters of

The Traveling Woman's Pet Peeves

women polled expressed displeasure at finding a less than warm greeting at check-in.

Why is this, especially since so many "front desk" personnel are female? The answer may lie in the vestiges of a societal position that dates back to Abraham: The man should be the out-of-home (read out-of-office) explorer. Every indication suggests we're less than a single generation away from eliminating this nasty syndrome, but why wait?

(Gender aside, men complain almost as much as women **do**, which may be a potent damning of the way front desk personnel are trained in the first place, but women's complaints are more likely to be based on being treated as "the little woman" and less on the professionalism of the desk personnel.)

The businesswoman of the 1990s retains a sensitivity parallel to that of a prisoner recently released because late evidence found her innocent. Certainly schools with courses in hospitality management should consider the temper of the times . . . which includes genuine hospitality, or at least the appearance of genuine hospitality.

Second on the list of pet peeves is "Rooms that Smell Stale," followed closely by "Unfriendly and Inefficient Service Personnel." Here we can't draw a gender-conclusion, because equal numbers of men and women voiced this complaint. But consider: We're in the first generation—or, even in the most sophisticated business setting, the second generation—of female business travelers. Think back to when *you* were first on the road. Weren't you less than likely to register a complaint, if only because you hadn't enough background to assess what the accommodations *should* be?

This suggests that even though statistics indicate gender equivalence, hotels actually continue to demonstrate greater deference to the traveling man than to the traveling woman.

Add an obbligato theme to this mix: The typical woman business traveler, according to the U.S. Travel Data Center, is both older and less-educated than the typical traveling man. Now stir this

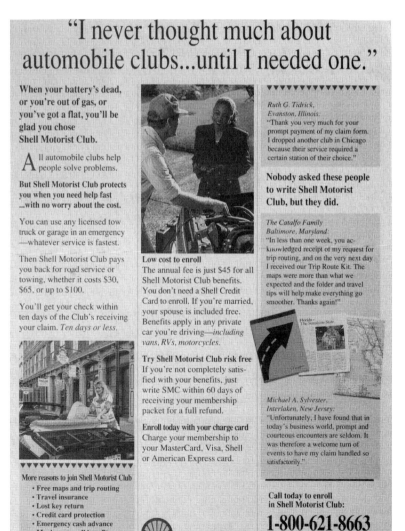

Figure 13-1
This ad for Shell Motorist Club plays up to a woman's need for security when she's on the road.

into the professional and psychological stew, and recognize what it does to the question:

So what do traveling businesswomen want?

Before drawing even an empirical conclusion, ask yourself a second question: Will today's answer be valid in the year 2025? Or for that matter, in 2010?

The sexual harassment issue is the tip of the iceberg, but when women travel it's a considerably bigger tip because the corporate cocoon has vanished. Misplaced sensitivity may be a problem, and misinterpretation of attitude *on both* sides of a negotiation — in the boardroom and across the check-in desk — can skew any answer to a survey question.

A recent poll by *Working Woman* magazine leaves little doubt about what this magazine's traveling readership wants *right now:* luxury, security, and service. (But then, who doesn't?)

What Does She Want Right Now? Topping the luxury list were the following: remote control TV, a thick terry robe, toiletries in the bath, complimentary limo service, two-line phones, overnight shoeshine service, 24-hour room service, and a business center equipped with fax machines, copiers, and secretaries.

Suppose the magazine were called *Working Man.* Would that list differ at all? In fact, as you read this, regardless of your gender, can you think of a logical addition to this list? That's why the differential may be a non-factor even sooner than the year 2010.

A footnote to the security aspect: Trade advertising has begun to follow the consumer lead. Take, for example, VingCard. This company manufactures the perforated key-cards that have replaced metal keys in many hotels. VingCard uses as its illustration in *Hospitality*—a hotel trade magazine—a woman, attaché case in hand, using the VingCard to enter her hotel room (figure 13-2). The headline: "With Our Name on the door, you and your Guests rest easier."

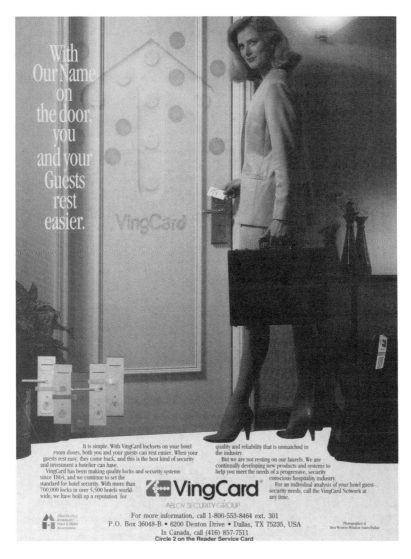

Figure 13-2
Consumer advertisers aren't the only ones to benefit by aiming their messages at women; trade ads are also hopping on the bandwagon.

We can ignore the semiprofessional random capitalization and the type reversed out of a light-colored background, but we can't ignore the logic of showing a female business traveler in an ad tied to hotel security. Women are—and should be, given the sex, strength, and nature of the typical intruder—more concerned about hotel security than men.

So trade advertising is catching on. Women do rent hotel rooms, in considerable numbers. Suppliers give customers (hotels) the same benefits those hotels give *their* customers (hotel guests) in order to convince the hotels to choose that supplier . . . who is marketing to women even when women aren't the direct target of the campaign.

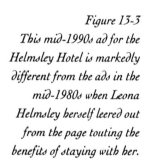

Figure 13-3
This mid-1990s ad for the Helmsley Hotel is markedly different from the ads in the mid-1980s when Leona Helmsley herself leered out from the page touting the benefits of staying with her.

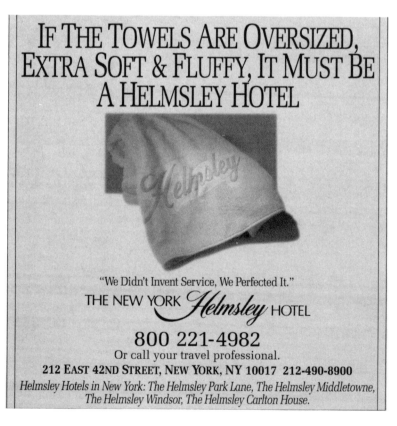

IF THE TOWELS ARE OVERSIZED, EXTRA SOFT & FLUFFY, IT MUST BE A HELMSLEY HOTEL

"We Didn't Invent Service, We Perfected It."

THE NEW YORK *Helmsley* HOTEL

800 221-4982

Or call your travel professional.

212 EAST 42ND STREET, NEW YORK, NY 10017 212-490-8900

Helmsley Hotels in New York: The Helmsley Park Lane, The Helmsley Middletowne, The Helmsley Windsor, The Helmsley Carlton House.

The 1980s ads for the Helmsley Palace, rigidly supervised by "The Queen of Mean," Leona Helmsley, were famous not only for their glorification of Leona Helmsley above the glorification of the hotel. They were also notorious because the various advertising agencies that placed these ads pointed out (sometimes in self-defense) that Mrs. Helmsley was the generating force behind them.

Mean, Miserable, and Far Ahead of Her Time

Yes, Leona Helmsley went down in flames. Yes, her queenly image dissolved like Dorian Gray when she wanted to appear old and infirm in court. That may be of interest to social historians (and to the Internal Revenue Service). In this chronicle of women's roles as initiators and recipients of advertising messages, Leona Helmsley has a special place; her ads were far ahead of their time.

What qualifies her ads as "breakthrough?"

First, the obvious difference was that the hotel's icon was female. After the suave Conrad Hilton and Bill Marriott, this was an invasion into hallowed male ranks by a gutsy, hard-spoken outsider.

Second, unlike other hotel spokespeople, Leona Helmsley used the word "Queen" in the taglines. By using "I won't settle for skimpy towels. Why should you?" she made it clear to all ad readers that her position wasn't that of queen; she was the Empress. Female dominance in a hotel catering primarily to men! Oh, yes, this was a breakthrough campaign.

Could Ivana Trump, sometime titular "president" of the fallen Plaza Hotel, have succeeded in a parallel series of ads? Not likely, because Ivana Trump symbolized plastic-surgery glamour, not chutzpah. She was a throwback-image, a sort of nineteenth-century play-toy of a rich real estate baron husband who gave his play-toy wife a toy of her own.

What hath Leona wrought?

History will not treat this woman kindly. But she is the Daniel Boone of female spokespersons. Others have followed—others less abrasive, less megalomaniacal, and, yes, less effective. Leona blazed a trail that has widened into a promotional superhighway. In the mid-1990s, we accept women as imperious heads of organizations *without* devoting attention to their womanhood. Would this have happened so soon without Leona?

Caution: The Artificial World

You heard it here first; attitude surveys are suspect.

They're suspect because too often they have no relationship with reality. A parallel: The real estate company asks, in its ad for vacant land, "Do you prefer waterfront? Wooded? Rolling meadow? All three?" But the ad doesn't point out the obvious; each of these options means a big jump in cost.

So the results of the survey by *Working Woman,* which "asked more than 100 frequent travelers to name the hotels that truly cater to businesswomen," were no more surprising than would be

Women on Business and Pleasure Trips

Total business and pleasure trips in millions and percent female travelers, 1987–1991.

Characteristic	Business Trips			Pleasure Trips		
	1987	1988	1991	1987	1988	1991
Total trips, in millions	7.5	155.6	150.6	444.9	455.3	495.0
Female travelers, in percent	32%	31%	38.2%	53%	50%	47%

Source: U.S. Travel Data Center, Washington, DC, *National Travel Survey,* annual; and unpublished data.

the results of a survey asking whether these women preferred to travel economy or first class.

Example: The 15 "preferred" hotels include the Ritz-Carlton in Atlanta, Boston, and Chicago . . . the Four Seasons in Beverly Hills . . . well, you get the idea. A bargain-priced *commercial* hotel? You'd have to add a clinker-question into the survey, relating choice to cost.

As women become more and more entrepreneurial, their decisions regarding where to stay, where to dine on the road, what class of travel to choose, and how much to spend on entertainment become as implicit as which clothes to take. A survey of this type, in 2010, will surely relate its results to reality.

An indication of the increase in distaff travel is exemplified in a late 1992 study by Simmons Market Research Bureau. The study showed a dramatic increase in percentile share of car rentals by women, which climbed from 30 percent in 1980 to 42 percent in 1991.

Driving Into the Mainstream

In preparing this book neither I nor my researcher could find a pre-1984 car rental ad aimed directly at women. Figures 13-4, 13-5, and 13-6 show how the 1990s have wrought a major change. Car rental ads are unisex or female-aimed, and that goes for general-interest and inflight magazine insertions as well.

Figure 13-4, the Avis ad, in a *general interest* magazine, is 120 percent female-oriented, without once singling out our gender. The illustration is of a woman. The narrated circumstance has no gender, but the headline (weak in my opinion) — "Avis. We make the road a little less lonely."—would make a male reader feel less masculine.

One can fault Avis for subliminal alienation of the macho male reader and the aggressively independent woman by emphasizing loneliness rather than security; still, we recognize the purpose of this ad.

Figure 13-4
The headline for this ad isn't as strong as it might have been, but we can't argue the emphasis on security when aiming an ad to the traveling woman.

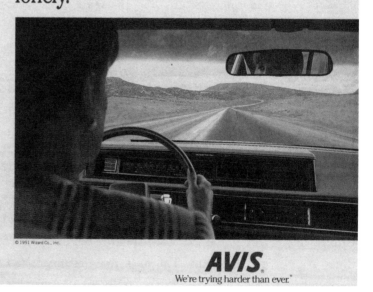

You've been on the road since 5 a.m. You haven't seen another car for miles. You never expected this was the road to success. But you're in control.

Because, when you rent an Avis car, we make sure that it's completely roadworthy. With our 49-Step Quality Control Program. Checking that things work the way they're supposed to. Brakes stop. Seat belts buckle. And the wipers wipe. Because no matter where you are, it does rain sometimes.

Whatever you need to know about the car and local driving conditions, we'll show you. Just look at our handy "Avis Cares℠" guides. They tell you where to find the brights when you need them. Whether you can make a right turn on red. Even what radio station to tune in for local driving conditions and weather reports. It's how we make driving a strange car on a strange road a little more familiar.

And, just in case something unexpected happens, we're ready to help you out. Just call our 24-Hour Hotline telephone number for assistance. It's printed right on your rental folder. Even if you just locked the keys inside your car, give us a call.

So, when we say, "We're trying harder than ever," that means a lot more than just our low rates. A lot more than free unlimited mileage no matter how far you drive. A lot more than getting you in and out of airports fast. When you travel with us, it's a not-so-lonesome road.

For reservations or information, call Avis at **1-800-331-1212** or your travel consultant today.

Avis.
We make the road a little less lonely.

© 1991 Wizard Co., Inc.

AVIS
We're trying harder than ever.

"The Avis Comfort Factor" (figure 13-5) is a more conventional approach to car rentals. The driver is a woman, but the pitch—a free upgrade—is commercial. Throughout the ad, the word "business" complements the clever psychology behind having a woman driver. Men won't object because the text is unisex; women might not sense themselves as a target if the driver were a man.

Figure 13-5
A more conventional ad.
The model is a woman,
and the ad works for
either gender.

"Discover the Avis Corporate Account Program" (figure 13-6) shows a businessman and a businesswoman. Could anyone possibly object to having the man entering the car on the driver's side? Probably not. On the other hand, some might object if the woman were the driver, because some vestige of the Age of Chivalry would jar a few memories on both sides.

Figure 13-6
Even stronger dual-gender
appeal, since both a man
and a woman are featured.

The Budget ad (figure 13-7), too, appeared in a general interest magazine. Budget's appeal is wide open: with such statements as "Beth Williams knows how to raise her standard of travel without raising her travel costs" and "as travel-savvy as Beth Williams." The ad places her in a position of absolute equivalence with the most sophisticated male car renter.

Figure 13-7
Testimonial-style ad starts
by building the credibility of
the woman, then uses her as
testimonial to build the
credibility of the product.

Budget has persistently pursued women's business. The "Smart Money Is On Budget" theme is subtly female-oriented, since "smart" is slightly more feminine than masculine. (The masculine counterpart: "shrewd.") The company's sponsorship of women's sports events has reached the $1 million level. The percentage of women renting cars from Budget has increased every year.

Stress: A Natural Evolution? Women's share of the stress factor seems to have jumped, too—a natural evolution (or devolution) as they take their places in the various chains of command. For example, while men's share of cigarettes purchased has dropped, women's share has increased. Women now buy more wine and tequila than men, they're running dead even on rum, and their market share has leaped from 30 percent to 42 percent for scotch.

These increases may be due as much to equality of buying decisions as to stress, and, like so many statistics, they may be better-positioned as curiosities than as market indicators. But unquestionably *some* portion of the leap in percentages has to be the result of greater targeting of women for these products. Wine is an obvious example, because this is one product whose changing ratios have to be tied to independent choice. For decades, table wines had been the province of the housewife. Now, in many households (and at many dinner tables at the Ritz-Carlton), the woman is at least as likely as her male dinner partner to choose the wine, and to do so knowledgeably.

Just Who IS the Frequent Flyer? A dependable chronicle of the changing face (and figure) of frequent flyers is the group of magazines nesting in the seat-pockets of every major airline.

Comparing the advertising in the pages of these magazines 10 years ago with today's ads powerfully demonstrates how women have surged to the forefront as comparable seatmates. For example, AT&T ran figure 13-8 to near-saturation in 1993. The headline: "Getting to gate 87 in two minutes isn't always easy. Calling AT&T is." Illustration? — a heel broken off a woman's shoe.

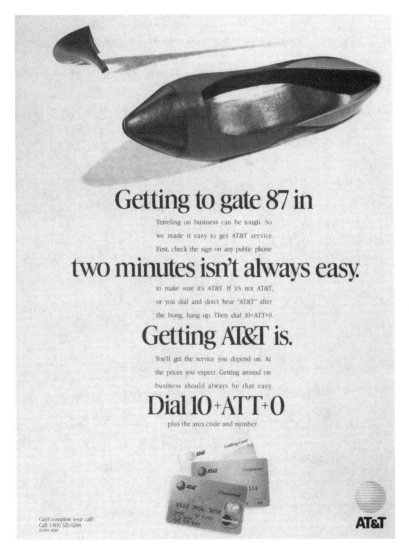

Figure 13-8
The problem, getting to the gate on time, has no gender. The illustration used is definitely woman-specific.

Will men read this ad? Why not? The *problem* has no gender; that AT&T chose a totally female exemplar indicates a desire to recruit a new cadre of AT&T traveler-users. (First line of copy: "Traveling on business can be tough.")

Critics might fault AT&T for suggesting it takes two minutes to get the AT&T operator—a lifetime for the busy traveler. We

Figure 13-9
No mistaking who the
intended target here is.

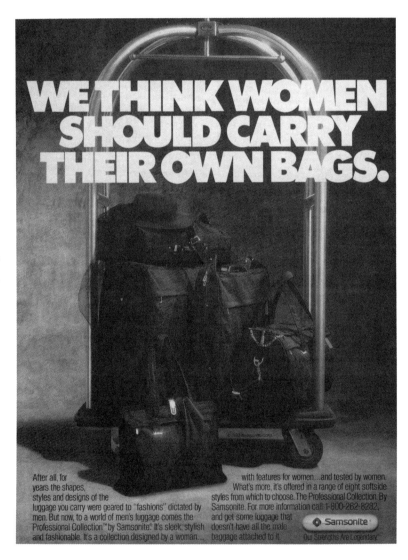

WE THINK WOMEN SHOULD CARRY THEIR OWN BAGS.

After all, for years the shapes, styles and designs of the luggage you carry were geared to "fashions" dictated by men. But now, to a world of men's luggage comes the Professional Collection™ by Samsonite. It's sleek, stylish and fashionable. It's a collection designed by a woman... with features for women...and tested by women. What's more, it's offered in a range of eight softside styles from which to choose. The Professional Collection. By Samsonite. For more information call 1-800-262-8282, and get some luggage that doesn't have all the male baggage attached to it.

◆ Samsonite

Our Strengths Are Legendary

might also note that the relationship between the illustration and concept is muddy. Our concern isn't with execution but with intent.

Samsonite also consistently advertises in frequent flyer magazines. Whose clothing hangs in a Samsonite case, under the heading, "Fly Through The Air With The Greatest Of Ease" (figure 13-9)? You guessed it: a woman's.

Emphasis on women as models and prototypes, in advertising aimed at the traveler, may ease as any recognition of a differential eases.

Planes, Trains, and Automobiles

Old-timers recall when politicians, courting the newly enfranchised woman voter, tailored messages to "My little lady." Cigarette manufacturers in the 1920s contributed to lung cancer statistics by showing "smart" women smoking. As society absorbed the change, however, the rationale for appealing to change disappeared.

Eventually, automobile rental agencies, hotels, and suitcase manufacturers will regard the gender a traveler represents as a nonissue.

Meanwhile, women are enjoying the attention!

☐ 1. Nearly 40% of business travelers are women. Is that much of your travel advertising tailored to the woman of the 1990s?

Marketing Checklist— Chapter 13

☐ 2. Security is a big concern to the traveling woman of the 1990s. Has your advertising put her fears to rest?

☐ 3. The percentage of women travelers has increased in the 1990s as well as the percentage of women decisionmakers in the hotel and travel trade. If you're a trade advertiser, do you target the woman of the 1990s in your business-to-business advertising?

☐ 4. Often women spend as much on business travel as men. Have you placed the female traveler in a position of absolute equivalence to the male traveler?

☐ 5. Have you selected women's business media to advertise your travel product or service?

CHAPTER

*"If American men
are obsessed with
money, American
women are obsessed
with weight. The
men talk of gain,
the women talk
of loss."*

— MARYA MANNES

Health and Fitness

Advertising: One Size

Doesn't Fit All

A 1992 study commissioned by the Pharmaceutical Manufacturers Association told us 79 drug makers were in the process of developing more than 250 drugs specifically for women.

How many of these drugs have a valid *raison d'être*? How many of these—of the hundreds that have already followed, and of the thousands more we'll see before the year 2001—will survive because they can project a sound reason to continue existing?

Obviously, the sales success of any drug or pharmaceutical depends on developing persuasive communications targeted not only to women, but, in the case of prescription drugs, at the targets' doctors as well.

From aspirin as a heart attack preventive to zinc as a nutritional supplement, medications are big business . . . and they're getting bigger.

**The Dual Target:
You Can't Reach One
Without the Other**

Two generations ago, doctors' recommendations weren't recommendations at all; they were edicts. "Take this twice a day, and I'll see you in two weeks."

Today, *more often than not*, the patient tells the doctor, "I want you to give me a prescription for Retin-A." The doctor meekly complies—not because doctors have lost their professionalism but because media exposure of even borderline medical developments has generated a sharing of information. Shared information equals partnership. Who can be a dictator in a partnership?

So the giant pharmaceutical companies have discovered that their secondary targets are now their primary targets. Consumer media regularly carry advertising—big, glossy, full-color advertising—for prescription drugs and medications the reader can't buy without a prescription from her doctor (figure 14-1).

Follow this twenty-first century logic:

The ratio of *elective* to mandatory surgery rises every year. What once was the province of fading movie stars ("tummy tucks," blepharoplasty, rhinoplasty) has moved to Main Street. Is it the physician who says, "You'd better schedule liposuction for those thighs?" Heck, no. The individual chooses a liposuction source from a plethora of medical candidates who hawk their services in almost every medium.

Follow this twenty-first century logic:

A woman calls her doctor to ask about a new "stop smoking" or "lose weight" drug—one available only by prescription. The doctor hasn't heard much about it.

How is that possible? Simple. In the mid–late 1990s, doctors may be immersed in professional publications that are loaded with

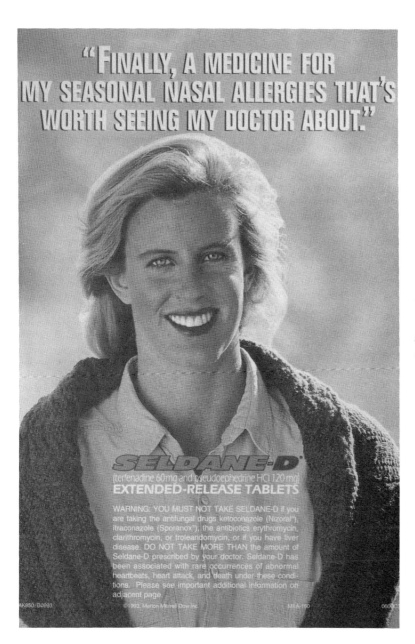

Figure 14-1
Seldane-D: just one type of
prescription product women
demand from their doctors.

arcane, off-the-beaten-path developments. The patient, on the other hand, is exposed to mainline advertising by shrewd pharmaceutical houses. So targeted advertising reaches the decision-maker — which, after all, is the whole idea behind targeted advertising.

The woman of the 1920s wouldn't have dared to make a bold suggestion to her doctor. Today, she feels guilty if she doesn't.

Doctors Join the Gold Rush Some readers may regard the above subhead as a satire, based on the reputation of doctors (paralleling lawyers) as greed-motivated; but who isn't?

Doctors compete, just as any other professional competes. Figure 14-2, an insert in *Lear's*, delivers an exemplary pitch:

■

Putting your face in hands you can trust
Finding a facial plastic surgeon

■

And who placed and paid for this insert? The American Academy of Facial Plastic and Reconstructive Surgery (a group of more than 3,000 physicians) did. Some 87 AAFPRS members participated in the insert, which listed their names, addresses, and phone numbers. How does this differ from a designer listing stores where a fashion is available?

(A more pertinent question to ask, given the role reversals of the 1990s, is: Why didn't those doctors put a similar ad in *Esquire*?)

Since the walls isolating doctors, lawyers, and accountants from the rest of us crumbled in the 1970s, advertising by these groups has become more and more aggressive — and competitive.

Now, follow this logic:

What good is advertising if the women at whom you aim it don't know what you're talking about? So, in a competitive milieu, doctors can't resent the latter-day medical education of those they once dominated through their intramural set of mysteries. In fact, they *have to* welcome it.

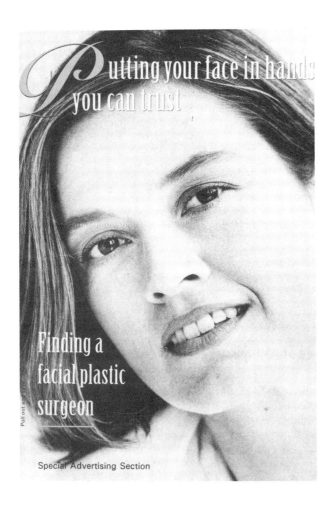

Figure 14-2
Ads for doctors were
unheard of in the early
1980s. In the 1990s doctors
form advertising coalitions.

Health and Fitness:
Moving Beyond
Equality

Equal opportunity has made some fields *super*-equal for women. No, not in football or tennis, but they do enjoy parity in health-related awareness and the determination to act on that awareness.

The research firm Louis Harris & Associates, Inc. reported that women pay more attention to the state of their health than men do. They scrutinize nutritional labeling in their buying decisions

Women's Health Trends

	Total female frequent participants (000)	Percent of all women
Total frequent participants: at least one fitness sport	23,792	27.7%
Aerobic exercising	4,514	5.3%
Bicycle riding	2,054	2.4%
Calisthenics	1,311	1.5%
Exercise walking	16,706	19.4%
Exercising with equipment	5,147	6.0%
Running/jogging	1,190	1.4%
Swimming	1,488	1.7%

Note: Frequent participation is defined as 110 or more days per year. *Source: Marketing to Women,* January, 1993 (Boston, MA: About Women, Inc., 1993). *Primary source:* National Sporting Goods Association.

more than men do (48 percent of women do so compared to just 28 percent of men). They monitor their stress levels more often (36 percent vs. 28 percent of men), and women are more likely to admit to being overweight than their male counterparts (75 percent compared to 59 percent).

A nonscientific addendum: Women are more likely than men to *discuss* such situations. This addendum can be of great significance to the advertiser, not only because of the "trickle-down" value of startling and/or sinister health-related statements, but also because almost no bugaboos are left in the closet in the wide-open 1990s.

Today, every bump on the skin, every flush, every tiny irregularity is monitored as though it were an approaching comet from outer space. Our grandmothers would have said, "It's nothing," until they expired quietly from an ailment that might have been treated. Today we say, "It's something" and we demand treatment for an ailment that may not, in fact, require it.

Awareness is the symbol of our time. In fact, *super*-awareness is often the sign of our time. The media have done their job. (Most television newscasts now have a regular "Health" feature, and most of the content of that feature is female-oriented.)

Are we breeding a generation of hypochondriacs through overattention to medical trivia? Women have health concerns men don't have, of course, resulting in a *booming* women's health care industry.

Compare these figures from the same Louis Harris study. In 1979, just 20 percent of women had mammogram tests. By 1990, that figure had risen to 65 percent. A full 80 percent have Pap smear tests at least every two years.

Controlling health costs was among the top three priorities named by women voters in the 1992 election, along with reducing unemployment and reducing the budget deficit.

Seriousness Begets Seriousness

Advertising copywriters enjoy being clever and funny. That may be why so much advertising misses its target. In the case of medical advertising, cleverness can be suicidal. Even the most flippant individual takes personal health seriously.

How do you sell a brand to women who take their health concerns very, very seriously? —with very, very serious ads.

Figure 14-3
Most health care
advertising reflects the
reader's attitude as
she's reading: serious. But
some ads can be so
off-the-wall, they work.

Granted, sometimes an ad can be so goofy it works (figure 14-3). But even so, some will resent it—not because the ad is clever but because they feel betrayed. Take a look at figure 14-3, a blatantly sexist message. By appealing to a strongly opinionated *segment* of the marketplace, the ad excludes those who don't share a militant attitude. The headline, "Imagine talking to him about your period," is followed by the snide, "Let's face it, he's never had one." (I'd like to add a parenthetical point: Any message that begins, "Let's face it," is either a cliché or imaginatively sterile.)

That the majority of women prefer women doctors for ob/gyn examinations is both obvious and logical; that there now exists a prevalence of women doctors for this specialty is a symbol of how far we've come since 1920.

Figure 14-4 shows an ad for Monistat 7. Take a look at the format: It's what the trade calls "advertorial"—a blend of advertising and text designed to look like magazine editorial. It is seldom accepted in most magazines without the damning label "Advertisement" at the top of the page.

This ad, from its headline—"WOMEN'S HEALTH NEWS"—through the text, is loaded with classic advertorial gimmicks. It features carefully directed page layout, a sidebar testimonial, and "myth-busting" editorial-type opinion. Where does this ad get its power? It involves the reader in apparent information, rather than a conventional sales pitch. (In my opinion, this ad's information/sales pitch ratio is slightly out of whack. To be really effective, advertorial should maintain its masquerade by having about 7/8 apparent editorial information, 1/8 sales pitch.)

Compare the Monistat ad with figure 14-5. The headline:

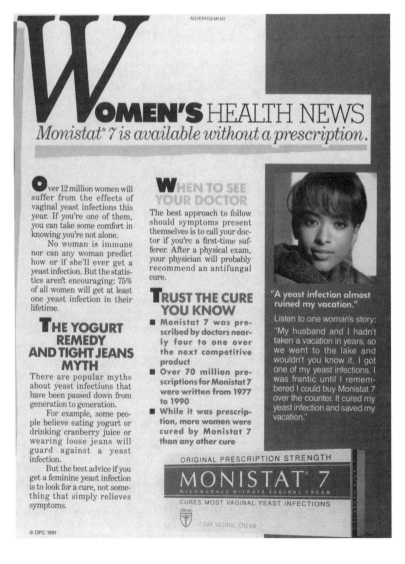

Figure 14-4
This ad gets its
message across using
an "advertorial" format —
mixing editorial with an
advertising sales pitch.

■

"How much moisture does your dry skin really need?"

■

This ad, which relics on careful art direction for its "official" editorial look, features a graph comparing the product, Neutrogena Emulsion, with "Leading Lotions."

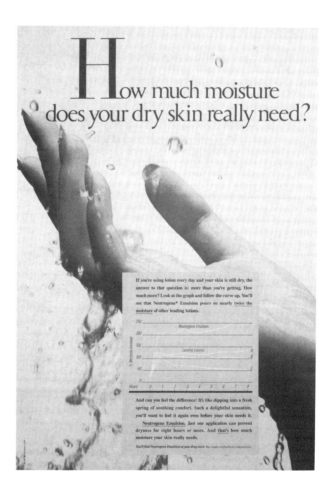

Figure 14-5
Another advertorial-type
ad with very little overt
product-sell.

No picture of the product, which would be a dead giveaway that this is an ad. No glaringly obvious call to action. Just a tiny reference in 6-point type at the bottom of the ad: "You'll find Neutrogena Emulsion at your drug store."

Figure 14-6 is another advertorial selling the nutritional virtues of Royal Jelly as a diet supplement. Told in first-person voices, in the son's and then in the mother's voice, it concludes with an actual byline. This ad appeals both to a woman's interests in her own health and in the health of her child.

Whatever Happened to the Male Authority-Figure?

Notice that Jason Balletta listened to "Mom's advice," not "Dad's advice," even though he "watched other kids playing ball." Does this make Jason less masculine? The issue is of no consequence because the ad ran in a woman's magazine, which certainly embraces the concept of female dominance.

Figure 14-7 capitalizes on the growing women's health care market . . . not by selling medications or products, but by selling information. After centuries of male-oriented medical studies, distributing up-to-date and targeted women's health care information is like showering manna onto the desert. The mailer knows this, and, as a public-interest nonprofit organization, suggests it is a dispassionate research-based headquarters.

Pure 1990s! Could an organization with the name National Women's Health Network have established itself in the 1950s? Does a parallel National *Men's* Health Network exist? Feminists would say it doesn't have to; old-timers would say this is another indication of growing female assertiveness.

The marketers here turn the lack of available women's health care to their advantage by creating exclusivity when they offer a booklet called *The Diet Your Doctor Won't Give You* as a premium. They subtly suggest that it's a male doctor who refuses to optimize your approach to a diet that might prevent breast cancer.

In Diets, Women Reign Supreme   Bring up the word "diet" and most people think not of a nutritional diet, but a weight-loss diet.

*Figure 14-6
Pure advertorial,
including personal
stories, testimonials,
and mom's advice.*

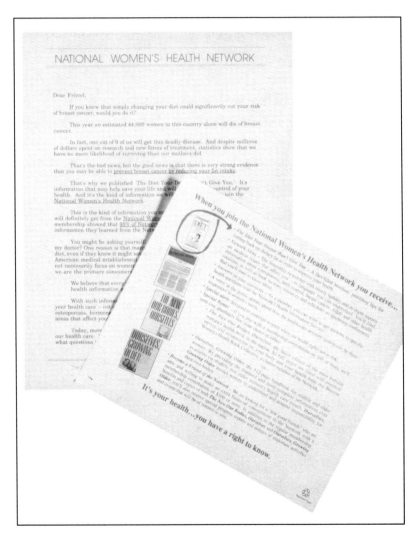

Figure 14-7
This fund raiser appeals
to a woman's demand for
health care information.
Could this organization
have garnered enough
support to survive in
the 1950s?

In fact, 46 percent of American adults—56 percent of whom are women—say they feel they're overweight, according to Mediamark Research, Inc. The same study reports that nearly half—46 percent—of all American women are on a diet.

Health is hot for many women. Four of the "10 hottest small magazines" in a 1993 *Adweek* listing were health-oriented: *Walking, Health, Cooking Light, and American Health.*

Figure 14-8 is an ad in a trade magazine selling mailing lists for health- and diet-conscious Americans. What's the illustration in the ad for "avid diet, health, fitness and cosmetic buyers?" A trim woman. Where's the male diet, health, and fitness buyer? Buried

Women's Dieting Methods

Method	Total women on diets
Exercise program	33%
Doctor's care	22%
Meal supplements	13%
Diet pills	8%
Diet organization or club	8%
Diet control book	8%
Candy-type appetite suppressants	1%

Note: Sample size: 20,000 U.S. adults. *Source: Marketing to Women,* January 1993 (Boston, MA: About Women, Inc., 1993). *Primary source:* The Source newsletter, Mediamark Research, Inc.

in the lists. Women are where it's at when selling fitness in the 1990s.

Women are in. Thin is in. No wonder the frozen prepared dinner brand Lean Cuisine now considers itself a mainstream brand instead of a diet brand. Its television campaign (at press time) doesn't even mention calories or the word "diet." It sells taste.

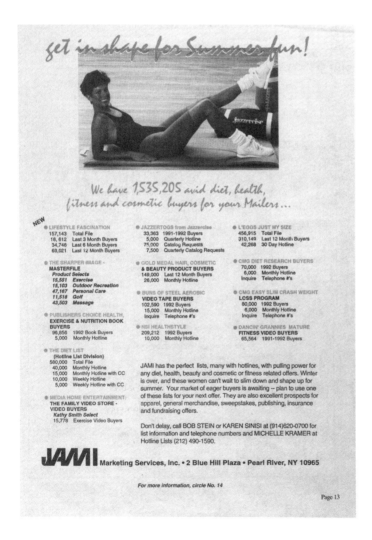

Figure 14-8
Even though this is an ad selling a mailing list for men and women, the marketer knows enough about targeting in the 1990s to feature a trim woman in the photo.

Dining on a Lean Cuisine is no more self-depriving than drinking a Diet Pepsi. Result: In the last measured period Lean Cuisine increased its market share by about 14 percent.

The mailer in figure 14-9 takes advantage of our natural aversion to dieting. The headline on the brochure: "At last . . . say goodbye to dieting and say hello to The Real You . . . "

The brochure describes a "weight-loss system that surpasses diets . . . designed for people who hate to exercise." The response card is a Guaranteed Success Certificate touting Kathy Smith's Fat Burning System.

Figure 14-9
A direct mailer capitalizing on the women's health and fitness craze of the '90s.

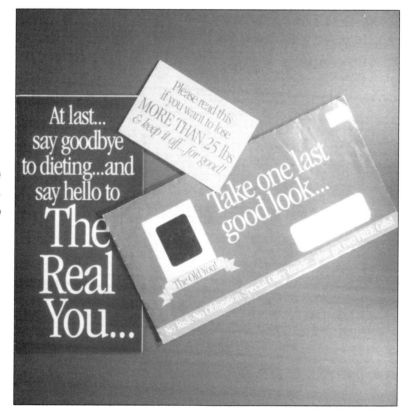

Okay, 46 percent of American women are on a diet. What about the other 54 percent? Every action has a reaction. To one huge group of skeptical and/or unable-to-keep-to-a-diet women, "diet" always has been a four-letter word. Mention the word and watch these women run in the other direction. Miracle liquid diets showed dramatic results in the elasticized waistlines of high-profile celebrities such as Oprah Winfrey and Tommy Lasorda. But as the celebrities weaned themselves off pseudo-chocolate shakes or tired of them, those rail-profile success stories gradually lost their girth-control, reverting into balloon-profile failures in front of TV audiences of millions.

Girth Control? Who Needs It?

The diet industry commands about $33 billion a year, but as the population ages, it's gaining, not losing avoirdupois. About 40 percent of American women over the age of 40 wear a size 14 dress or bigger.

So is it any wonder that an entire market group of women out there has chucked their dusty diet and exercise videos into the fire, grabbed the Godiva chocolates, and made peace with their cellulite?

No reason they shouldn't. Clothing manufacturers finally recognize girth has nothing to do with net worth. In 1982, clothing sales for the large-sized woman amounted to less than $6 billion. Today, it's a growing $10 billion industry.

The zaftig woman no longer settles for a closet brimming with muumuus to hide her size. She's demanding fashionable clothes *in her size*—and designers are scrambling all over each other to oblige her.

Givenchy's "En Plus" line of large-sized clothing features larger versions of the season's regular-size designs. This line commands as much as $250 for a blouse and $600 for a dress. Harvé Benard's "Pour la Femme" line lets out the seams and adds elastic waistbands to the designer's regular season's offerings.

Sales of Liz Claiborne's large-sized clothing line, dubbed "Elisabeth," reached $100 million in 1991, and sales are still breaking records.

Saks Fifth Avenue has carved out a big (in every way) marketing niche with its Salon Z, a boutique for women sized 14 and larger. No tent overblouses here. Salon Z is stocked with large-sized fashions from the likes of Albert Nipon, Pauline Trigère, and Adrienne Vitadini.

Bloomingdale's features Gianni Versace and Marina Rinaldi in generous proportions. Spiegel has established a high-fashion catalog (figure 14-10), "For You—The Fashion Collection for Sizes 14 and Up." The catalog sells a video of the same title, billed as a fashion primer for "fashion, *career,* makeup, and more." Note the inclusion of career. Large women don't have to feel they're less qualified because they carry more weight. They *can* compete on equal terms.

Fitting Pretty Queensize Pantyhose (figure 14-11) and Just My Size bras, panties, and hosiery (figure 14-12) are solid, fashion-oriented lines whose market is the larger woman. These companies don't feel they have (as bridal magazines have) a transitory buyership; they go for the permanent customer, and the permanent customer is there for them.

Actually, appealing to hyper-targets is the trend anyway. The larger-woman market is one of a great many markets that have broken away from the kind of generalized marketing that killed the once-mighty Sears, Roebuck & Co. catalog. What interests

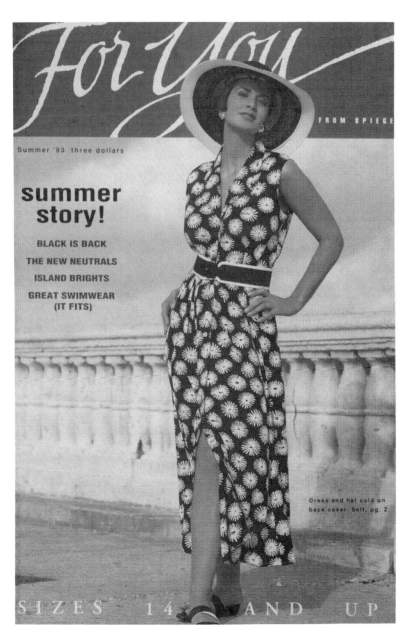

Figure 14-10
Spiegel's targeted "For You"
catalog is high-fashion for
sizes 14 and more.

us, in this specialized analysis, isn't the existence of companies whose marketing strategy targets the full-size woman; it's the number of such companies.

Safety On Both Sides of the Health & Fitness Street

Was it Wallis Simpson, the Duchess of Windsor, who said "You can never be too rich or too thin?" She may have had a point in

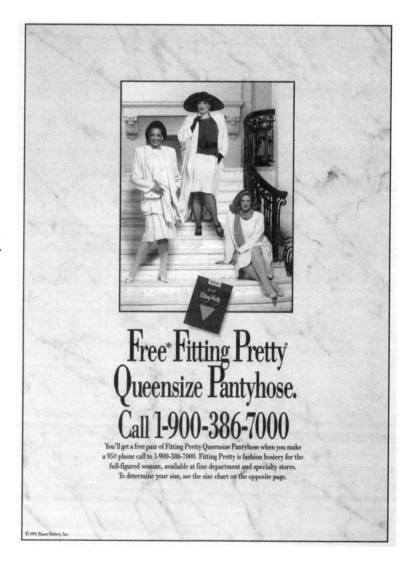

Figures 14-11 and 14-12
A growing number of advertisers in the 1990s are zeroing in on a formerly-ignored target group, the large-sized woman.

her day, but today, the thins and the pudgies co-exist . . . in a remarkably peaceable kingdom.

That's the ultimate point of female social evolution. Everybody has her own thing, and everybody is supposed to respect everybody else's thing, rather than say—as generations of frustrated

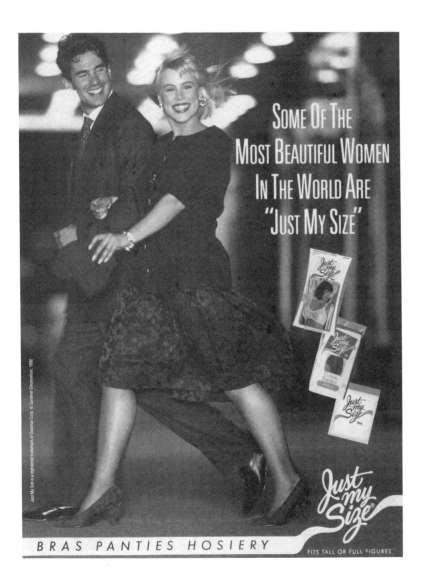

SOME OF THE
MOST BEAUTIFUL WOMEN
IN THE WORLD ARE
"JUST MY SIZE"

Just my Size

BRAS PANTIES HOSIERY   FITS TALL OR FULL FIGURES

moms said—"Dear, don't you think you ought to lose a little weight?"

Today's mom might be the one shopping merrily at Salon Z, chomping her high-calorie Godivas. The 1990s woman—and her reeducated male counterpart—says, with both wisdom, diplomacy— and if they're suppliers of either camp, profitability—"It's her business."

Marketing Checklist—
Chapter 14

☐ 1. The success of healthcare advertising depends on a targeted message, and patients now take an aggressive position in healthcare, surgical, and prescription decisions. Have you targeted women as well as their doctors in your campaign?

☐ 2. If you're a healthcare professional, have you looked into forming an advertising "alliance" to reach several markets at once?

☐ 3. On the whole, women pay more attention to their health (and the health of their families) than men do. Are you contributing to her education by making health information readily accessible to her in your advertising?

☐ 4. Have you tried an "advertorial" format in your campaign?

☐ 5. Even though nearly half of all American women are on a diet, "diet" is still a 4-letter word to most of them. Have you tested positioning your diet product as an everyday, non-diet product for better health?

☐ 6. To many women, big is beautiful and they've made their peace with cellulite. Have you considered the over-size-14 woman as a separate healthcare target group and a separate group for a new line extension?

CHAPTER 15

"We haven't come a long way, we've come a short way. If we hadn't come a short way, no one would be calling us 'baby'."

— ELIZABETH JANEWAY

Evolution, Devolution and Revolution — The Stratification of Society: Where Does the 1990s Woman Fit In?

Since the dawn of primitive society, when the beginnings of reason replaced the bludgeon—a trend the 1990s seems to have reversed—human beings have built layer upon diverse layer of artificial ethics, artificial morality, and artificial societal customs, all of which have been dictated by the social necessities and mores of the time.

These layers accelerated their construction in exact ratio to the speed with which information could be passed hand to hand. The weary messenger was replaced by homing pigeons whose legs were taped with terse notes. The telegraph made regional, then national, then international news available quickly to printing presses whose volume and speed increased to match.

Electronic communication brought changes that took place in a matter of days rather than decades. World War I was reported to a handful of military and governmental leaders by an astounding new development—radio, which had enabled ships at sea to pick up survivors of the *Titanic*.

Then came television. We know the marital troubles of the royal house of England before members of the family do. We're tuned in.

That's the point; we're tuned in. Would the troubles of the royal house of England have existed at all if its own members—and I'm referring to the *female* members whose contacts were worldly before marrying into the once-secluded halls of Buckingham Palace—hadn't been able to see what was going on in the rest of the world?

Market loyalties, like personal loyalties are subject to outside influences unheard of a century ago.

So society evolves . . . devolves . . . and revolves.

Our Evolving Target: Marketing Schizophrenia

We can't ignore the fact that our customer changes from year to year as she moves through different times and different periods, in her life and in society. Marketers who are stuck in treacle because they had success with a campaign back in the antediluvian days of 1975 are, quite realistically, bewildered because the campaign is laughable today. Marketers who isolate themselves from the accelerated changes in both public taste and public acceptability simply don't belong in the world of 1990s marketing.

Both types of marketers do exist. They're costing themselves or their clients a lot of money. They're firing arrows at a Sherman tank.

All right, here we are in the mid-1990s. Should we significantly adapt our approach to influencing women from, say, the mid-1980s?

You better believe it.

Women are an ever-more-fragmented market. The 1980s approach still motivates a portion of the previously unified target. You want to reach all of us? Tailor your message to suit the most responsive *fragment* through each type of multiple media.

Take a look at figure 15-1 and figure 15-2. 15-1 appeared in 1988: "The Man's Diamond. When a Woman Loves a Man." The woman is *partly* emancipated, but she's carefully posed in a submissive position, and she recognizes that her man is surprised by the gift. "He never expected a diamond," she says, "But, I never expected to love him so much."

Figure 15-2 ran in 1993, just five years later. Here, the woman holds the superior position. The caption, "Watching his face told me that this had been the right year to give him a diamond," tells the reader the man might have expected a diamond—a reversal from the tradition of men giving diamonds to women—and she made the *when* decision.

Are these two ads mutually exclusive? Certainly not. Are they *widely* different? If they were, they couldn't be useful examples. They symbolize the evolutionary trend toward total equality. As totality is achieved, some marketers will inevitably push beyond for *super*-equality, creating yet another level of potential sales appeal.

Midway down the line separating the woman of yesterday from the woman of tomorrow is an ad (figure 15-3) for a deodorant called Secret. The headline:

■

"First we made it strong enough for a man.
Then we faced a bigger challenge."

■

*Figures 15-1 and 15-2
Careful art direction of
an ad can make a subtle
difference in targeting.
15-1 ran in a men's
magazine. 15-2 ran in a
women's magazine.*

A deodorant "strong enough for a man," for a woman? Can you see how this might appeal to the *transitional* woman? Had the headline ended with " . . . strong enough for a man" it surely would annoy the belligerently liberated woman; by adding the second sentence the ad manages to serve both camps.

Figure 15-3
A carefully-worded
contemporary ad for
the transitional woman
of the 1990s.

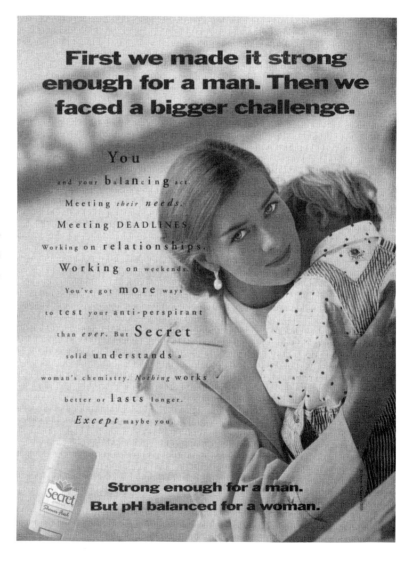

Might this ad run 10 years from now? Probably not. Alertness to attitudinal change is the key to marketing change.

What influences each stratum of 1990s womanhood? What guides the purchasing decisions of each segment?

Determinants of Selling Levels

Marketing success already requires us to know the answers to those questions . . . and we're a generation away from the complete stratification of society.

The availability of multiple channels on cable TV contributes to this stratification. With 500 channels, pinpointed programming will be another sundering factor. Each societal segment and sub-segment will — as the result of contagious intramural militancy — demand its own singular appeal. Most budgets will object to this ongoing rebellion, and will produce one or two messages to cover the gender. So no twenty-first century mass message will be perfect . . . or totally imperfect.

Society changes; psychology doesn't. A woman's responsibilities determine her major purchases. Her level of security determines her impulse buys. Her available time determines her buying method. Her nose for value, balanced against her social position, determines the price she'll pay. Is this a change from 1920? Nope.

If you were in the marketplace in 1960, you might have been mildly startled to see a torso mannequin, clad in a brassiere, for an "unmentionables" ad. A few years later, when Preparation H broke ground with its television commercial, you might have said, "What'll they advertise next?" A dramatic show on the Kraft Theatre used the word "broad" to refer to a woman, and the

Think Back to 1960

phone lines lit up. Planned Parenthood was widely regarded as an "extremist" group.

Today, "So what?" is the prevalent attitude, even among the most conservative viewers, with one exception.

Brassieres on torso mannequins? Quaint.

Maidenform, renowned in the 1960s for its fixed-position ads ("I dreamt I was Cleopatra on the Nile in my Maidenform bra") in the 1990s has become an archetype of the new bold approach to advertising. The approach derives its effectiveness from a sound principle: If you don't grab their attention, you ain't gonna sell. During the 1992 political campaigns, Maidenform ran a series of television spots (figure 15-4) using the theme "If you've got something to say, now's the time to get it off your chest." The ads featured well-supported women wearing campaign buttons with slogans such as "Pro-Choice," "Fight Racism," and "Quayle for President."

Preparation H? So what? Even the most conservative 1990s woman doesn't blush at Gyne-Lotrimin or Massengill. A 1993 ad in Parade—a magazine whose polyglot readership is second to none—bears the headline "Discover the Replens® difference for long-lasting vaginal moisture" (figure 15-5).

Even Planned Parenthood is staid enough to attract high society doyennes on its local boards of directors.

The New Female Dominance

So what's the exception? The word "broad," which generates a rash of phone calls—*but not for the same reason.*

In 1960, the word offended sensibilities. Nice people didn't use that word, and parents didn't want their children to hear it.

While it doesn't present a united front, 'If you've got something to say, now's the time to get it off your chest,' is the idea behind this :30 PSA from Maidenform urging women to vote. It's also Ogilvy & Mather/New York's first Maidenform spot since it won the account in March. Creative director/copywriter Julie Newton-Cucchi teamed with art director Beth Kosuk and executive creative director Vel Richey-Rankin

Figure 15-4
The call to action from Maidenform's campaign-button television ad during the 1992 presidential campaign was "If you've got something to say, now's the time to get it off your chest."

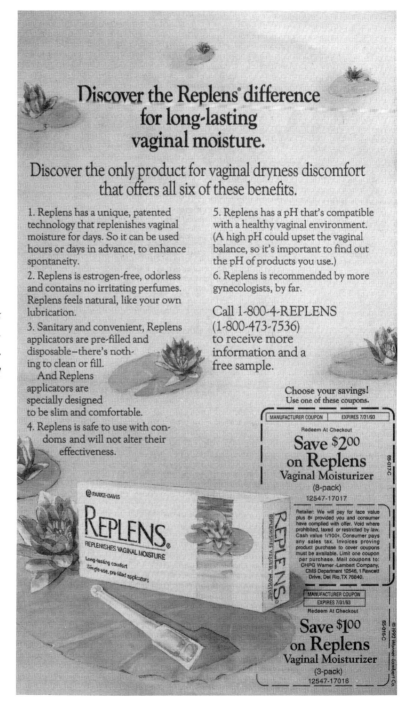

Figure 15-5
Even the most conservative
1990s woman is no longer
embarrassed by personal
care ads like these.

In the 1990s, the reason is that women just don't like being called "broads," and they have the clout to make their disdain stick. Women spray-paint a wall with "Dead men don't rape" and the message is not erased for days. Female talk show hosts say they're "pissed off" and the phone doesn't ring at all. A generation of new activists repeat lyrics from "songs" by the female punk bands Bikini Kill and Bratmobile — "Don't need you to tell me I'm cute."

The organization Riot Grrl, hyper-militant about such issues as *Roe v. Wade* and sexual harassment, brags that some of its members are "as old as 25."

Okay, what happens when these women are *over* 25? Or over 35? How do we advertise to them, rebels who wear body paint?

Many advertisers will choose to ignore them; mainstream advertisers traditionally ignore extremists. From a marketing point of view, this smacks of wisdom, because appealing to extremists invariably alienates a larger group of potential customers than it attracts.

Militancy is an aberration in civilized society, regardless of rationale or gender. *Dominance* is a different ball game.

What better example do we have of emerging female dominance than a *Playboy* ad that ran in an advertising publication in 1993, (figure 15-6)? The ad, designed to attract advertisers for the magazine's fortieth anniversary issue in 1994, showed a "memo" from the publisher to one of the staff members. The memo begins with these words:

∎

"It's hard to believe that three of us—you,
me and the magazine—are celebrating our

40th birthdays in the same year. I tried to
keep mine fairly low key, but the
magazine's—that's another story."

■

Every person, male or female, who is even remotely conversant
with the magazine, knows Christie Hefner, a woman, is the publisher.

Oh, sure, Christie Hefner is the daughter of the magazine's
founder and might not be publisher except for the genetic affiliation. But she is publisher. Men, *at a men's magazine,* work for her
and toady to her. And she has no compunctions about telling her

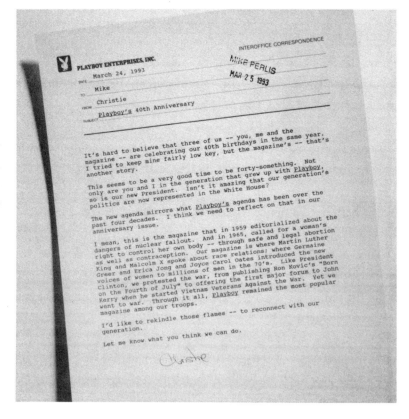

Figure 15-6
A woman, Christie Hefner
now runs and operates the
formerly male-dominated
Playboy Enterprises
and doesn't hesitate to
mention her age.

age in print. (Kind of funny that she says she's keeping her birthday "low key" in a space ad.)

Donna Karan ran an *eight-page* ad in a women's magazine with the single line of text: "In Women We Trust" (figure 15-7). The eight full-page illustrations chronicled a woman who won an election for president of the United States. Her Secret Service aides, her cabinet, her assistants, her acolytes — all are men.

Is anyone outraged over this ad? Only the grossest redneck males might be — and they'd never see the ad. The concept of "uppity woman" isn't just dormant; it's dead, the happy victim of social evolution/devolution/revolution.

And In the Other Corner . . .

Members of Riot Grrl would probably throw rocks through the windows of marketers who flourish by hawking products aimed at women who want to maximize their traditional roles as sex objects. (In fact, they regularly picket beauty contests.)

But as I pointed out earlier in this chapter, and in other chapters of this book, advertising to women is now far from merely appealing to a single market segment. So publications whose readership is more comfortable with their traditional roles have mirrored a different kind of evolution — augmentation of what once was whispered but now, within that group, is common table talk. They focus on women who seek to be more attractive to men by artificially improving on natural assets.

The Frederick's of Hollywood catalog is no longer hidden in the drawer. Groups of women enter mass orders; a wife or girlfriend shows her husband or boyfriend what she's about to order. Victoria's Secret, even a few years ago regarded as slightly naughty,

Figure 15-7
Another election-year
campaign, showing a
woman as president, from
Donna Karan.

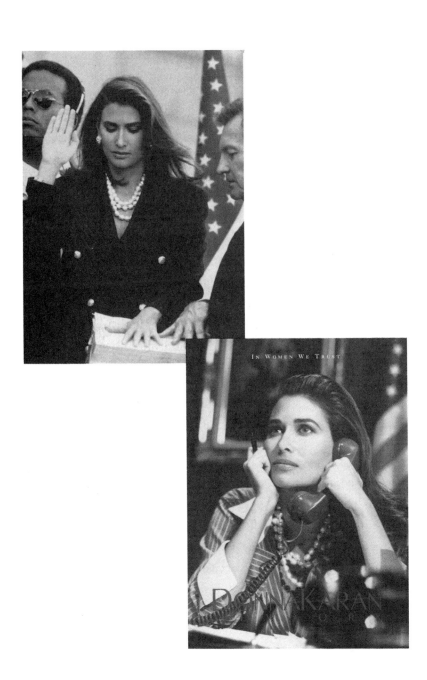

has stores in shopping malls, and our neighbors of both sexes wander down its aisles.

Full-page ads for breast enlargement devices and creams are commonplace (figure 15-8). Some magazines carry half a dozen or more. Look at a typical sales pitch:

■

"Let's **be honest.** There's no substitute for **firm, round, beautiful breasts.** No matter what anyone says, **LARGER BREASTS DO MAKE A BIG DIFFERENCE.** You know how much **ATTENTION** women with large breasts demand from men. And you also know how it feels to see **OTHER WOMEN** get all that attention just because their breasts are larger than yours. Now you can **fight back** with MACROCELL-D58™, the ultimate breast enhancer . . . .

■

What better example could exist of the dichotomy within women's ranks today?

Glamour commissioned a survey of its readers, to study the motivations behind buying patterns. Asked the number one factor determining clothing budget priorities, 56 percent named work; 35 percent named everyday, not work; 16 percent named leisure; and 8 percent named social occasions and parties. And this was *Glamour,* not *Working Woman* or the female readers of *Forbes.* Career *über alles.* What might a similar survey have shown before World War II?

The same survey compared *Glamour* with *Cosmopolitan.* While these two publications are by no means at opposite poles of the

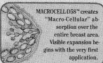

Figure 15-8
The ubiquitous breast-enlargement advertising, virtually unchanged through the past two decades, still pulls in responses today.

fragmentation continuum, they exemplify why an advertiser who attempts to motivate generic "women" might be nonplussed. The category: "Two most important reasons for reading the magazine." The answers: Beauty and Fashion for *Glamour;* and Male Relationships and Personal Relationships for *Cosmopolitan.*

Remembering that a published commercial survey has to be self-serving or it wouldn't be published, we see additional differences between the two publications. Under the category "Magazine turned to more often for information in the following areas," *Glamour* outdistanced *Cosmopolitan* 74.5 percent to 23.4 percent for Fitness and Exercise, and 69.8 percent to 28.9 percent for Beauty. On the other hand, *Cosmopolitan* ran away from *Glamour* 82.1 percent to 16.2 percent for Sex Advice, and 78.3 percent to 19.6 percent for Male Relationships.

All right, why would *Glamour* publish *any* statistic giving a competitor (for advertising dollars) an edge? One reason is obvious and the other isn't so obvious. The obvious reason is that the survey positions the publication in the minds of advertising agency space buyers. If you're buying space for Nordic Track or Revlon, the statistical evidence is persuasive.

The less obvious reason is the vestige of pre-1990s morality. Are "nice" women readers interested in sex advice? You bet they are — but *Glamour* subtly suggests otherwise.

Actually, many women read both publications, and many advertisers include both in their media schedules. Come the year 2010, when market segmentation is more profound, this may not be so. We may see women hiding *one publication or the other* in a drawer, lest visitors conclude that an out-of-sync interest exists.

Advertising to women is not only a complex puzzle, but the complexity seems to be increasing exponentially.

No book short of a dozen volumes can pretend to isolate all the market segments, all the motivators, all the past, present, and future trends. What we can do—and what this book has tried to do—is to alert those whose professional positions depend in whole or in part on their ability to stimulate *the most buying impulses per advertising dollar spent* to be aware of ongoing evolution . . . devolution . . . revolution.

What a fascinating marketplace this is!

And are we lucky to be here to analyze it and try to profit from it? Well, yes and no. But I vote yes.

L'Envoi

☐ 1. Society — and our marketing targets — continually evolve. Are you keeping up in your positioning year to year?

☐ 2. Because the women's market group gets more fragmented each year, no advertising message will be completely perfect. Have you determined what guides the marketing decisions of each segment of your market group?

☐ 3. Even though society changes, basic selling psychology remains constant. Have you taken a step back to analyze the motivating power of your message?

☐ 4. Media coverage will often give extremist groups more than their fair share of air time. Are you taking care to recognize extremist groups for what they are — aberrations — and avoiding undue influence on your advertising?

**Marketing Checklist—
Chapter Fifteen**

Who to Call for What:

Mini Sourcebook

■ *Consultants*

CAROL ANN VALENTINE
2607 S. Forest Ave.
Tempe, AZ 85282
(602) 967-2187

Type of Consultation: Conducts seminars and other training programs on communication. Frequent programs focus on non-verbal communication, listening skills, interviewing and communication among women. Serves private industries as well as government agencies. Small, women-owned firm. **Founded:** 1975. **Principal Executive:** Carol Ann Valentine. **Seminars:** Effective Listening; Family Communication. **Staff:** 2.

CONSULTANTS ON TODAY'S WOMEN
361 S. Commonwealth Ave.
Elgin, IL 60123
(708) 741-1739

Type of Consultation: Provides consulting service to businesses seeking to develop educational materials and newsletters in consumer interest areas, with emphasis on foods and textiles; to governmental agencies requiring knowledge of women's consumer interests; and to women's organizations in program development areas. **Founded:** 1976. **Principal Executive:** Barbara J. Schock, Managing Director. **Staff:** 1.

NEW FUTURES ENTERPRISES
4502 Broad Rd.
Syracuse, NY 13215
(315) 469-3902

Type of Consultation: Specializes in issues relating to women, male-female dynamics, and gender equity serving education, government, and business. Provides training, research, surveys, program development, evaluation, problem identification and solving, and video production. Active in New York and the northeastern United States. Women-owned firm. **Founded:** 1983. **Principal Executive:** Rosemary Agonito. **Publications and/or Videos:** R. Agonito, *All About Grants: Training Video*, provides an introduction to successful grant seeking. **Seminars:** Positive Male-Female Communications Skills; Overcoming Sexual Harassment; Women's Leadership/Management Training; Women and Minority Business Ownership Training; Sex Equity in Schools. **Staff:** 3.

PROCUREMENT RESOURCES, INC.
111 Petrol Point, Ste. 204
Peachtree City, GA 30269
(404) 631-3633

Type of Consultation: Management consultants with specialized expertise in minority/women's purchasing programs. Services focused on: staff training, supplier sourcing, needs evaluation, and program design and development. Serves private industries as well as government agencies. Active in continental United States. Minority-owned firm. **Founded:** 1973. **Principal Executive(s):** Reginald Williams, President; Carla Greenlee, Vice President. **Seminars:** Doing Business with Minority Vendors. **Staff:** 7.

WOMANHOOD MEDIA
2701 Durant Ave., Ste. 14
Berkeley, CA 94704-1733
(510) 549-2970

Type of Consultation: Consultant in academic affirmative management, with specializations in areas of women studies/women's services, media, libraries, and community college, through counseling-consulting in research structure and projects, course and program innovation, staff and professional development. Professional development services include tailor made training and workshops mainly for women in academe and in management. Also offers expert witness services. Small women-owned firm. **Computer Services:** Prepares unique "Pathfinders" for individual researchers. **Founded:** 1975. **Principal Executive:** Helen R. Wheeler. **Publications and/or Videos:** H. Wheeler, *Getting Published in Women's Studies: An International Interdisciplinary, Professional Development Guide Mainly for Women.* McFarland (1989). **Seminars:** How to Write and Market Your First Nonfiction Book; Getting the Right Job; Women and the Media; Women and Aging; Herstory-Why Women's History; Response to Sexual Harassment; Women's Health Issues; Working with the Mass Media to Get Publicity for your Organization, Event, and Self; Women and Politics; Women and Leadership; Censorship in U.S.A.

 *Directories*

AMERICAN NEWS WOMEN'S CLUB-DIRECTORY
1607 22nd St. NW
Washington, DC 20008
(202) 232-6770

Approximately 450 women employed by or associated with the news media industry. **Frequency:** Annual.

ANNOTATED GUIDE TO WOMEN'S PERIODICALS
PO Box E-62
Richmond, IN 47374
(317) 983-1268

DIRECTORY OF NATIONAL WOMEN'S ORGANIZATIONS
The Sara Delano Roosevelt Memorial House
47-49 E. 65th St.
New York, NY 10021
(212) 570-5001

Describes 500 U.S. national women's organizations and groups, including research centers and discipline caucuses, policy and activist organizations, foundations, government agencies, libraries and archives, political action committees and unions, sororities and religious groups, women of color organizations, and more.

DIRECTORY OF ORGANIZATIONS FOR WOMEN
PO Box 190 B
Garrett Park, MD 20896
(301) 946-2553

Hundreds of national and regional professional, service, and other organizations of women. **Frequency:** Periodic.

DIRECTORY OF WOMEN ENTREPRENEURS
PO Box 450827, Northlake Branch
Atlanta, GA 30345
(404) 496-5986

Approximately 3,200 women-owned businesses; companies with minority and women professional development programs, women's groups and organizations, and minority business assistance offices. **Frequency:** Annual, February.

DIRECTORY OF WOMEN'S MEDIA
47-49 E. 65th St.
New York, NY 10021
(212) 570-5001

More than 1300 women's media resources, including print and electronic media, publishers and news services, art groups, productions, and distributors (for film, video, cable, theater, dance, music, and multimedia), writers' groups and speakers' bureaus, media organizations, bookstores, libraries, museums, and archives.

DIRECTORY OF WORK-IN-PROGRESS AND RECENTLY PUBLISHED RESOURCES
47-49 E. 65th St.
New York, NY 10021
(212) 570-5001

More than 1400 citations of works-in-progress and recently-published research and resources that encompass a broad range of work by and about women, including journal articles, books, conference presentations, data collections, policy guidelines, reports, art, and media.

FEMINIST BUSINESS AND PROFESSIONAL NETWORK-DIRECTORY
PO Box 91214
Washington, DC 20090-1214
(703) 836-5325

Frequency: Annual.

FEMINIST PERIODICALS: A CURRENT LISTING OF CONTENTS
Memorial Library, Rm. 112A
728 State St.
Madison, WI 53706
(608) 263-5754

Over 100 periodicals of national or midwestern readership focusing on women's issues, particularly from a feminist standpoint. **Frequency:** Quarterly.

HOW TO GET MONEY FOR RESEARCH
311 E. 94th St.
New York, NY 10128
(212) 360-5790

About 85 organizations, associations, foundations, and institutions offering grants and fellowships for research studies conducted by or about women; about 90 libraries or publishers offering research grant information. **Frequency:** Irregular; latest edition 1983; new edition expected; date not set.

INTERNATIONAL CENTERS FOR RESEARCH ON WOMEN

The Sara Delano Roosevelt Memorial House
47-49 E. 65th St.
New York, NY 10021
(212) 570-5001

Lists over 150 research and documentation centers in 47 countries, including the U.S. member centers of the National Council.

INTERNATIONAL DIRECTORY OF GAY AND LESBIAN PERIODICALS

4041 N. Central, No. 700
Phoenix, AZ 85012
(602) 265-2651

Over 2,000 publishers of gay and lesbian newspapers, newsletters, journals, magazines, and other publications. **Frequency:** Published March 1987.

NATIONAL COUNCIL OF CAREER WOMEN–MEMBERSHIP DIRECTORY

3203 Gemstone Ct.
Oakton, VA 22124
(703) 591-4359

Covers 450 members. **Frequency:** Annual, summer. Available to members only.

NATIONAL DIRECTORY OF WOMEN-OWNED BUSINESS FIRMS

2 E. 22nd St., Ste. 202
Lombard, IL 60148
(708) 495-8787

Over 20,000 women-owned businesses. **Frequency:** Irregular, latest edition January 1990.

NATIONAL WOMEN'S MAILING LIST

Box 68
Jenner, CA 95450
(707) 632-5763

Frequency: Supplied upon demand.

NWSA DIRECTORY OF WOMEN'S STUDIES PROGRAMS, WOMEN'S CENTERS, AND WOMEN'S RESEARCH CENTERS

University of Maryland
College Park, MD 20742-1325
(301) 405-5573

Over 600 academic programs in women's studies. **Frequency:** Biennial, even years.

PLANNING CONSULTANT ROSTER

1313 E. 60th St.
Chicago, IL 60637
(202) 872-0611

Firms that specialize or are active in planning; includes women- and minority-owned planning firms.

REGIONAL DIRECTORY OF MINORITY & WOMEN-OWNED BUSINESS FIRMS

2 E. 22nd St., Ste. 202
Lombard, IL 60148
(708) 495-8787

Frequency: Irregular; previous editions May 1988; latest edition January 1990.

A WOMAN'S YELLOW BOOK

2001 S St., Ste. 540
Washington, DC 20009
(202) 328-1415

About 575 national organizations, government agencies, research institutes, clearinghouses, and publishers concerned with women's issues. **Frequency:** Irregular; latest edition spring 1990.

WOMEN IN COMMUNICATIONS, INC.–NATIONAL MEMBERSHIP AND RESOURCE DIRECTORY

2101 Wilson Blvd., Ste. 417
Arlington, VA 22201
(703) 528-4200

12,500 professional and student members. **Frequency:** Biennial, January of odd years.

WOMEN DIRECTORS OF THE TOP CORPORATE 1,000

1440 New York Ave. NW, Ste. 300
Washington, DC 20005
(202) 393-5257

About 400 women serving on the boards of Fortune 1,000 corporations, compiled from surveys of Fortune 500 Industrial and Fortune 500 Service corporations. **Frequency:** Annual, January.

WOMEN'S INFORMATION DIRECTORY

835 Penobscot Bldg.
Detroit, MI 48226
(313) 961-2242

Nearly 10,800 entries covering national, regional, state, and local women's organizations; battered women's services; displaced homemaker programs; family planning services; university-related women's centers; library collections; museums and galleries; women's colleges and universities; women's studies programs; scholarships, fellowships, and loans; awards, honors, and prizes; research centers; federal government agencies; federal domestic assistance programs; state and local government agencies; top U.S. women-owned businesses; consultants and consulting organizations; directories; journals and magazines; newsletters; newspapers; publishers; booksellers; videos; and electronic resources. **Frequency:** Biennial.

A WOMEN'S MAILING LIST DIRECTORY

47-49 E. 65th St.
New York, NY 10021
(212) 570-5001

Over 100 women's organizations offering their mailing lists for sale or exchange. **Frequency:** Irregular; latest edition 1990.

WOMEN'S ORGANIZATIONS: A NATIONAL DIRECTORY

Box 190F
Garrett Park, MD 20896
(301) 946-2553

Covers 2,000 national and local women's organizations including professional and trade associations, government commissions, and research centers specializing in women's issues. **Frequency:** Irregular; latest edition 1986.

■ *Electronic Resources*

DATA RESOURCES OF THE HENRY A. MURRAY RESEARCH CENTER OF RADCLIFFE COLLEGE

Radcliffe College
Garden St.
Cambridge, MA 02138
(617) 495-8140

Contains social science data on the lives and experiences of American Women. **Format:** Diskette; magnetic tape. **Language used in database:** English. **Subject coverage:** American women in sociology.

FAMILY RESOURCES DATABASE

3989 Central Ave. NE, Ste. 550
Minneapolis, MN 55421
(612) 781-9331

Provides references and abstracts of journal and nonjournal literature covering marriage and the family as well as descriptions of the programs and services offered by research centers and other organizations in the field. Includes the Human Resource Bank, which lists family specialists willing to be contacted by the general public; and the Idea Bank, which covers research work in progress. **Format:** Online; magnetic tape. **Language used in database:** English. **Subject coverage:** Marriage and family, including trends and changes; organizations and services for families; family relationships and dynamics; mate selection; marriage and divorce; issues related to reproduction; sexual attitudes and behavior; families with special problems; psychology and sociology; counseling, therapy, and education; minority groups; and aids for theory and research.

FEMAIL

Provides a forum for discussing issues of interest to women. **Electronic mail address:** FEMAIL-REQUEST%HPDLH@ HPLABS.HP.COM. **Format:** Electronic bulletin board.

Language used in database: English. **Subject coverage:** Women's issues.

GENDER

Provides a forum for the discussion of questions and issues pertaining to the study of communication and gender from an academic perspective. **Electronic mail address:** COMSERVE@ RPIECS (BITNET); COMSERVE@VM.ECS.RPI.EDU. (Internet). **Format:** Electronic bulletin board. **Language used in database:** English. **Subject coverage:** Communications and gender.

KINSEY INSTITUTE FOR RESEARCH IN SEX, GENDER, AND REPRODUCTION BIBLIOGRAPHIC DATABASE

Indiana University
Morrison Hall, 4th Fl.
Bloomington, IN 47405
(812) 855-7686

Provides full bibliographic descriptions of books received by the Kinsey Institute's library. **Format:** Producer provides search services. **Language used in database:** English. **Subject coverage:** Sex, gender, reproduction, and sexual behavior.

MARGUERITE RAWALT RESOURCE CENTER DATABASE

2021 Massachusetts Ave. NW
Washington, DC 20036
(202) 293-1200

Contains information dealing with the status of women in the United States, workplace trends, economic issues affecting women workers, and balancing work and family life. **Format:** Producer provides search services. **Language used in database:** English. **Subject coverage:** Women in the United States.

MARKETING TO WOMEN

33 Broad St.
Boston, MA 02109
(617) 723-4337

Contains the complete text of *Marketing to Women*, a monthly newsletter discussing market studies aimed at women. Covers such topics as demographics, women's attitudes, family issues, consumer products, fashion, media preferences, health care, employment, recreation, food and nutrition, shopping, working women, travel, and reproduction. Includes interviews, research news, and book reviews. **Format:** Online. **Language used in database:** English. **Subject coverage:** Advertising and marketing directed towards women.

THE NATIONAL REPORT ON WORK AND FAMILY

1231 25th St. NW
Washington, DC 20037
(202) 452-4132

Provides information on social issues concerning work and family, including related court cases and legal requirements. **Format:** Online; producer provides search services. **Language used in database:** English. **Subject coverage:** Work and family issues, including day care, alternative work schedules, paternity and maternity leave, relocation, sick child care, pay equity and nondiscrimination insurance, and elder care.

NATIONAL WOMEN'S MAILING LIST
PO Box 68
Jenner, CA 95450
(707) 632-5763

Contains names and addresses of individuals and groups interested in women's and feminist issues. **Format:** Producer provides search services. **Language used in database:** English. **Subject coverage:** Women's and feminist issues.

PREGNANT PROFESSIONALS: BALANCING CAREER & FAMILY
1231 25th St. NW
Washington, DC 20037
(202) 452-4132

Contains the complete text of *Pregnant Professionals: Balancing Career and Family*, a special report providing information on problems associated with balancing a professional career, pregnancy, and family. Includes possible solutions to given problems. **Format:** Online. **Language used in database:** English. **Subject coverage:** Family and family life.

PROMOTING MINORITIES & WOMEN
1231 25th St. NW
Washington, DC 20037
(202) 452-4132

Contains the complete text of *Promoting Minorities & Women*, a special report on affirmative action policies in the 1990s. Includes information on changing demographics of the U.S. labor pool, with projections of labor force growth by sex and race. Provides examples of major corporate affirmative action programs and reviews of several case studies. **Format:** Online. **Language used in database:** English. **Subject coverage:** Employment of women and minorities and family life.

RESEARCH-IN-PROGRESS
Sara Delano Roosevelt Memorial House
47-49 E. 65th St.
New York, NY 10021
(212) 570-5001

Contains citations to books, articles, dissertations, working papers, curricula, art, software, and reports pertaining to research in the field of women's studies. **Format:** Online. **Language used in database:** English. **Subject coverage:** Women's studies.

ROPER CENTER FOR PUBLIC OPINION RESEARCH
University of Connecticut
U-164 R
Storrs, CT 06268
(203) 486-4440

Contains a collection of more than 9000 survey data sets covering information from some 75 countries dealing with domestic political attitudes and behavior, public policy, market research, and mass media. **Format:** Diskette; magnetic tape. **Language used in database:** English. **Subject coverage:** Global sociology and demographics.

SEXUAL HARASSMENT IN THE FEDERAL WORKPLACE, 1978-1980
1120 Vermont Ave. NW
Washington, DC 20419

Contains the responses to a mail survey on sexual harassment. Provides demographic information on the respondent, attitudinal and demographic information on the respondent's workplace, attitudes regarding sexual behavior that may occur at work, respondent definition of sexual harassment, general data on the incidence level of sexual harassment, and information about whether the respondent has been accused of sexual harassment. **Format:** Producer provides search services. **Language used in database:** English. **Subject coverage:** Sexual harassment.

SURVEY OF WOMEN-OWNED BUSINESSES
Washington, DC 20233
(301) 763-5470

Covers basic economic data on businesses owned by women in the United States. **Format:** CD-ROM. **Language used in database:** English. **Subject coverage:** U.S. women-owned businesses.

■ *Journals and Magazines*

MINORITIES AND WOMEN IN BUSINESS
PO Drawer 210
Burlington, NC 27216
(919) 229-1462

Magazine networks with major corporations and small businesses owned and operated by minority and female entrepreneurs. **First published:** October 1984. **Frequency:** 6/yr. **Subscription:** Free to qualified subscribers; $15; $36 three years.

NATIONAL BUSINESS WOMAN
2012 Massachusetts Ave. NW
Washington, DC 20036
(202) 293-1100

Magazine for working women. **First published:** 1919. **Frequency:** 4/yr. **Subscription:** $10.

THE PROFESSIONAL COMMUNICATOR
2101 Wilson Blvd., Ste. 417
Arlington, VA 22201
(703) 528-4200

National magazine features communications management practices, how-to material, membership news, communications trends, features, opinion columns, and information about women and communications issues. **Frequency:** 5/yr. **Subscription:** $15; $3/single copy.

SUCCESSFUL WOMAN IN BUSINESS
1429 Walnut St.
Philadelphia, PA 19102
(215) 563-6005

Magazine containing advice on resources, management strategies, personal finance, and career development for professional and executive women. **First published:** 1979. **Subscription:** $48 (included in membership dues).

WOMAN ENTREPRENEUR
641 Lexington Ave., 9th Fl.
New York, NY 10022
(212) 688-1900

Magazine for women in business. **Frequency:** Monthly.

WOMAN'S ENTERPRISE
28210 Dorothy Dr.
Box 3000
Agoura Hills, CA 91301
(818) 889-8740

Small business magazine for women who own or would like to start their own business. **First published:** December 1987. **Frequency:** 6/yr. Subscription: $9.95.

WOMEN IN BUSINESS
9100 Ward Pkwy.
PO Box 8728
Kansas City, MO 64114-0728
(816) 361-6621

Women's business magazine for member of the American Business Women's Association. **First published:** 1949. **Frequency:** 6/yr. **Subscription:** $12; $2/single issue.

WOMEN & WORK
Office of Information and Public Affairs
200 Constitution Ave. NW
Washington, DC 20210
(202) 523-7323

Government publication covering women's legal, educational, and employment issues. **Frequency:** Monthly.

■ National Women's Organizations

AFL-CIO COMMITTEE ON SALARIED AND PROFESSIONAL WOMEN
Department for Professional Employees
815 16th St., NW, No. 707
Washington, DC 20006
(202) 638-0320
Gloria Johnson, Chair.

Explores the problems facing women in professional and technical occupations and encourages organizing and union participation among white collar women workers. **Founded:** 1974. **Publications:** *Interface.* Also publishes statistics on white collar women.

ALLIANCE OF MINORITY WOMEN FOR BUSINESS AND POLITICAL DEVELOPMENT
c/o Brenda Alford
Brassman Research
PO Box 13933
Silver Spring, MD 20911-3933
(301) 565-0258
Brenda Alford, President.

Minority women who own businesses in industries including manufacturing, construction, service, finance, insurance, real estate, retail trade, wholesale trade, transportation, and public utilities. Objectives are to unite minority women entrepreneurs and to encourage joint ventures and information exchange for political influence. **Formerly:** (1982) Task Force on Black Women Business Owners. **Founded:** 1982. **Members:** 650.

AMERICAN BUSINESS WOMEN'S ASSOCIATION
9100 Ward Pkwy.
PO Box 8728
Kansas City, MO 64114
(816) 361-6621
Carolyn B. Elman, Executive Director.

Women in business, including women owning or operating their own businesses, women in professions, and women employed in any level of government, education, retailing, manufacturing, and service companies. Provides opportunities for businesswomen to help themselves and others grow personally and professionally through leadership, education, networking support, and national recognition. Presents national Top Ten Business Women of ABWA, and Local Woman of the Year awards to outstanding businesswomen. Offers leadership training and discounted CareerTrack programs, a resume service, credit card and member loan programs, and various travel and insurance benefits. Annually awards more than $2.5 million to women students through chapter scholarship programs; also awards scholarships nationally through the Stephen Bufton Memorial Educational Fund. Sponsors American Business Women's Day annually on Sept. 22. **Founded:** 1949. **Local groups:** 2000. **Members:** 90,000. **Publications:** *CONNECT,* quarterly.

Newsletter. *Women in Business*, bimonthly. General interest magazine for businesswomen. Also publishes training materials.

AMERICAN COUNCIL FOR CAREER WOMEN

c/o Joan Savoy
PO Box 50825
New Orleans, LA 70150
(504) 529-1116
Joan Savoy, President.

Computerized services: Accounting and mailing list. Corporations, organizations representing 5000 individuals, and individuals concerned about the interests of career women. Purpose is to promote leadership and professional development among women. Seeks to enhance opportunities for career women in all educational and employment endeavors. Provides a forum for the discussion of issues, opportunities, and problems concerning women in business. Encourages higher business standards and improved business methods among men and women; works to maintain the integrity of and improve the business conditions for working women. Promotes heightened public awareness of and the demand for opportunities, products, and services for women; seeks to educate the public to the opportunities available to women. Bestows Achievers Award to outstanding business woman. Sponsors annual professional seminar. **Founded:** 1979. **Members:** 5175. **Publications:** *American Council for Career Women Membership Roster*, annual. *News/Views*, quarterly. Also publishes *Women's Career Calendar*.

AMERICAN SOCIETY OF PROFESSIONAL AND EXECUTIVE WOMEN

1429 Walnut St.
Philadelphia, PA 19102
(215) 563-4415
Laurie Wagman, Executive Director.

Computerized Services: Data base. To promote, through practical information and benefits, a positive attitudinal environment for career women involved in all areas of American enterprise. Conducts seminars; provides discount library services and executive recruitment. **Founded:** 1979. **Members:** 25,200. **Publications:** *Successful Woman in Business*, quarterly. Membership magazine for professional and executive women. Includes list of books and other resources on management, leadership, and business issues. Also publishes guides.

ASSOCIATION OF EXECUTIVE AND PROFESSIONAL WOMEN

The International Alliance
8600 LaSalle Rd., Ste. 308
Baltimore, MD 21204
(410) 321-6699
Marian Goetze, Executive Vice President.

The Alliance serves worldwide as an umbrella organization that unites, supports, and promotes executive and professional women and their networks in the business, not-for-profit, and government sectors. It also maintains a speakers' bureau and a Directors Resource Database. **Publications:** *The Alliance*, bimonthly. The group also publishes an annual member directory.

BUSINESS AND PROFESSIONAL WOMEN'S FOUNDATION

2012 Massachusetts Ave. NW
Washington, DC 20036
(202) 293-1200
Linda Colvard Dorian, Executive Director.

Dedicated to improving the economic status of working women through their integration into all occupations. Conducts and supports research on women and work, with special emphasis on economic issues. Provides Lena Lake Forrest Fellowship research at the doctoral and postdoctoral level; Sally Butler Memorial Fund for Latina Research for women of Latin American descent/citizenship. Awards educational scholarships to mature women, including Clairol Loving Care Scholarship, Avon Products Foundation Scholarship, and New York Life Foundation Scholarship for women in health professions and health product sales careers. Sponsors BPW Foundation Loan Fund for Women in Engineering and BPW/Sears-Roebuck Loan Fund for Women in Graduate Business Studies. Maintains Marguerite Rawalt Resource Center of 20,000 items on economic issues involving women and work and provides public reference and referral service. Established by BPW/USA and the National Federation of Business and Professional Women's Clubs. **Founded:** 1956. **Publications:** *Annual Report.* Also issues publications list.

CATALYST

250 Park Ave., S.
New York, NY 10003
(212) 777-8900
Felice N. Schwartz, President.

A national research and advisory organization that helps corporations foster career and leadership development of women. Works to: identify and analyze human resource issues such as impediments to women's progress in the corporation, balancing work and family, and managing a diverse work force. Develops cost-effective and transferable models that help employers manage the two-gender work force. **Services include:** Corporate Board Resource to assist employers in locating qualified women for board directorships; speakers' bureau; Information Center, which holds current statistics, print media, and research materials on women in business. **Founded:** 1962. **Publications:** *Perspective on Current Corporate Issues*, monthly. Also publishes research reports, career guidance books and pamphlets, policy planning tools for managing a diverse work force, and other publications on leadership development and career and family issues.

COALITION OF LEADING WOMEN'S ORGANIZATIONS

825 8th Ave.
New York, NY 10019
(212) 474-5000
Marcella Rosen, Chairperson.

COMMITTEE OF 200

625 N. Michigan Ave., Ste. 500
Chicago, IL 60611-3108
(312) 751-3477
Lydia Lewis, Executive Director.

Women executives who are recognized as leaders in their industries. (Though originally intended to have a membership of 200 top-ranking businesswomen, the committee is no longer limited to 200.) Encourages successful entrepreneurship by women and the active participation of women business owners and senior corporate executives in business, economic, social, and educational concerns. Seeks to strengthen the influence of women business leaders. Provides forum for exchange of ideas and enhancement of business opportunities for women. **Founded:** 1982. **Members:** 320. **Publications:** *Network,* monthly. Flier. *Update,* semiannual. Newsletter.

CORNELL UNIVERSITY INSTITUTE FOR WOMEN AND WORK

New York School of Industrial and Labor Relations
15 E. 26th St., 4th Fl.
New York, NY 10010
(212) 340-2800
Francine Moccio, Director.

IWW promotes education and applied research. Also sponsors conferences and seminars on working women's issues. Programs may be conducted in association with unions, government, or other universities. Topics include training for union leadership positions and research on health care occupations, nontraditional work, women in trades, and work and family issues. **Founded:** 1972.

EXECUTIVE WOMEN INTERNATIONAL

515 South, 700 East, Ste. 2E
Salt Lake City, UT 84102
(801) 355-2800
Lois Trayner-Allinder, President.

Individuals holding key positions in business professions. **Formerly:** (1977) Executives' Secretaries. **Founded:** 1938. **Local groups:** 86. **Members:** 5000. **Publications:** *Executive Women International Directory,* annual. *Pulse,* quarterly. Newsletter. Also publishes brochures.

FEDERATION OF ORGANIZATIONS FOR PROFESSIONAL WOMEN

2001 S St. NW, Ste. 500
Washington DC 20009
(202) 328-1415
Dr. Viola Young-Horvath, Director.

Computerized services: Mailing list (for members only). Affiliation of groups (30) and associates (200). Women's groups concerned with economic, educational, and social equality for women; interested individuals. Works to enhance the educational and employment status of women. Acts as a forum for the exchange of ideas and to provide mutual support. Provides information on selected public policy issues to affiliate groups. Offers research and policy analyses. Accepts internships. Conducts seminars and training programs; compiles statistics. Maintains speakers' bureau and referral service. Sponsors networking events. **Founded:** 1972. **Members:** 230. **Publications:** *A Woman's Yellow Book,* periodic. Directory. *ALERT,* bimonthly. Newsletter; *Washington Women Directory,* periodic. Also publishes booklets.

FEMINIST BUSINESS AND PROFESSIONAL NETWORK

PO Box 91214
Washington, DC 20090-1214
Chris Lundburg, President.

Individuals and companies promoting cooperation, nurturing, and increased visibility of women in business and the professions. Provides technical assistance and networking support. Facilitates the sharing of information, problems, and successes among members. Offers community education and referral service. Believes that "feminism as a world-view of cooperation, equality, peace, and nurturing" can be part of a business philosophy, and that feminist businesses provide jobs and allow women the opportunity to realize individual goals and work in a nonoppressive atmosphere. Operates speakers' bureau. Although its activities are primarily local, the group plans to expand nationally. **Founded:** 1986. **Members:** 85. **Publications:** *FBPN Directory,* quarterly. Also publishes brochure.

FORUM FOR WOMEN BUSINESS OWNERS

703 Third St., SW
Washington, DC 20024

FOUNDATION FOR WOMEN'S RESOURCES

Leadership America Program
700 N. Fairfax St., Ste. 202
Alexandria, VA 22314
(703) 549-1102
Kae B. Dakin, Executive Director.

National, non-profit leadership development program of the Foundation for Women's Resources for women of achievement. Goal is to develop more women leaders and to link them to the expanding network of their peers across the nation. Each year the program brings together a new group of 100 accomplished women from across the nation to participate in a year-long series of three professional development seminars. Through discussions with some of the country's most influential leaders, participants explore critical national and international issues while connecting with other women of achievement. **Founded:** 1988.

THE INTERNATIONAL ALLIANCE, AN ASSOCIATION OF EXECUTIVE AND PROFESSIONAL WOMEN

8600 LaSalle Rd., Ste. 308
Baltimore, MD 21204
(301) 321-6699
Marian E. Goetze, Executive Vice President.

20 Local networks comprised of 5000 professional and executive women; individual businesswomen without a network affiliation (100) are alliance associates. **Seeks to:** promote recognition of the achievements of women in business; encourage placement of women in senior executive positions; maintain high standards of professional competence among members. Facilitates communication on an international scale among professional women's networks and their members. Represents members' interests before policymakers in business and government. Sponsors programs that support equal opportunity and enhance members' business and professional skills. Operates appointments and directors service. Conducts seminars, symposia, and workshops; maintains speakers' bureau. **Formerly:** (1986) National Alliance of Professional and Executive Women's Networks. **Founded:** 1980. **Members:** 120. **Publications:** *Membership Directory*, annual. *The Alliance*, bimonthly. Association professional newsletter. Includes calendar of events and research updates.

MS. FOUNDATION FOR WOMEN

141 5th Ave., Ste. 6-S
New York, NY 10010
(212) 353-8580
Marie C. Wilson, Executive Director.

Goals are to eliminate sex discrimination and to improve the status of women and girls in society. Provides funds and technical assistance to activist, community-based self-help feminist projects working on issues of economic development, nonsexist multicultural education, reproductive rights, health and AIDS, and prevention of violence to women and children. Evaluates community-based women's groups and helps them strengthen their programs. **Founded:** 1972. **Projects:** Ad Hoc Sexual Harassment Coalition, a broad-based coalition of women's and civil rights groups organized in response to the sexual harassment charges brought by Anita Hill against Justice Clarence Thomas during the U.S. Supreme Court nomination hearings. List of supporters. **Publications:** *Newsletter*, quarterly. *Report*, annual. Also publishes periodic grant listings and summary brochures.

NATIONAL ALLIANCE OF HOMEBASED BUSINESSWOMEN

PO Box 306
Midland Park, NJ 07432
(201) 423-9131
Marie MacBride, Administrator.

Computerized services: Mailing list. Men and women who operate or plan to operate a homebased business; supporting members are interested individuals. Supports the right of every individual to operate a homebased business. Conducts national and local networking to combat the image of homebased businesses as "cottage industries" by emphasizing, encouraging, and stimulating personal, professional, and economic growth of members. Believes that homebased businesses deserve respect and should enjoy the same privileges and obligations as other businesses. Seeks the removal of federal, state, and local restrictions on homebased business. Keeps members abreast of legal, political, and business developments affecting homebased businesses. Serves as a forum for the discussion and exchange of information and experiences; provides a network of professional and educational contacts. **Seeks to:** influence planning boards to adopt zoning laws that are fair to homebased business; eliminate laws prohibiting homebased business; gain recognition of the legitimacy of homebased business; provide educational and business resources. Arranges and provides life insurance, car rentals, and hotel discounts for members; publicizes members' goods and services; conducts seminars. **Founded:** 1981. **Local groups:** 15. **Members:** 600. **Publications:** *Alliance*, bimonthly. Professional and association newsletter. Book reviews; classified ads. *National Alliance of Homebased Businesswomen-Directory of Members*, annual in July with January update. Membership directory arranged by personal name, by company name, and geographically. Also publishes *Zoning for Homebased Business* and *Planning for Homebased Business* (pamphlets).

NATIONAL ASSOCIATION OF COMMISSIONS FOR WOMEN

YWCA Bldg., 6th Fl.
624 9th St. NW
Washington, DC 20001
(202) 628-5030
Claire Bigelow, Director.

State, city, and county commissions that focus on the status of women. Seeks to strengthen and coordinate the vital work of the state and local commissions, and to further the legal, social, political, economic, and educational equality of American women, that they may make their fullest contribution in our nation. Works to: eliminate discrimination based on sex, race, age, religion, national origin, or marital status in all areas of American society; foster the dissemination of information and provide counsel on opportunities for the effective participation of women in the private and public sector; create greater public awareness of the role and function of commissions on the status of women and provide a national focus on issues affecting women; strengthen commissions, coordinate their efforts nationwide, and provide a unified voice; act as a central clearinghouse and networking resource for information and activities of commissions across the country; foster a closer relationship and fuller exchange of ideas among members. Offers guidance in the designing of new strategies and programs on critical contemporary issues of concern to women; assists efforts to broaden the base of involvement of women of color and those of different backgrounds; works with other national women's groups on issues requiring collective action. Presents testimony at public hearings; monitors legislation of special interest to women. Maintains speakers' bureau; compiles statistics. Conducts research, workshops, and leadership training programs. Operates resource library. **Formerly:** (1975) Interstate Association of Commissions for Women. **Founded:** 1970. **Local groups:** 200. **Regional Groups:** 33. **State Groups:** 40. **Members:** 128. **Publications:** *Breakthrough*, quarterly. Newsletter reporting on news and activities of regional, state, and local commissions; includes legislative updates. *Directory of National, Regional, State and Local Commissions*, periodic. Also publishes informational pamphlets, organizational handbook, and federal legislative alerts.

NATIONAL ASSOCIATION OF MINORITY WOMEN IN BUSINESS
906 Grand Ave., Ste. 200
Kansas City, MO 64106
(816) 421-3335
Inez Kaiser, President.

Minority women in business ownership and management positions; college students. Serves as a network for the exchange of ideas and information on business opportunities for minority women in the public and private sectors. Conducts research and educational programs, as well as workshops, conferences, seminars, and luncheons. Maintains speakers' bureau, hall of fame, and placement service; compiles statistics; bestows awards to women who have made significant contributions to the field. **Founded:** 1972. **Members:** 5000. **Publications:** *Today*, bimonthly. Newsletter. Also publishes brochures.

NATIONAL ASSOCIATION OF WOMEN BUSINESS OWNERS
600 S. Federal St., Ste. 400
Chicago, IL 60605
(312) 922-6222
Natalie Holmes, Executive Director.

Computerized services: Data bank of women-owned businesses. Women who own and operate their own businesses. **Purposes are:** to identify and bring together women business owners in mutual support; to communicate and share experiences and talents with others; to use collective influence to broaden opportunities for women in business. **Services offered include:** workshops and seminars; information clearinghouse, referral service, and reader service; representation before governmental bodies; liaison with groups of similar orientation. Bestows awards. **Formerly:** (1976) Association of Women Business Owners. **Founded:** 1974. **Local groups:** 44. **Members:** 3000. **Publications:** *Annual Membership Roster. Statement*, bimonthly. Association and membership activities newsletter. Includes calendar of events.

NATIONAL ASSOCIATION FOR WOMEN IN CAREERS
PO Box 81525
Chicago, IL 60681-0525
(312) 938-7662
Pat Surbella, CEO & President.

Service organization for women representing various economic sectors including corporations, personally-owned businesses, nonprofit and sales organizations, retail outlets, financial institutions including government and health agencies, educational institutions, and associations. Provides support, networking, and skill-development services for all women to enhance their potential for greater success and enable them to meet future challenges for personal and career growth. Attempts to help women integrate who they are with what they do and to balance the demands of career growth and private life. Conducts seminars; provides job referral, career planning, and professional speakers. **Formerly:** (1985) National Association of Future Women. **Founded:** 1981. **State Groups:** 8. **Members:** 1500. **Publications:** *Directory*, periodic.

NATIONAL COUNCIL OF CAREER WOMEN
3202 Gemstone Ct.
Oakton, VA 22124
(703) 591-4359
Patricia Whittaker, President.

Women interested in achieving maximum potential in the business world and individual careers (350); corporate sponsors (5). Seeks to enhance the image and role of women in the business and professional world, through professional skill development, education, mentoring, and networking. Bestows awards; operates placement services. **Founded:** 1975. **Members:** 355. **Publications:** *Membership Directory*, annual. *NCCW News*, bimonthly. Also publishes brochure.

NATIONAL COUNCIL FOR RESEARCH ON WOMEN
Sara Delano Roosevelt Memorial House
47-49 E. 65th St.
New York, NY 10021
(212) 570-5001
Mary Ellen Capek, Executive Director.

National network of organizations representing the academic community, policymakers, and others interested in women's issues. Purpose is to bring institutional resources to bear on feminist research, policy analysis, and educational programs addressing legal, economic, and social inequities. Conducts and promotes collaborative research on women in development, and race, class, and gender issues; acts as clearinghouse. Houses the National Network of Women's Caucuses and Committees in the Disciplinary and Professional Associations. Operates the National Council Database Project that coordinates the development and application of current technology, software, and index standards to improve access to existing research, programs, and work in progress; is developing an online data base. Sponsors seminars. **Founded:** 1981. **Members:** 60. **Publications:** *Annual Report. Directory of Members*, periodic. *Women's Mailing List Directory*, periodic. *Women's Research Network News*, 3-4/year. Newsletter reporting on member centers' activities, women's caucuses, and research; includes information on new books, fellowships, study and job opportunities, and conference announcements. Also publishes *A Declining Federal Commitment to Research About Women, 1980-1984, International Centers for Research on Women, Mainstreaming Minority Women's Studies, Opportunities for Research and Study, 1989, Third World Women in Agriculture, an Annotated Bibliography, Transforming the Knowledge Base, Women in Academe: Progress and Prospects, A Task Force Report, Women in Development: Theory and Practice, Women's Thesaurus: An Index of Language Used to Describe and Locate Information By and About Women, Sexual Harassment: Research and Resources, A Report-in-Progress.*

NATIONAL FOUNDATION FOR WOMEN BUSINESS OWNERS

1825 I St. NW, Ste. 800
Washington, DC 20006
(202) 833-1854
Sharon Hardary, Executive Director.

NFWBO is the nonprofit educational branch of the National Association of Business Owners. NFWBO is concerned with the leadership and career training of women entrepreneurs and women in management. Performs data collection and disseminates facts and statistics on women business owners; offers management and technical assistance programs; and provides work force training and monitoring programs. **Publications:** *Newsletter of the National Foundation for Women Business Owners,* quarterly.

NATIONAL WOMEN'S ECONOMIC ALLIANCE FOUNDATION

1440 New York Ave. NW, Ste. 300
Washington, DC 20005
(202) 393-5257
Patricia Harrison, President.

Computerized services: Data base of women on corporate boards. Executive-level women and men. Promotes dialogue among men and women in industry, business, and government. Focuses on professional, economic, and career concerns and how to address these issues within the framework of the free enterprise system. Conducts research programs and leadership seminars; offers placement service; maintains biographical archives; bestows awards. **Founded:** 1983. **Members:** 750. **Publications:** *NWEA Outlook,* semiannual. *Policy Papers,* periodic. *Women Directors of the Top 1000 Corporations,* annual. Directory of women who serve on corporate boards of Fortune 1000 companies. Also publishes *America's New Women Entrepreneurs* (book). **Telecommunications services:** telex, 756546.

NETWORK FOR PROFESSIONAL WOMEN

c/o JoAnne P. Smith
City Personnel
100 Committee Plaza, Ste. 220
Hartford, CT 06103
(203) 727-1988
JoAnne P. Smith, President.

To educate and motivate professional women in all facets of their lives. Sponsors seminars and workshops on topics including management of credit, employment networking, IRAs, and reentering the work force. **Founded:** 1979.

9 TO 5 WORKING WOMEN EDUCATION FUND

614 Superior Ave. NW
Cleveland, OH 44113
(216) 566-1699
Tami O'Dell, Executive Director.

Conducts research on the concerns of women office workers. **Topics include:** the future of office work; automation; health and safety issues; affirmative action; family and medical leave; pay equity; flex-time; job-sharing. Conducts public presentations and seminars upon request; provides speakers. Compiles statistics; has conducted a national survey on women and stress. Maintains biographical archives and library on the history of working women. **Formerly:** (1989) Working Women Education Fund. **Founded:** 1973. **Publications:** Reports.

WOMEN IN ADVERTISING AND MARKETING

4200 Wisconsin Ave. NW, Ste. 106-238
Washington, DC 20016
(301) 369-7400
Hilary Levine, President.

Professional women in advertising and marketing. Serves as a network to keep members abreast of developments in advertising and marketing. Fosters professional contact among members. Conducts periodic seminar. Operates speakers' bureau and job bank. **Founded:** 1980. **Local groups:** 1. **Members:** 225. **Publications:** *Membership Directory,* periodic. *Newsletter,* quarterly.

WOMEN ENTREPRENEURS

1275 Market St., Ste. 1300
San Francisco, CA 94103
(415) 929-0129
Sharon Cannon, President.

Computer Services: Data base. Women who actively own and operate a business (retail, service, manufacturing, consulting, publishing or other); associate members are persons with plans to start a business or who support the organization's goals. Offers the woman business owner support, recognition, and access to vital information and resources. Has participated in government studies and in the 1980 White House Conference on Small Business. Conducts monthly programs featuring speakers and technical assistance educational seminars and workshops; sponsors Advice Forum, providing business and problem-solving information; bestows Appreciation Awards. **Founded:** 1974. **Members:** 150. **Publications:** *Membership Roster,* annual. *Prospectus,* monthly.

WOMEN EXECUTIVES IN PUBLIC RELATIONS

PO Box 20766
New York, NY 10025-1516
(212) 721-9661
Alyce K. Noonan, Administrator.

Women and men senior-level executives in public relations (membership by invitation). Purposes are to: provide a support network for women in public relations; cooperate for mutual advancement and broaden professional knowledge; foster equality of opportunity, management development, training, promotion, and remuneration in public relations. Offers grants and scholarships for courses in public relations and internships to college students majoring in communications. **Formerly:** (1971) Committee on Women in Public Relations. **Founded:** 1946. **Members:** 110. **Publications:** *Network*, quarterly. Newsletter.

WOMEN IN INFORMATION PROCESSING

Lock Box 39173
Washington, DC 20016
(202) 328-6161
Janice H. Miller, President.

Computer Services: Resumé bank. International organization of women who are professionals in computer fields, office automation, robotics, telecommunications, artificial intelligence, and related disciplines. **Seeks to:** advance the industry by helping women benefit from opportunities created by automation; attract additional qualified women; aid women in building professional contacts. Sponsors product demonstrations and exhibits. Offers speakers' bureau, career counseling, monthly seminar, resume guidance, discussions, and scholarship programs. Compiles statistics; bestows awards; offers group rate medical insurance. Presents annual award for meritorious achievements. **Founded:** 1979. **Regional Groups:** 5. **Members:** 4827. **Publications:** *Forumnet*, quarterly. *Salary and Perception Survey*, annual.

WOMEN'S BUSINESS DEVELOPMENT CENTER

205 Gurley Hall
Russell Sage College
Troy, NY 12180
(518) 270-2302
Ruth Leverett, Chair, Board of Directors.

The Center acts as a catalyst for women to recognize and increase their business skills and ownership and to influence the business environment by providing access to a variety of resources.

WOMEN'S INFORMATION EXCHANGE

PO Box 68
Jenner, CA 95450
(707) 632-5763
Jill Lippitt, Executive Officer.

Computer Services: Data base on women and women's service providers organized into categories such as health centers, women's centers, women's studies programs, and newspapers; data is available to organizations on peel-and-stick labels through the National Women's Mailing List. Feminist women computer specialists who believe that computer technology may be used to support the efforts of women and women's organizations nationwide. Promotes networking and communication between women and women's organizations. Provides speakers on such topics as gender-based learning differences, office automation, and women and technology. **Founded:** 1980.

WOMEN'S INSTITUTE

5225 Pooks Hill Rd., Ste. 1718-N
Bethesda, MD 20814
(301) 530-9192
Rita Z. Johnston, President.

Serves as a vehicle for the development and presentation of programs on special problems and major issues of concern to women. Provides an educational and political forum for women's roles in economic, family, political and social life on a local, national, and international level. Conducts research. Presents the Myra E. Barrer Journalism Award for excellence and commitment to feminist journalism to a senior or graduate students at American University in Washington, DC. Maintains library. **Founded:** 1975. **Publications:** *Winds of Change: Korean Women in America, Convention on the Elimination of All Forms of Discrimination Against Women*, and *United Nations Decade for Women Plans of Action* (books).

WOMEN'S INTERNATIONAL NETWORK

187 Grant St.
Lexington, MA 02173
(616) 862-9431
Fran P. Hosken, Coordinator/Editor.

Goal is to encourage cooperation and communication between women of all backgrounds, beliefs, nationalities, and age groups through the compilation and dissemination of information on women's development. Participants voluntarily contribute news and information on women and health, environment, media, violence, female genital mutilation, and United Nations events of concern to women. The Network's Women and International Affairs Clearinghouse surveys career opportunities for women interested in working in international and development agencies. Conducts research on women's health and on women's development throughout the world. Maintains library of women's publications. **Founded:** 1975. **Publications:** *WIN News*, quarterly. Journal providing information on women and women's groups worldwide. Has also published *Hosken Report: Genital and Sexual Mutilations of Females, Action Guide*, and *The Childbirth Picture Book* (series in Arabic, English, French, and Spanish), including flip charts and color slides.

WOMEN'S MEDIA PROJECT

1333 H St., NW, 11th Fl.
Washington, DC 20005
(202) 682-0940
Rosanna Landis, Contact.

A project of the NOW Legal Defense and Education Fund. Feminist activists united to eliminate sex role stereotyping of women and men in the media and to increase the participation of women and minorities in broadcasting. Purposes are to: conduct public education campaigns with up-to-date information on issues that affect women; guide individuals and groups in developing effective dialogues with local broadcasters and publishers through community action campaigns; monitor compliance with equal employment legislation in the communications industry; encourage development and distribution of quality television and radio programming that offers realistic and contemporary images of women. Identifies programming promoting equality between women and men. Conducts research in broadcast employment. **Formerly:** (1987) Media Project. **Founded:** 1979. **Publications:** *Women's Media Campaign Workbook*, annual. Also publishes research reports.

■ *Newsletters*

THE GP REPORTER
Box 060377, N.D. Sta.
Staten Island, NY 10306-0004
(718) 981-5703

Focuses on journalism, mass communication, advertising, and marketing "to promote the growth of a professional journalistic approach to the legitimate concerns of Gay men and women." Recurring features include editorials and news briefs. **First published:** June 1982. **Frequency:** Bimonthly. **Price:** $9/yr.

MARKETING TO WOMEN
33 Broad St.
Boston, MA 02109
(617) 723-4337

Discusses market studies aimed at women. Covers such topics as demographics, women's attitudes, family issues, consumer products, fashion, media preferences, health care, employment, recreation, food/nutrition, shopping, working women, travel, and reproduction. **Edited by:** E. Janice Leeming. **Frequency:** Monthly. **Former title:** *Woman Scope*. **Price:** $230/yr. for individuals and $200 for institutions, USC; $255 and $225 elsewhere.

MEDIA REPORT TO WOMEN
10606 Mantz Rd.
Silver Spring, MD 20903-1228
(301) 445-3230

Discusses concerns of media women and news of current women's media events. Carries documents and reports on women's actions worldwide in areas such as devising new communications structures, the employment of women in the media, and the portrayal of women in the media. Focuses on how to increase the effectiveness of media to keep the public aware of women's news and information. **First published:** 1972. **Frequency:** Bimonthly. **Price:** $35/yr. for individuals; $50 for institutions.

MS. FOUNDATION FOR WOMEN NEWSLETTER
141 5th Ave., Ste. 6S
New York, NY 10010-7105
(212) 353-8580

Reports efforts the foundation has made in the areas of funding and assistance to women's self-help initiatives, changes in public consciousness, law, philanthropy, and social policy, and the direction of resources toward activities that discourage racial, class, age, sexual orientation, and cultural barriers.

THE MURRAY RESEARCH CENTER NEWS
10 Garden St.
Cambridge, MA 02138
(617) 495-8140

Reports on the Center's research initiatives and archival collection of social and behavioral research data. The center houses data with an emphasis on the lives of American women. **Frequency:** 2/yr.

NATIONAL ASSOCIATION OF WOMEN BUSINESS OWNERS–STATEMENT
600 S. Federal St., Ste. 400
Chicago, IL 60605
(312) 922-0465

Serves as a forum for women business owners to communicate and share experiences with others and to use their collective influence to broaden opportunities for women in business. Monitors trends and legislative developments affecting women in business, and provides news of the Association's services and activities on the behalf of women business owners. **Frequency:** Bimonthly. **Price:** Included in membership.

THE NATIONAL REPORT ON WORK & FAMILY
1350 Connecticut Ave. NW
Washington, DC 20036
(202) 862-0993

Examines the changes in family structure and their impact on the workplace. Covers parental leave, elder care, care for sick children, flexible worktime, and other related issues. **First published:** December 15, 1987. **Frequency:** Biweekly. **Price:** $475/yr.

NEWSLETTER OF THE GEOGRAPHIC PERSPECTIVES ON WOMEN SPECIALTY GROUP
Department of Geography
Lucy Stone Hall
New Brunswick, NJ 08903
(201) 932-4013

Discusses topics relating to women and gender.

OSCLG NEWS
Communication Department
2607 S. Forest Ave.
Tempe, AZ 85282
(602) 967-2817

Information on creative projects in the areas of communication, language, and gender. **Frequency:** Quarterly. **Price:** $6/yr.

THE SEX AND GENDER NEWSLETTER

Sociology Department
PO Box 5072
New Brunswick, NJ 08904-5072
(908) 932-2897

Contains information on gender relations.

SUCCESSFUL SALESWOMEN

PO Box 2606
Novato, CA 94948
(415) 898-2606

Reports on the status of women in sales and marketing.

UCLA CENTER FOR THE STUDY OF WOMEN NEWSLETTER

236A Kinsey Hall
Los Angeles, CA 90064
(213) 825-0590

Covers activities of the Center, which encourages and supports research on women and gender issues. **Frequency:** Quarterly.

WOMEN AND GENDER RESEARCH INSTITUTE NEWSLETTER

College of Natural Resources
Logan, UT 84322-5200
(801) 750-2580

Encourages the involvement of women in research and promotes research on gender-related issues.

WOMEN & LANGUAGE

Communication Department
Fairfax, VA 22030
(703) 993-1099

Presents interdisciplinary research in the field of language and gender. Discusses theory, language use, acquisition, and attitudes. Coordinates information on sex-differentiated language research in linguistics, anthropology, speech communication, sociology, psychology, literature, education, medicine, women's studies, and other disciplines. **First published:** January 1976. **Frequency:** 2/yr. **Price:** $8/yr. for individuals, U.S.; $10 for individuals, Canada; $13 elsewhere. $15 for institutions, U.S. and Canada.

WOMEN WITH WHEELS-NEWSLETTER

1718 A Northfield Sq.
Northfield, IL 60093
(708) 501-3519

Provides information on cars and their maintenance. Features articles on anti-lock brakes, safety, leasing, purchasing, and deal-

ing with car salespeople. **First published:** Spring 1989. **Frequency:** Quarterly. **Price:** $15/yr. for individuals; $20 for institutions.

WOMEN AT WORK

1325 G St., NW
Washington, DC 20005
(202) 638-3143

Combines information devoted to increasing economic independence and equality of opportunities for women. **Frequency:** Quarterly.

THE WOMEN'S CAUCUS NEWSLETTER

5105 Backlick Rd., Ste. E
Annandale, VA 22003
(703) 750-0533

Disseminates information on women in communications. Supports scholarly research on women and gender. **Frequency:** Semiannual.

■ *Newspapers*

THE OWL OBSERVER

730 11th St. NW, Ste. 300
Washington, DC 20001
(202) 783-6686

National. Includes news, views, and concerns of mid-life and older women activists. **Frequency:** 6/yr. **Subscription:** $15.

RIVETING NEWS

PO Box 93384
Cleveland, OH 44101
(216) 961-4449

Tabloid reporting on racism, affirmative action, child care, the environment, housing, and other issues relating to women. Includes book reviews. **Frequency:** Quarterly. **Subscription:** $7.

SAN DIEGO LESBIAN PRESS

PO Box 8666
San Diego, CA 92102

Newspaper providing a forum and focus for lesbian ideas and issues. **Frequency:** 6/yr.

TODAY'S CHICAGO WOMAN

233 E. Ontario St., Ste. 1300
Chicago, IL 60611
(312) 951-7600

Magazine (tabloid) providing information to working women in Chicago. **First published:** October 1982. **Frequency:** Monthly. **Subscription:** Free to qualified subscribers.

TODAY'S WOMAN

PO Box 1048
Peoria, IL 61653-1048
(309) 672-2722

Newspaper focusing on women's issues, news, and profiles.
First published: 1985. **Frequency:** Monthly.

WOMANEWS

PO Box 220 Village Sta.
New York, NY 10014
(212) 674-1698

New York City feminist newspaper and calendar. Provides a
forum for the NYC feminist community while focusing on issues
of interest to women everywhere. **Frequency:** Monthly.
Subscription: $1.25/sample issue.

WOMEN'S NEWS

PO Box 829
Harrison, NY 10528
(914) 835-5400

Feminist newspaper geared toward women's issues, problems,
events, and causes. Features pull-out event calendar, news
briefs, follow-ups, classifieds, displays, letters, and special cultural
issues. **First published:** December 1979. **Frequency:**
Monthly. **Subscription:** $15.

THE WOMEN'S RECORD

55 Northern Blvd.
Greenvale, NY 11548
(516) 625-3033

Business newspaper for professional women. **First published:**
August 1985. **Frequency:** Monthly. **Subscription:** $10;
$16.95 two years.

■ *Research Centers*

ALVERNO COLLEGE RESEARCH CENTER ON WOMEN

3401 S. 39th St.
Milwaukee, WI 53215
(414) 382-6084
Austin Doherty, Vice President for Academic Affairs

Founded: 1970. **Library Holdings:** Maintains books,
research reports, pamphlets, periodicals, and audiovisual
resources. Lola Stuller, librarian. **Meetings/Seminars:**
Cosponsors Woman to Woman Conference (annually).
Publications: *RCD Reporter* (irregularly). **Research
Interests:** Status and role of women in American society and
economic, political, psychological, social, physiological, and religious factors that have influenced the past history of women
and contribute to contemporary lifestyles. Mainstreams
women's studies in the college curriculum and monitors
women's contributions in academic disciplines.

BUSINESS AND PROFESSIONAL WOMEN'S FOUNDATION

2012 Massachusetts Ave. NW
Washington, DC 20036
(202) 293-1200

Contact: Sandra Shastel, Executive Director
Founded: 1956. **Library Holdings:** 6,000 volumes and
other materials on economic issues affecting U.S. women.
Publications: *Research Summaries; Information Digests on
Women and Work.* **Research Interests:** Women's economic
issues, including wage work, family work and life, and pay equity.
Awards research fellowships for doctoral and postdoctoral
research on women's economic issues and for women
researchers of Latin American descent or citizenship.

CITY UNIVERSITY OF NEW YORK CENTER FOR THE STUDY OF WOMEN AND SOCIETY

33 W. 42nd St.
New York, NY 10036
(212) 642-2954

Contact: Dr. Sue Rosenberg Zalk, Director
Formerly: Center for the Study of Women and Sex Roles.
Founded: 1978. **Meetings/Seminars:** Holds seminars and
conferences on topics related to women and society.
Publications: *Newsletter* (biannual); *Feminist Directory;
Gender-Balancing Handbook.* **Research Interests:** Issues
related to women in health and women and work. Projects
include revision of college curricula to reflect scholarship on
gender, race, ethnicity, and class, a study of women and substance abuse, an investigation of gender and crime, and an evaluation of women internationally.

COLUMBIA UNIVERSITY INSTITUTE FOR RESEARCH ON WOMEN AND GENDER

763 Schermerhorn Extension
New York, NY 10027
(212) 854-3277

Contact: Martha Howell, Director
Research Interests: Women as related to race and class.

EQUITY POLICY CENTER

2000 P St. NW
Washington, DC 20036
(202) 872-1770

Contact: Dr. Irene Tinker, President
Founded: 1978. **Library Holdings:** 6,000 titles on women,
fugitives, development policy, urban development, employment
and income generation, rural development, agriculture and food,
education, communications, natural resources, energy, science,
population, migrations and refugees, and youth. Putting all text
on CD ROM. **Research Interests:** Studies and promotes
more equitable distribution of income and resources world-

wide, with particular attention to women. Programs concentrate on the food system, micro-enterprise, population, household energy, futures, and development policy.

THE FEMINIST PRESS AT THE CITY UNIVERSITY OF NEW YORK

311 E. 94 St.
New York, NY 10128
(212) 360-5790

Contact: Prof. Florence Howe, Director
Founded: 1970. **Library Holdings:** Several thousand books, a vertical file on women's studies programs, and a major collection of international materials on women. **Meetings/Seminars:** Sponsors programs at the annual meetings of the National Women's Studies Association and at international meetings. **Publications:** *Women's Studies Quarterly*. **Meetings/Educational Activities:** Sponsors programs at the annual meetings of the National Women's Studies Association and at international meetings. **Research Interests:** Women's lives and patterns of education for women, including "lost" literature by and about women (fiction, autobiography, biography, and history). Also studies the status and treatment of women in colleges and universities and the history and status of women's studies programs and centers for research on women, both nationally and internationally. Specific projects focus on literature by and about disabled women, about disabled women and lost women writers and lost women writers of India.

NATIONAL MUSEUM OF WOMEN IN THE ARTS

Library and Research Center
1250 New York Ave. NW
Washington, DC 20005
(202) 783-5000

Contact: Krystyna Wasserman, Director
Founded: 1981. **Research Interests:** Women in the arts. Research is mostly related to the visual arts.

OHIO STATE UNIVERSITY
CENTER FOR WOMEN'S STUDIES

207 Dulles Hall
230 W. 17th Ave.
Columbus, OH 43210-1311
(614) 292-1021

Contact: Dr. Susan M. Hartmann, Director
Formerly: Office of Women's Studies (1980). **Founded:** 1975. **Meetings/Seminars:** Sponsors a visiting lecture series and a colloquium/symposium series. **Publications:** *Feminisms* (quarterly review of new scholarship, fiction, poetry, films, and art by and about women); Research Directory (covering approximately 50 faculty members at the University pursuing work in women's studies). **Research Interests:** Develops, coordinates, and conducts interdisciplinary research projects in

women's studies with focus on cultural identities, gender issues, collective history, social roles, literary and artistic productions, and individual experiences. Administers research grants program yearly for faculty, staff, and students conducting scholarly research on women and women's issues.

RADCLIFFE COLLEGE
HENRY A. MURRAY RESEARCH CENTER

10 Garden St.
Cambridge, MA 02138
(617) 495-8140

Contact: Dr. Anne Colby, Director
Formerly: Radcliffe Data Resource and Research Center (1979). **Founded:** 1976. **Meetings/Seminars:** Sponsors workshops, colloquia, and occasional conferences during the academic year. **Publications:** *Murray Center News* (two times per year); *Guide to the Data Resources of the Murray Center*. **Research Interests:** National repository for data on American women collected by social scientists. Houses both computer and raw data, including interview transcripts, questionnaires, and projective tests for secondary analysis, follow-up, replication, and other research purposes. Acts as a catalyst for and sponsors scholarly research, including dissertation and postdoctoral research on women. Grants awards to eligible researchers.

SIMMONS COLLEGE
INSTITUTE FOR CASE DEVELOPMENT AND RESEARCH

Graduate School of Management
409 Commonwealth Ave.
Boston, MA 02215
(617) 536-8289

Contact: Cinny Little, Director
Founded: 1974. **Library Holdings:** Maintains a collection on management; Jane Nash, librarian. **Publications:** *Catalogue of Cases on Women in Management* (revised annually). **Research Interests:** Researches, publishes, and distributes case studies on organizational behavior issues in management. All cases feature women in middle and senior management. Cases address a variety of management situations as well as the issues of career planning and development, minority women in management, and balancing family and career.

SMITH COLLEGE
PROJECT ON WOMEN AND SOCIAL CHANGE

138 Elm St.
Northampton, MA 01063
(413) 585-3591

Contact: Dr. Susan C. Bourque, Director
Founded: 1978. **Library Holdings:** Contact organization for more information. **Research Interests:** Women, including studies in the areas of health and technology, cross-cultural issues, adult development, public policy, gender, and international development.

STATE UNIVERSITY OF NEW YORK COLLEGE AT BROCKPORT
Community Research Center
Brockport, NY 14420
(716) 395-2682

Contact: Margaret Blackman, Dept. Head
Specialty: Gender and Cultural Diversity.

SYRACUSE UNIVERSITY WOMEN'S STUDIES PROGRAM
307 Hall of Languages
Syracuse, NY 13244-1170
(315) 443-3707

Contact: Diane Lyden Murphy, Director
Founded: 1975. **Meetings/Seminars:** Coordinates conferences and sponsors a lecture series, weekly lunch seminars, and faculty seminars. **Publications:** *Newsletter* (semiannually). **Research Interests:** Women, including studies on women's work in the U.S. and comparative perspectives, images, and traditions of women in literature; the gendering of knowledge and the academic profession; sex role socialization; feminist theory; women's history; and women and public policy. Activities focus on feminist analysis for social change.

UNION INSTITUTE THE WOMEN'S PROJECT
1731 Connecticut Ave., NW, No.300
Washington, DC 20009-1146
(202) 667-1313

Contact: Dr. Judith Arcana

UNIVERSITY OF CONNECTICUT INSTITUTE FOR THE STUDY OF WOMEN AND GENDER
U-181
Stoors, CT 06268-1181
(203) 486-2186

Contact: Patricia A. Carter, Coordinator
The institute's purpose is the development of research projects that have "both a theoretical and applied nature," including gender equity in education, women and technology, women and international development, women and labor force participation, and women and disability. **Publications:** *Annual Report*; *Working Paper Series*.

UNIVERSITY OF ILLINOIS AT CHICAGO WOMEN'S STUDIES PROGRAM
Box 4348, M/C 360
Rm. 1022 C BSB
Chicago, IL 60680
(312) 413-2300

Contact: Stephanie Riger, Director
Founded: 1973. **Research Interests:** Interdisciplinary studies concerning the history and role of women in society. Studies have included the development of curricula especially appropriate to women's studies in an urban area.

UNIVERSITY OF SOUTHERN CALIFORNIA INSTITUTE FOR THE STUDY OF WOMEN AND MEN
734 W. Adams Blvd., 208
Los Angeles, CA 90007
(213) 743-3683

Contact: Judith Glass, Ph.D., Director
Founded: 1987. **Meetings/Seminars:** Sponsors an affiliated scholars program, a distinguished visitors program, and outreach programs, including a mentoring project with minority high school girls. **Publications:** *Bi-Annual Newsletter; Faculty Research Directory.* **Research Interests:** Gender issues, feminism, ethnicity, and sexuality. Also studies media and its feminist movement.

UNIVERSITY OF TEXAS AT ARLINGTON WOMEN AND MINORITY WORK RESEARCH AND RESOURCE CENTER
Box 19129
Arlington, TX 76019
(817) 273-3131

Contact: Kathleen Underwood, Director
Research Interests: Women and work, particularly the interrelationships between work and family, women entrepreneurs and owners of small businesses, and the effect of on-site child care facilities on employee, family, company, and child. Activities encompass studies of demographic trends and projections, education, reentry of mature women to higher education, and sex equity.

WOMEN EMPLOYED INSTITUTE
22 W. Monroe, Ste. 1400
Chicago, IL 60603-2505
(312) 782-3902

Contact: Anne Ladky, Executive Director
Founded: 1973. **Research Interests:** Economic status of working women, working women and the law, sexual harassment in the workplace, equal employment opportunity, women's access to vocational education and job training, comparable worth, working mothers, and career development.

■ *Top 25 Women-Owned Businesses*

AXEL JOHNSON GROUP
110 E. 59th St.
New York, NY 10022
Antonia Axson Johnson, Chair

Number of Employees: 2,000 **Founded:** 1873 **Rank in 1991:** 1 **Sales:** $829 million **Type of Business:** Specialty metals, water-treatment and telecommunications equipment.

MINYARD FOOD STORES
PO Box 518
Coppell, TX 75019
Gretchen Minyard Williams, Co-Chair

Number of Employees: 6,100. **Founded:** 1932 **Rank in 1991:** 2 **Sales:** $700 million **Type of Business:** Supermarket chains.

WARNACO GROUP INC.
90 Park Ave.
New York, NY 10016
Linda J. Wachner, Chair, CEO, President

Number of Employees: 11,800 **Founded:** 1874 **Rank in 1991:** 3 **Sales:** $548 million **Type of Business:** Apparel manufacturer.

JOCKEY INTERNATIONAL
2300 60th St.
Kenosha, WI 53140
Donna W. Steigerwaldt, Chair, CEO

Number of Employees: 5,000 **Founded:** 1876 **Rank in 1991:** 4 **Sales:** $450 million **Type of Business:** Apparel manufacturer.

ESPRIT DE CORP
900 Minnesota Ave.
San Francisco, CA 94017
Susie Tompkins, Creative Director

Number of Employees: 1,400 **Founded:** 1968 **Rank in 1991:** 5 **Sales:** $450 million **Type of Business:** Women's, children's apparel manufacturer and wholesaler.

ASTRONAUTICS
41115 N. Teutonia
Milwaukee, WI 53209
Norma Paige, Chair and Executive Vice President

Number of Employees: 4,700 **Founded:** 1959 **Rank in 1991:** 6 **Sales:** $415 million **Type of Business:** Aircraft and navigation equipment manufacturer.

JENNY CRAIG, INC.
445 Marine View Ave., Ste. 300
Del Mar, CA 92014
Jenny Craig, Vice Chair

Number of Employees: 7,000 **Founded:** 1983 **Rank in 1991:** 7 **Sales:** $412 million **Type of Business:** Weight-loss centers and diet foods.

COPLEY PRESS
7776 Ivanhoe Ave.
La Jolla, CA 92307
Helen K. Copley, Chair, CEO

Number of Employees: 3,500 **Founded:** 1905 **Rank in 1991:** 8 **Sales:** $405 million **Type of Business:** Newspaper publishing and printing.

CHARLES LEVY CO.
1200 N. Northbranch St.
Chicago, IL 60627
Barbara Levy Kipper, Chair

Number of Employees: 1,700 **Founded:** 1893 **Rank in 1991:** 9 **Sales:** $350 million **Type of Business:** Book, magazine, newspaper and video wholesaler.

LUNDY PACKING CO.
PO Box 49
Clinton, NC 28328
Annabelle Lundy Fetterman, Chair

Number of Employees: 900 **Founded:** 1950 **Rank in 1991:** 10 **Sales:** $350 million. **Type of Business:** Pork processing

GEAR HOLDINGS, INC.
127 7th Ave.
New York, NY 10011
Bettye Martin Musham, CEO, President

Number of Employees: 30 **Rank in 1991:** 11 **Sales:** $280 million **Type of Business:** Furniture design, home furnishings.

JOHNSON PUBLISHING
820 S. Michigan Ave.
Chicago, IL 60605
Linda Johnson Rice, CEO, President

Number of Employees: 2,753 **Founded:** 1942 **Rank in 1991:** 12 **Sales:** $252 million **Type of Business:** Black media conglomerate.

OWEN HEALTHCARE, INC.
9800 Centre Pkwy., Ste. 1100
Houston, TX 77036
Dian Graves Owen, Chair, Co-CEO

Number of Employees: 2,000 **Founded:** 1970 **Rank in 1991:** 13 **Sales:** $250 million **Type of Business:** Cost-control company for hospital pharmacies.

CAROLE LITTLE, INC.
102 E. Martin Luther King Blvd.
Los Angeles, CA 90011
Carole Little, Co-Chair, Co-Founder

Number of Employees: 600 **Founded:** 1975 **Rank in 1991:** 14 **Sales:** $205 million **Type of Business:** Women's apparel manufacturer.

SUNSHINE-JR. STORES, INC.
PO Box 2498
Panama City, FL 32402
Lana Jane Lewis-Brent, President, Vice Chair

Number of Employees: 1,800 **Founded:** 1944 **Rank in 1991:** 15 **Sales:** $203 million **Type of Business:** Convenience food stores, supermarkets, and gasoline service stations.

TOOTSIE ROLL INDUSTRIES
7401 S. Cicero Ave.
Chicago, IL 60629
Ellen R. Gordon, President

Number of Employees: 1,400 **Founded:** 1917 **Rank in 1991:** 16 **Sales:** $200 million **Type of Business:** Candy manufacturer.

DONNA KARAN CO.
550 7th Ave., 14th Fl.
New York, NY 10018
Donna Karan, CEO

Number of Employees: 750 **Founded:** 1984 **Rank in 1991:** 17 **Sales:** $200 million **Type of Business:** Women's apparel manufacturer.

OWEN STEEL CO.
PO Box 18
Columbia, SC 29202
Dorothy Owen, Chair

Number of Employees: 1,500 **Founded:** 1936 **Rank in 1991:** 18 **Sales:** $192 million **Type of Business:** Structural and reinforcement steel.

RESORT CONDOMINIUMS INTERNATIONAL
3502 Woodview Trace
Indianapolis, IN 46268
Christel Dehaan, CEO & President

Number of Employees: 2,300 **Rank in 1991:** 19 **Sales:** $180 million **Type of Business:** Real estate, time share trading.

ADRIENNE VITTADINI, INC.
1441 Broadway, 1st Fl.
New York, NY 10018
Adrienne Vittadini, Chair

Number of Employees: 200 **Founded:** 1979 **Rank in 1991:** 20 **Sales:** $160 million **Type of Business:** Apparel.

LILLIAN VERNON CORP.
510 S. Fulton Ave.
Mt. Vernon, NY 15150
Lillian Vernon, CEO

Number of Employees: 1,000 **Founded:** 1951 **Rank in 1991:** 21 **Sales:** $160 million **Type of Business:** Mail-order gifts and novelties.

COPELAND LUMBER YARDS INC.
901 NE Glisan
Portland, OR 97232
Helen Jo Whitsell, Chair, CEO

Number of Employees: 800 **Founded:** 1913 **Rank in 1991:** 22 **Sales:** $152 million **Type of Business:** Retail lumber and building materials.

SOFTWARE SPECTRUM
2140 Merritt Dr.
Garland, TX 75741
Judy Sims, CEO

Number of Employees: 260 **Founded:** 1983 **Rank in 1991:** 23 **Sales:** $146 million **Type of Business:** Software retailer.

REDKEN LABORATORIES
6625 Variel Ave.
Canoga Park, CA 91303
Paula Kent Meehan, Chair, CEO

Number of Employees: 830 **Founded:** 1960 **Rank in 1991:** 24 **Sales:** $140 million **Type of Business:** Hair and skin care products manufacturer.

ROSE ACRE FARMS
6874 N. Base Rd.
Seymour, IN 47274
Lois Rust, President

Number of Employees: 500 **Rank in 1991:** 25 **Sales:** $127 million **Type of Business:** Egg farm.

■ *Videos*

THE AMERICAN PARADE: WE THE WOMEN
468 Park Ave., S.
New York, NY 10016
(212) 684-5910

1974. Narrated by Mary Tyler Moore, the program traces the history of the women's movement. **Acquisition:** Purchase. **Format:** Beta, VHS, 3/4" U-matic. **Length:** 30 mins.

AND BABY MAKES TWO
1320 Braddock Pl.
Alexandria, VA 22314-1698
(703) 739-5380

1982. This program follows the lives of five single women who are raising their children alone. **Acquisition:** Rent/Lease, Purchase, Duplication, Off-Air Record. **Format:** Beta, VHS, 3/4" U-matic. **Length:** 30 mins.

...AND EVERYTHING NICE

468 Park Ave., S.
New York, NY 10016
(212) 684-5910

1974. The program shows the process of consciousness-raising (CR) during which women develop new expectations. In an actual CR group, Gloria Steinem and Shirley Chisholm provide insights. **Acquisition:** Purchase. **Format:** Beta, VHS, 3/4" U-matic. **Length:** 20 mins.

ARE YOU LISTENING?

PO Box 246
Hillsdale, NY 12529
(518) 325-3900

197?. This program series is an in-depth look at women in all phases, positions, and stages in life. Each program concerns itself with women's role and function in the structures of society. Programs are available individually. **Acquisition:** Rent/Lease, Purchase. **Format:** 3/4" U-matic, 2" Quad. **Length:** 28 mins.

AT THE HOUSTON WOMEN'S CONFERENCE

PO Box 246
Hillsdale, NY 12529
(518) 325-3900

1977. Participants active in women's issues discuss the media's impact on the women's movement. **Acquisition:** Rent/Lease, Purchase. **Format:** 3/4" U-matic, 2" Quad. **Length:** 29 mins.

THE BEAUTY QUEENS

5547 N. Ravenswood Ave.
Chicago, IL 60640
(312) 878-2600

1989. A documentary series examining three women who helped shape the beauty industry. The first tape tells the history of Helena Rubinstein's rise from poverty. The second tape discusses Elizabeth Arden and her introduction of the health-farm concept. The final tape shares the life of marketing genius Estee Lauder. **Acquisition:** Purchase. **Format:** VHS. **Length:** 60 mins.

THE BEST TIME OF MY LIFE: PORTRAITS OF WOMEN IN MID-LIFE

1251 Avenue of the Americas, 16th Fl.
New York, NY 10020-1173
(212) 586-5131

1987. This film attempts to deal with the so called mid-life crisis by examining the lives of a group of women, ages 40-60, who feel they are experiencing the best period of their lives. **Acquisition:** Rent/Lease, Purchase, Duplication. **Format:**

Beta, VHS, 3/4" U-matic. **Length:** 59 mins.

CAUTION: WOMEN WORKING

University of Michigan
400 4th St.
Ann Arbor, MI 48109
(313) 764-8228

1980. A musical portrayal of the role of American women in society and as members of the work force. Folksinger-composer Sheila Ritter weaves a story about women through rich comic and serious songs. **Acquisition:** Rent/Lease, Purchase. **Format:** 3/4" U-matic, Other than listed. **Length:** 29 mins.

CLORAE AND ALBIE

39 Chapel St.
Newton, MA 02160
(617) 969-7100

197?. Film deals with the need for women to prepare for the responsibilities of life in or out of marriage, with or without children. The program underscores the need for young women to grow up assuming that they will be self-supporting; that they have options with regard to education and careers and should consider them carefully. Students can compare their own lives to those documented in the program and learn a great deal from the experiences of others who have been or are in similar situations. Part of the "Role of Women in American Society" series. **Acquisition:** Rent/Lease, Purchase. **Format:** 3/4" U-matic, Other than listed. **Length:** 36 mins.

ENTERPRISING WOMEN

6901 Woodley Ave.
Van Nuys, CA 91406-4878
(818) 785-4111

1989. Profiles of five different businesses and the women who run them. **Acquisition:** Purchase, Duplication License. **Format:** Beta, VHS, 3/4" U-matic. **Length:** 27 mins.

EQUALITY

1573 Parkside Ave.
Trenton, NJ 08625
(609) 292-5252

1977. This study of age, sex, race, and economic equality features interviews with Gloria Steinem, the Rev. Jesse Jackson and Marabel Morgan. **Acquisition:** Rent/Lease, Purchase. **Format:** VHS, 3/4" U-matic. **Length:** 60 mins.

FROM PREGNANT WORKER TO WORKING MOTHER

930 Pitner Ave.
Evanston, IL 60202
(708) 328-6700

1984. The attitudes and emotional reactions of the future mother and her business associates during all stages of pregnancy are discussed. **Acquisition:** Rent/Lease, Purchase,

Trade-in, Duplication License. **Format:** 3/4" U-matic, Other than listed. **Length:** 22 mins.

GIRLS AT 12
39 Chapel St.
Newton, MA 02160
(617) 969-7100

1975. The video program looks at three capable youngsters for whom many avenues are open as they make the transition from the end of childhood into adolescence and womanhood. This tape is also concerned with specific socialization processes they are experiencing. Part of the "Role of Women in American Society" series. **Acquisition:** Rent/Lease, Purchase. **Format:** 3/4" U-matic, Other than listed. **Length:** 30 mins.

HAIRPIECE: A FILM FOR NAPPY-HEADED PEOPLE
225 Lafayette St., Ste. 212
New York, NY 10012
(212) 925-0606

1985. An irreverent, animated satire on the standards of beauty imposed on black women in our society. **Acquisition:** Purchase, Rent/Lease. **Format:** Beta, VHS, 3/4" U-matic. **Length:** 10 mins.

THE HIDDEN ARMY
Box 29035
Chicago, IL 60629
(312) 436-8051

1944. A salute to the "hidden army" of women who worked in American industry during World War II, replacing the men who were fighting overseas. Made as a morale booster to bolster sagging production in the last year of the war. **Acquisition:** Purchase. **Format:** Beta, VHS, 3/4" U-matic. **Length:** 17 mins.

I'M NOT A FEMINIST, BUT. . .
930 Pitner Ave.
Evanston, IL 60202
(708) 328-6700

1986. A tongue-in-cheek view of traditional and contemporary roles for women in marriage. Animated. **Acquisition:** Purchase. **Format:** Beta, VHS, 3/4" U-matic, Other than listed. **Length:** 9 mins.

LIES
225 Lafayette Street, Ste. 212
New York, NY 10012
(212) 925-0606

1983. This is a comic, yet dramatic video study of the lies women tell in order to negotiate the hurdles of everyday living in a sexist world. **Acquisition:** Rent/Lease, Purchase. **Format:** Beta, VHS, 3/4" U-matic. **Length:** 30 mins.

MRS. BREADWINNER
108 Wilmot Rd.
Deerfield, IL 60015-9990
(708) 940-1260

1982. A look at the increasing number of women who work and out-earn their husbands and how it affects their families. **Acquisition:** Rent/Lease, Purchase. **Format:** Beta, VHS, 3/4" U-matic. **Length:** 12 mins.

OF SNAKES, MOONS, AND FROGS
School of the Art Institute of Chicago
37 S. Wabash Ave.
Chicago, IL 60603
(312) 443-3793

1991. This unique, mind-expanding video focuses on woman's role in society throughout history. It becomes apparent that woman's status is reaching an all-time low. What happened to the days of goddesses and high priestesses? More than just a Woman's Studies film, the process of history, religion, and the modifications of time are captured. **Acquisition:** Purchase. **Format:** VHS, 3/4" U-matic. **Length:** 27 mins.

ON EQUAL TERMS: SEX EQUITY IN THE WORKFORCE
1800 30th St., Ste. 207
Boulder, CO 80301
(303) 444-1166

1987. This video explores how young women can be brought to understand and accept the fact that they will need self-supporting careers. **Acquisition:** Purchase. **Format:** Beta, VHS, 3/4" U-matic. **Length:** 29 mins.

READY, WILLING AND ABLE. . .
964 Educational Sciences Building
1025 W. Johnson St.
Madison, WI 53706
(608) 263-2929

1987. A set of programs about the difficulties and struggles that women today experience when trying to have both a family and a job. **Acquisition:** Purchase. **Format:** VHS. **Length:** 30 mins.

THERE'S NO SUCH THING AS WOMAN'S WORK
7738 Bell Rd.
Windsor, CA 95492
(707) 838-6000

1987. Photographs, cartoons and newsreels depicting womens' changing influence in the U.S. workforce. **Acquisition:** Purchase. **Format:** VHS. **Length:** 30 mins.

A TRUCK DRIVER NAMED GRET
260 5th Ave., Rm. 705
New York, NY 10001
(212) 683-1660

1983. A look at a 38-year-old woman who is a wife, a mother and a truck driver, yet manages to juggle all three careers at once. **Acquisition:** Purchase. **Format:** Beta, VHS, 3/4" U-matic. **Length:** 11 mins.

WHAT DOES SHE WANT?

School of the Art Institute of Chicago
37 S. Wabash Ave.
Chicago, IL 60603
(312) 443-3793

1986. A series of experimental, free-form video pieces by and about women. Each title in the series includes approximately seven shorts dealing with feminist issues. Experimental short titles include "Suburban Queen," "A Chevrolet Impala," "Kleenex Napkins Cling Like Cloth," "A Crack in the Tube," "In My Merry Oldsmobile," "Christine Choy," and numerous others by Mindy Faber, Julie Dash, Cecelia Condit, Laurel Chiten, and many other contemporary artists. **Acquisition:** Rent/Lease, Purchase. **Format:** Beta, VHS, 3/4" U-matic. **Length:** 60 mins.

WHAT YOU TAKE FOR GRANTED

225 Lafayette St., Ste. 212
New York, NY 10012
(212) 925-0606

1983. A creative look at women's experiences in jobs traditionally held by men. **Acquisition:** Purchase, Rent/Lease. **Format:** Beta, VHS, 3/4" U-matic. **Length:** 75 mins.

WHEN MOM HAS TO WORK

930 Pitner Ave.
Evanston, IL 60202
(708) 328-6700

1988. Women should be able to have a family and a job without feeling exhausted or guilty about it. **Acquisition:** Purchase, Rent/Lease. **Format:** Beta, VHS, 3/4" U-matic. **Length:** 23 mins.

WINDOWS ON WOMEN

7755 16th St. NW
Washington, DC 20012
(301)588-4095

1986. A look through interviews and statistics at the changing role of women in today's world. **Acquisition:** Purchase. **Format:** Beta, VHS, 3/4" U-matic. **Length:** 60 mins.

WOMAN ENTREPRENEUR: DO YOU HAVE WHAT IT TAKES?

4111 S. Darlington St., Ste. 600
Tulsa, OK 74135
(918) 622-6460

1987. A motivational look at starting a business for women, featuring interviews with a half dozen women who have made it. **Acquisition:** Purchase. **Format:** Beta, VHS. **Length:** 55 mins.

WOMEN AND THE AMERICAN FAMILY

29 Bramble Ln.
Melville, NY 11747
(516) 367-4250

1987. The role of women—past, present, and future—is examined from a historical perspective. **Acquisition:** Purchase. **Format:** VHS. **Length:** 28 mins.

WOMEN IN AMERICAN LIFE–VIDEO SERIES

7738 Bell Rd.
Windsor, CA 95492
(707) 838-6000

1989. This five-part series features over 700 historical photographs selected from dozens of photo archives throughout the United States. Each video focuses on a particular time in the country's history and emphasizes women's daily life experiences, work and involvements with social issues. Also available individually. **Acquisition:** Purchase. **Format:** VHS. **Length:** 88 mins.

WOMEN IN BUSINESS

Box 69799
Los Angeles, CA 90069
(213) 652-8000

1984. Six different women discuss their business problems and successes. **Acquisition:** Rent/Lease, Purchase. **Format:** Beta, VHS, 3/4" U-matic, Other than listed. **Length:** 24 mins.

WOMEN IN BUSINESS: THE RISKS, REWARDS & SECRETS OF RUNNING YOUR OWN COMPANY

PO Box 2
Wilmot, WI 53192
(800) 888-9355

1990. Five successful businesswomen give insights and advice on the business world. **Acquisition:** Purchase. **Format:** VHS. **Length:** 75 mins.

WOMEN AND FAMILY

Instructional Media Center
Chico, CA 95929
(916) 895-6112

1979. This program includes role models of egalitarian marriage, a call for change from traditional male-female roles, child care, and communication skills. **Acquisition:** Purchase. **Format:** Beta, VHS, 3/4" U-matic. **Length:** 50 mins.

WOMEN, POWER, AND POLITICS

1573 Parkside Ave.
Trenton, NJ 08625
(609) 292-5252

1988. This documentary examines the history of women's rights from the early 20th century to Geraldine Ferraro's nomination for the Vice Presidency of the country. **Acquisition:** Rent/Lease, Purchase. **Format:** VHS, 3/4" U-matic. **Length:** 30 mins.

WOMEN AND SOCIETY

930 Pitner Ave.
Evanston, IL 60202
(708) 328-6700

1988. The history of women in a male-dominated society is chronicled. **Acquisition:** Purchase, Rent/Lease. **Format:** Beta, VHS, 3/4" U-matic. **Length:** 26 mins.

A WORD IN EDGEWISE

225 Lafayette St., Ste. 212
New York, NY 10012
(212) 925-0606

1986. An inventive, necessary video which insightfully exposes the numerous biases against women in the English language. **Acquisition:** Purchase, Rent/Lease. **Format:** Beta, VHS, 3/4" U-matic. **Length:** 26 mins.

THE WORKING MOM'S SURVIVAL GUIDE

300 Brickstone Sq.
Andover, MA 01810
800-228-2495

1990. Successful career women with families give tips for survival to working moms. Expectant mothers who plan a return to the office will find this useful. A 15-minute workout is included. **Acquisition:** Purchase. **Format:** VHS. **Length:** 30 mins.

YOU'VE COME A LONG WAY, MAYBE?

Indiana University Audio-Visual Center
Franklin 004
Bloomington, IN 47405-5901
(812) 855-4848

1981. A documentary based upon the question "Are women paid less than men because of marketplace factors, or because of subtle, historical patterns of discrimination?" **Acquisition:** Rent/Lease, Purchase, Duplication License. **Format:** 3/4" U-matic. **Length:** 55 mins.

Figures at Your Fingertips:

A Statistical Profile

■ *Education and Employment*

Age of Women College Students: 1980-2000

Percentage distribution of women enrolled in institutions of higher education, by age group: Fall 1980, 1988, and 2000.

Age	1980	1988	2000
Under 25	60.5%	56.1%	56.9%
25-29	14.1%	13.7%	11.0%
30-34	10.7%	10.6%	9.0%
35+	14.7%	19.6%	23.1%

Source: "Percentage Distribution of Women Enrolled in Institutions of Higher Education, by Age Group: Fall 1980, 1988, and 2000," *Projections of Education Statistics to 2000,* Figure 19, p. 25 (Washington, D.C.: National Center for Education Statistics, 1989). Primary source: data collected from many sources, including Federal and State agencies, private research organizations, and professional organizations. The age distribution for the year 2000 is based on the middle alternative projections.

Bachelors' Degrees, 1975-2000

Bachelors' degrees conferred 1975-1987; estimates 1988 and 1989; projections 1990-2000.

Year ending	Total	Women	Men
1975	922,933	418,092	504,841
1976	925,746	420,821	504,925
1977	919,549	424,004	495,545
1978	921,204	433,857	487,347
1979	921,390	444,046	477,344
1980	929,417	455,806	473,611
1981	935,140	465,257	469,883
1982	952,998	479,634	473,364
1983	969,510	490,370	479,140
1984	974,309	491,990	482,319
1985	979,477	496,949	482,528
1986	987,823	501,900	485,923
1987	991,339	510,485	480,854
1988	989,000	517,000	472,000
1989	994,000	521,000	473,000
1990	1,005,000	530,000	475,000
1991	995,000	532,000	463,000
1992	1,011,000	543,000	468,000
1993	1,016,000	548,000	468,000
1994	1,006,000	542,000	464,000
1995	990,000	534,000	456,000
1996	973,000	522,000	451,000
1997	962,000	512,000	450,000
1998	961,000	509,000	452,000
1999	968,000	507,000	461,000
2000	976,000	509,000	467,000

Source: Selected from "Bachelor's degrees, by sex of recipient, with projections: 50 States and D.C., 1974-75 to 1999-2000," *Projections of Education Statistics to 2000*, p. 67 (Washington, D.C.: National Center for Education Statistics, 1989). Primary source: U.S. Department of Education, National Center for Education Statistics, "Degrees and Other Formal Awards Conferred" survey, Integrated Postsecondary Education Data System (IPEDS), and Early National Estimates survey, 1987 and 1988. (This table was prepared April 1989.). Because of rounding, details may not add to totals.

Comparison of Undergraduate GPAs
(bachelor's degree recipients)

Major	Women	Men
All	3.07	2.92
Engineering & computer science	3.17	2.96
Science & math	3.18	2.98
Business	2.96	2.79
Education	3.05	2.89
Humanities	3.16	3.10
Arts	3.13	3.08
Social Sciences	3.08	2.95

Source: Marketing to Women, March 1992 (Boston, MA: About Women, Inc., 1993).
Primary Source: The U.S. Department of Education.

Doctors' Degrees, 1975-2000
[Continued]

Year ending	Total	Women	Men
1987	34,120	12,021	22,099
1988	34,000	12,000	22,000
1989	34,200	12,600	21,600
1990	34,400	12,900	21,500
1991	34,500	13,200	21,300
1992	34,600	13,700	20,900
1993	34,700	14,200	20,500
1994	34,800	14,700	20,100
1995	34,900	15,200	19,700
1996	34,900	15,700	19,200
1997	35,000	16,300	18,700
1998	35,000	16,900	18,100
1999	35,000	17,600	17,400
2000	35,100	18,400	16,700

Source: "Doctor's degrees, by sex of recipient, with projections: 50 States and D.C., 1974-75 to 1999-2000," *Projections of Education Statistics to 2000,* p. 69 (Washington, D.C.: National Center for Education Statistics, 1989). Primary source: U.S. Department of Education, National Center for Education Statistics, "Degrees and Other Formal Awards Conferred" survey, Integrated Postsecondary Education Data System (IPEDS), and Early Natijonal Estimates survey, 1987 and 1988. (This table was prepared April 1989.). Because of rounding, details may not add to totals.

Employment Status of the Adult Population

Employment characteristics, total, and female and male adult population, 1990.

Characteristic	Number (thousands)		
	Total	Female	Male
Total adults	180,974	94,667	86,307
Employed full time	98,104	40,087	58,017
Employed part time	16,795	11,616	5,180
Sole wage earner	32,480	11,803	20,677
Not employed	66,074	42,965	23,110
Professional	15,966	8,019	7,947
Executive/Admin./Managerial	14,845	5,871	8,974
Clerical/Sales/Technical	35,437	22,765	12,672
Precision/Crafts/Repair	13,595	1,207	12,388
Other employed	35,057	13,842	21,216

Source: Selected from *Mediamark Research Multimedia Audiences Report, Spring 1990* (New York: Mediamark Research Inc., 1990).

Masters' Degrees, 1975-2000

Masters' degrees conferred 1975-1987; estimates 1988 and 1989; projections 1990-2000.

Year ending	Total	Women	Men
1975	292,450	130,880	161,570
1976	311,771	144,523	167,248
1977	317,164	149,381	167,783
1978	311,620	150,408	161,212
1979	301,079	147,709	153,370
1980	298,081	147,332	150,749
1981	295,739	148,696	147,043
1982	295,546	150,014	145,532
1983	289,921	145,224	144,697
1984	284,263	140,668	143,595
1985	286,251	142,861	143,390
1986	288,567	145,059	143,508
1987	289,557	148,194	141,363
1988	292,000	150,000	142,000
1989	293,000	156,000	137,000
1990	301,000	158,000	143,000
1991	300,000	158,000	142,000
1992	302,000	159,000	143,000
1993	301,000	158,000	143,000
1994	299,000	157,000	142,000
1995	295,000	155,000	140,000
1996	292,000	153,000	139,000
1997	290,000	152,000	138,000
1998	289,000	151,000	138,000
1999	287,000	150,000	137,000
2000	286,000	150,000	137,000

Source: Selected from "Master's degrees, by sex of recipient, with projections: 50 States and D.C., 1974-75 to 1999-2000," *Projections of Education Statistics to 2000,* p. 68 (Washington, D.C.: National Center for Education Statistics, 1989). Primary source: U.S. Department of Education, National Center for Education Statistics, "Degrees and Other Formal Awards Conferred" survey, Integrated Postsecondary Education Data System (IPEDS), and Early Natijonal Estimates survey, 1987 and 1988. (This table was prepared April 1989.). Because of rounding, details may not add to totals.

Professional Degrees, 1975-2000

First-professional degrees conferred 1975-1987; estimates 1988 and 1989; projections 1990-2000.

Year ending	Total	Women	Men
1975	55,916	6,960	48,956
1976	62,649	9,757	52,892
1977	64,359	11,985	52,374
1978	66,581	14,311	52,270
1979	68,848	16,196	52,652
1980	70,131	17,415	52,716
1981	71,956	19,164	52,792
1982	72,032	19,809	52,223
1983	73,136	21,826	51,310
1984	74,407	23,073	51,334
1985	75,063	24,608	50,455
1986	73,910	24,649	49,261
1987	72,750	25,290	47,460
1988	72,000	25,000	46,000
1989	72,200	25,800	46,400
1990	72,400	26,400	46,000
1991	72,300	26,000	45,700
1992	72,100	26,600	45,500
1993	72,700	27,100	45,600
1994	72,200	27,800	44,400
1995	70,600	27,600	43,000
1996	69,200	27,000	42,200
1997	68,300	26,800	41,500
1998	67,800	26,800	41,000
1999	67,600	26,800	40,800
2000	67,100	26,800	40,400

Source: "First-professional degrees, by sex of recipient, with projections: 50 States and D.C., 1974-75 to 1999-2000," *Projections of Education Statistics to 2000,* p. 70 (Washington, D.C.: National Center for Education Statistics, 1989). Primary source: U.S. Department of Education, National Center for Education Statistics, "Degrees and Other Formal Awards Conferred" survey, Integrated Postsecondary Education Data System (IPEDS), and Early Natijonal Estimates survey, 1987 and 1988. (This table was prepared April 1989.). Because of rounding, details may not add to totals.

Unequal Pay

Occupation	Women	Men	Gap
Graphic Designer	$19,812	$32,032	38%
Insurance Underwriter	$25,116	$38,532	35%
Financial Manager	$28,016	$43,524	33%
Buyer, Wholesale or Retail	$20,436	$30,212	32%
Personnel Manager	$31,408	$45,812	31%
Property/Real Estate Manager	$19,916	$26,884	26%
Attorney	$45,500	$61,256	28%
Accountant/Auditor	$25,116	$33,488	25%
College Professor	$32,240	$42,016	23%
Editor/Reporter	$23,504	$30,576	23%
Public Administrator	$28,548	$36,920	23%
Educational/ Vocational Counselor	$29,278	$36,140	19%
Physician	$41,704	$50,856	18%
Computer Systems Analyst	$34,372	$41,548	17%
Public Relations Specialist	$27,248	$32,396	16%
Teacher	$25,260	$30,888	15%
Psychologist	$26,728	$31,460	15%
Secretary	$17,732	$20,124	12%
Engineer	$38,272	$42,744	11%
Advertising Salesperson	$24,804	$27,196	9%
Police/Detective	$25,116	$26,624	6%
Mechanic	$23,868	$24,804	4%
Registered Nurse	$31,616	$32,032	1%
Postal Clerk	$29,069	$28,392	2%

Source: Marketing to Women, March 1992 (Boston, MA: About Women, Inc., 1993).
Primary Source: Working Woman's 1992 salary survey.

Women Labor Force Indicators

Characteristics of women in the labor force, second quarter, 1990.

Characteristic	Number or %
Population and labor force	
Women, 16 years and over, in thousands	
Civilian noninstitutional population[1]	98,289
Civilian labor force	56,682
Civilian labor force participation rates	
Women, 16 years and over	57.7%
16 to 19 years	52.2%
20 years and over	58.1%
20 to 24 years	71.8%
25 to 54 years	74.3%
55 years and over	23.2%
White	57.6%
Black	58.5%
Employment status, in thousands	
Women, 16 years and over:	
Employed	53,730
Unemployed	2,952
Unemployment rates	
Women, 16 years and over	5.2%
16 to 19 years	13.9%
20 years and over	4.6%
White, 16 years and over	4.5%
White, 16 to 19 years	12.3%
Black, 16 years and over	10.0%
Black, 16 to 19 years	25.7%
Full-time workers	
Percent of employed women working full time	75.0%
Percent of unemployed women looking for full-time work	73.0%
Marital status	
Married women, husband present	
Civilian noninstitutional population, thousands[1]	53,048
Civilian labor force participation rate	58.4%
Unemployment rate	3.6%
Women who maintain families:	
Civilian noninstitutional population, thousands[1]	11,051
Civilian labor force participation rate	62.7%
Unemployment rate	7.6%

Source: Selected from "Summary indicators on women in the labor force, quarterly averages, 1989 and 1990," *Employment in Perspective: Women in the Labor Force*, Report 791, Second Quarter 1990, p. 2 (Washington, D.C.: U.S. Department of Labor, August 1990). Also in source: data for 1989 and first quarter 1990; data by other characteristics. Data are seasonally adjusted unless otherwise indicated. Due to rounding and independent seasonal adjustment, some components may not add to totals. *Note:* 1. Not seasonally adjusted.

■ *Health*

Effects of Menopause on Mental Health

Percentage of menopausal women reporting selected symptoms at *neither* baseline (premenopausal) *nor* follow-up (postmenopausal) examination. The authors concluded that natural menopaus did not have negative mental health consequences for most middle-aged healthy women.

Symptom	Percent
Body worry	
Natural menopause	67%
Hormone users	44%
Excitable	
Natural menopause	57%
Hormone users	78%
Aches in neck and skull	
Natural menopause	57%
Hormone users	41%
Depression	
Natural menopause	45%
Hormone users	44%
Nervous	
Natural menopause	33%
Hormone users	31%
Trouble sleeping	
Natural menopause	55%
Hormone users	41%

Source: Karen A. Matthews, Rena R. Wing, Lewis H. Kuller, Elaine N. Meilahn, Sheryl F. Kelsey, E. Jane Costello, and Arlene W. Caggiula, "Influences of natural Menopause on Psychological Characteristics and Symptoms of Middle-Aged Healthy Women," *Journal of Consulting and Clinical Psychology* 58:3, 1990, p. 345-351. Address correspondence to Karen A. Matthews, Dept. of Psychiatry, University of Pittsburgh, 3811 O'Hara Street, Pittsburgh, PA 15213. Related reading: "Study Suggests Menopause Doesn't Affect Mental Health," *New York Times,* July 26, 1990, p. B7. The study began with 541 initially premenopausal healthy women given an extensive evaluation at baseline. After 3 years, 69 women ceased cycling for 12 months; another 32 had ceased cycling and had taken hormone replacement therapy for 12 months. These women were reevaluated in a clinic examination identical to the baseline examination, as were 101 age-matched premenopausal control women.

Premenstrual Syndrome and the Media

Some physical conditions and behavior of premenstrual women, according to the popular press.

Symptom/Behavior	% of Articles
Water retention	
swelling/bloating	71%
painful/tender breasts	55%
weight gain	33%
skin blemishes/acne	29%
Negative affect	
depression/despair/sadness	72%
mood swings	51%
anxiety	42%
tension	35%
crying	31%
suicidal ideation/attempt	26%
Pain	
headache	58%
fatigue/lassitude	40%
Change in eating habits	
cravings for sugar/salt	44%
Impaired concentration	
poor motor coordination/clumsiness	13%
insomnia/sleep irregularities	12%
Behavior change	
violence	26%
lethargy	19%
Automonic reactions	
constipation	18%
dizziness/faintness	15%

Source: Joan C. Chrisler, PhD, and Karen B. Levy, BA, "The Media Construct a Menstrual Monster: A Content Analysis of PMS Articles in the Popular Press," *Women & Health* 16(2): 1990, p. 89+. Also in source: a discussion of the implications of negative coverage of menstrual cycle changes and recommendations to improve media reports. The authors' search of *Reader's Guide to Periodical Literature* from 1980 to 1987 turned up 81 articles on premenstrual syndrome.

Rise of Women's Services: 1970-1988

Some interesting facts about women's groups culled by the author from Susanna Downie's *Decade of Achievement*.

1. No one had heard of a battered women's shelter in 1970, but by 1988 there were at least 1,200 such establishments;

2. No one had heard of a "women's center" in 1970, but according to the National Association of Women's Centers, there were at least 4,000 such centers by 1988;

3. Few had heard of a rape crisis center in 1970; by 1988 there were 600 such centers;

4. The need for displaced homemakers groups, programs, or services, first recognized in the early 1970s, had resulted in the formation of more than 1,000 such groups, programs, or services by 1988.

Source: Sarah Harder, "Flourishing in the Mainstream: The U.S. Women's Movement Today," *The American Woman 1990-91*, 1990, p. 273+. Also: Downie, Susanna (editor). *Decade of Achievement: 1977-1987—A Report of a Survey Based on the National Plan of Action for Women*. Beaver Dam, Wisconsin: National Women's Conference Committee, 1988.

335

Walking Alone at Night and Safety at Home

Question: "Is there any area near where you live...where you would be afraid to walk alone at night? How about at home at night...do you feel safe and secure?"

Characteristic of respondent	Afraid to walk alone at night		Feel safe at home	
	Yes	No	Yes	No
Total United States	43%	57%	90%	10%
Sex				
Female	59%	41%	86%	14%
Male	25%	75%	94%	6%
Age				
18 to 29 years	45%	55%	89%	11%
30 to 49 years	32%	68%	91%	9%
50 years and older	52%	48%	89%	11%
Race				
White	41%	59%	91%	9%
Nonwhite	55%	45%	82%	18%
Black	53%	47%	81%	19%

Source: "Attitudes toward walking alone at night and safety at home," *Sourcebook of Criminal Justice Statistics - 1988,* 1989, p. 211. Primary source: George Gallup, Jr., *The Gallup Report,* Report Nos. 282-283 (Princeton, NJ: The Gallup Poll, March/April 1989), p. 8. Table adapted by SOURCEBOOK staff. Also in source: data by education, politics, income, and religion.

■ *Home and Family*

Effect of Working Wives on Family Income

Women in work force	57,798,000
Percent of work force that is female	45.5%
Percent of women 16 and over in the work force	57.8%
Of working women, percent part time	26.5%
Of working women, percent full time	73.5%
Median family income in the U.S.	$40,995
Median family income when wife is in work force	$48,169
Median family income when wife is not employed	$30,075

Source: Bureau of Labor Statistics, Women's Bureau, 1992. 1991 *Current Population Report* from the U.S. Census Bureau.

Household Composition

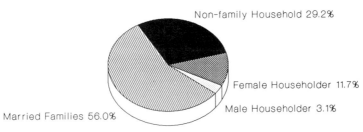

Non-family Household 29.2%

Female Householder 11.7%

Male Householder 3.1%

Married Families 56.0%

1990 composition of U.S. households, estimate, March 1990.

Type of household	Total
Total households, 1990	93.3 million
Married-couple families	56.0%
Non-family households	29.2%
Female householder (no husband present)	11.7%
Male householder (no wife present)	3.1%

Source: "Number of Two-Parent Family Households Still Decreasing," *Census and You,* Vol. 26,
No. 2, February 1991, p. 3. Primary source: *Household and Family Characteristics: 1990 and 1989,*
Current Population Reports P-20, No. 447.

Household Income by Female Age

Female adults, in thousands, by age group and annual household income.

Household Income	Total	Age 18-24	Age 25-34	Age 35-44	Age 45-54	Age 55-64	Age 65+
$75,000 or more	7,136	1,036	1,155	2,050	1,664	991	240
$60,000-74,999	6,633	872	1,460	2,002	1,456	475	367
$50,000-59,999	7,430	630	2,081	2,126	1,245	966	383
$40,000-49,999	10,943	1,232	3,204	2,908	1,911	1,076	612
$30,000-39,999	14,473	1,793	4,301	3,060	2,094	1,715	1,510
$20,000-29,999	15,927	2,395	4,140	3,057	1,763	1,915	2,656
$10,000-19,999	18,041	2,459	3,222	1,950	1,626	3,031	5,753
Less than $10,000	14,083	2,263	2,493	1,023	974	1,602	5,727

Source: Selected from *Mediamark Research Multimedia Audiences Report, Spring 1990*, p. 116-118 (New York: Mediamark Research Inc., 1990).

Household Income by Female Educational Attainment

Number of women in thousands, by educational attainment and annual household income, 1990.

Household Income	Total	Graduated College	Attended College	Graduated High School	Did Not Graduate HS
Total Women	94,667	14,333	17,363	39,830	23,142
$75,000 or more	7,136	3,054	1,852	1,959	272
$60,000-74,999	6,633	2,214	1,520	2,469	430
$50,000-59,999	7,430	1,941	1,811	2,978	701
$40,000-49,999	10,043	2,185	2,398	5,189	1,172
$30,000-39,999	14,473	2,117	3,171	6,922	2,264
$20,000-29,999	15,927	1,596	1,751	8,285	3,295
$10,000-19,999	18,041	866	2,407	7,843	6,926
Less than $10,000	14,083	361	1,454	4,185	8,082

Source: Selected from *Mediamark Research Multimedia Audiences Report, Spring 1990*, p. 114 (New York: Mediamark Research Inc., 1990).

Household Income by Female Household Status

Female adults, in thousands, by household status and income.

Household Income	Total	Heads of Households	Working Mothers	Mothers	Female Homemakers
$75,000 or more	7,136	753	1,894	2,503	5,950
$60,000-74,999	6,633	821	2,166	2,702	5,600
$50,000-59,999	7,430	1,210	2,373	3,220	6,353
$40,000-49,999	10,943	1,486	3,451	4,831	9,623
$30,000-39,999	14,473	2,984	4,240	6,167	12,677
$20,000-29,999	15,927	4,646	3,679	6,136	13,762
$10,000-19,999	18,041	8,185	2,474	5,041	16,448
Less than $10,000	14,083	9,844	1,267	3,660	12,953

Source: Selected from *Mediamark Research Multimedia Audiences Report, Spring 1990,* p. 112, 204, 206 (New York: Mediamark Research Inc., 1990).

Household Income by Female Marital Status

Female adults, in thousands, by marital status and annual household income.

Household Income	Total	Single	Married	All Others	Engaged
All Women	94,667	16,895	55,273	22,500	3,026
Household Income					
$75,000 or more	7,136	1,431	5,371	334	131
$60,000-74,999	6,633	1,096	4,960	577	346
$50,000-59,999	7,430	1,125	5,445	860	206
$40,000-49,999	10,943	1,645	8,210	1,089	380
$30,000-39,999	14,473	1,997	10,006	2,470	327
$20,000-29,999	15,927	2,855	9,511	3,561	575
$10,000-19,999	18,041	3,086	8,536	6,419	572
Less than $10,000	14,083	3,660	3,234	7,189	487

Source: Selected from *Mediamark Research Multimedia Audiences Report, Spring 1990*, p. 142 (New York: Mediamark Research Inc., 1990).

Household Size

Total and female and male adult households, by number of persons, 1990.

Characteristic	Number (thousands)		
	Total	Female	Male
Total adults	180,974	94,667	86,307
Household Size			
1 person	22,006	13,337	8,669
2 persons	56,768	29,035	27,732
3 or more persons	102,201	52,295	49,905

Source: Selected from *Mediamark Research Multimedia Audiences Report, Spring 1990* (New York: Mediamark Research Inc., 1990).

Household Types by Income Level

Households by total money income in 1989, by type of households, by female householder, by race, and by Hispanic origin of householder.

| Total money income | Total | Family households | | | Nonfamily households | |
		Total	Female householder no husband present	Total	Female householder	Living alone
			Numbers in thousands			
Total	93,347	66,090	10,890	27,257	15,651	13,950
Under $5,000	4,970	2,236	1,423	2,734	1,882	1,839
$5,000 to $9,999	9,622	4,022	1,826	5,601	4,038	3,963
$10,000 to $14,999	9,057	5,252	1,557	3,805	2,417	2,298
$15,000 to $19,999	8,620	5,502	1,263	3,118	1,825	1,677
$20,000 to $24,999	8,134	5,465	1,051	2,669	1,428	1,224
$25,000 to $29,999	7,778	5,583	879	2,195	1,160	978
$30,000 to $34,999	7,062	5,340	706	1,722	800	637
$35,000 to $39,999	6,154	4,940	546	1,214	535	410
$40,000 to $44,999	5,556	4,506	414	1,050	439	302
$45,000 to $49,999	4,472	3,745	258	727	265	160
$50,000 to $54,999	4,090	3,580	240	510	200	132
$55,000 to $59,999	2,972	2,617	150	354	143	79
$60,000 to $64,999	2,630	2,317	149	313	94	52
$65,000 to $69,999	2,148	1,892	88	255	114	46
$70,000 to $74,999	1,684	1,486	69	198	69	32
$75,000 to $79,999	1,403	1,289	60	114	50	25
$80,000 to $84,999	1,178	1,048	41	130	37	22
$85,000 to $89,999	857	788	29	69	26	13
$90,000 to $94,999	759	705	21	53	18	8
$95,000 to $99,999	570	541	27	29	6	3
$100,000 and over	3,631	3,236	94	396	104	51
White						
Total	80,163	56,590	7,306	23,573	13,622	12,161
Under $5,000	3,354	1,367	716	1,987	1,402	1,372
$5,000 to $9,999	7,532	2,785	1,039	4,747	3,519	3,463
$10,000 to $14,999	7,564	4,173	1,012	3,391	2,186	2,092
$15,000 to $19,999	7,288	4,529	857	2,759	1,667	1,534
$20,000 to $24,999	6,994	4,659	802	2,335	1,248	1,070
$25,000 to $29,999	6,792	4,861	646	1,931	1,029	870
$30,000 to $34,999	6,202	4,690	519	1,512	701	563
$35,000 to $39,999	5,413	4,334	406	1,078	464	368
$40,000 to $44,999	5,017	4,061	332	957	398	263
$45,000 to $49,999	4,055	3,376	206	679	250	149
$50,000 to $54,999	3,696	3,259	197	437	159	104
$55,000 to $59,999	2,669	2,342	106	327	130	76
$60,000 to $64,999	2,355	2,068	122	288	89	49
$65,000 to $69,999	1,934	1,700	64	235	101	46

[Continued]

Household Types by Income Level
[Continued]

| Total money income | Total | Family households | | | Nonfamily households | |
		Total	Female householder no husband present	Total	Female householder	Living alone
$70,000 to $74,999	1,531	1,353	54	178	62	29
$75,000 to $79,999	1,281	1,181	52	100	39	21
$80,000 to $84,999	1,098	976	33	123	33	22
$85,000 to $89,999	785	720	28	65	26	13
$90,000 to $94,999	702	653	16	49	16	8
$95,000 to $99,999	499	472	19	27	4	1
$100,000 and over	3,402	3,031	78	371	99	47
Black						
Total	10,486	7,470	3,275	3,015	1,702	1,525
Under $5,000	1,479	793	673	686	453	441
$5,000 to $9,999	1,802	1,075	712	727	453	433
$10,000 to $14,999	1,250	910	498	339	184	162
$15,000 to $19,999	1,111	820	378	291	127	113
$20,000 to $24,999	941	661	240	279	150	131
$25,000 to $29,999	786	573	206	213	104	87
$30,000 to $34,999	661	515	170	146	79	63
$35,000 to $39,999	552	461	118	91	54	31
$40,000 to $44,999	418	350	81	68	27	26
$45,000 to $49,999	284	253	43	31	11	7
$50,000 to $54,999	264	218	35	47	22	17
$55,000 to $59,999	198	174	38	25	12	2
$60,000 to $64,999	190	169	22	21	2	2
$65,000 to $69,999	148	136	17	13	9	-
$70,000 to $74,999	92	85	14	7	2	-
$75,000 to $79,999	65	61	6	4	4	4
$80,000 to $84,999	47	46	5	1	1	-
$85,000 to $89,999	43	39	-	4	-	-
$90,000 to $94,999	31	27	2	5	3	-
$95,000 to $99,999	43	41	6	2	2	2
$100,000 and over	81	65	12	16	5	3
Hispanic Origin[1]						
Total	5,933	4,840	1,116	1,093	506	442
Under $5,000	480	303	207	178	100	97
$5,000 to $9,999	793	549	253	244	143	143
$10,000 to $14,999	727	575	159	151	62	56
$15,000 to $19,999	705	586	130	120	55	42
$20,000 to $24,999	594	484	91	110	45	37
$25,000 to $29,999	515	441	78	74	31	23
$30,000 to $34,999	425	359	41	66	22	17
$35,000 to $39,999	341	303	31	38	12	11

[Continued]

Household Types by Income Level
[Continued]

Total money income	Total	Family households			Nonfamily households	
		Total	Female householder no husband present	Total	Female householder	Living alone
$40,000 to $44,999	298	270	37	28	7	2
$45,000 to $49,999	234	214	18	20	8	4
$50,000 to $54,999	203	189	21	15	7	3
$55,000 to $59,999	124	114	13	10	4	2
$60,000 to $64,999	114	105	6	9	3	2
$65,000 to $69,999	76	67	5	9	1	-
$70,000 to $74,999	55	51	7	4	1	-
$75,000 to $79,999	39	36	-	3	1	1
$80,000 to $84,999	39	38	6	1	-	-
$85,000 to $89,999	26	26	6	-	-	-
$90,000 to $94,999	31	30	1	1	1	-
$95,000 to $99,999	20	20	4	-	-	-
$100,000 and over	95	82	2	14	3	2

Source: Selected from "Type of Household—Households, by Total Money Income in 1989, Race, and Hispanic Origin of Householder," Current Population Reports, "Money Income and Poverty Status in the United States 1989 (Advance Data from the March 1990 Current Population Survey), September 1990, p. 23-24. Also in source: data for married-couple families, male householders, male nonfamily households. Households as of March 1990. Note: 1. Persons of Hispanic origin may be of any race.

Household Types: 1990-2000

Households by type: Series A projections 1990-2000.

Year	Total	Family				Nonfamily		
		Total	Married couple	Female house-holder[1]	Male house-holder[1]	Total	Female house-holder	Male house-holder
				Numbers in thousands				
1990	95,243	65,964	51,704	11,538	2,723	29,279	16,270	13,008
1995	102,785	68,219	52,178	12,765	3,276	34,565	18,463	16,102
2000	110,217	70,024	52,263	13,916	3,845	40,193	20,722	19,471

Source: Selected from "Households, by Type—Projections: 1990 to 2000," *Statistical Abstract of the United States 1990,* 1990, p. 45. Primary source: U.S. Bureau of the Census, *Current Population Reports,* Series P-25, No. 986. Also in source: Series B and Series C projections. As of July. Series A figures reflect the assumption that the recent moderation in marriage and divorce trends will continue, but that historical changes spanning the last 25 years must be taken into consideration. Series A assumes a continuation of past trends in householder proportions but changes in recent years are given more weight. *Note:* 1. With no spouse present.

Households with Children

Total and female and male adult households with children, by age of children, 1990.

Characteristic of children	Number (thousands)		
	Total	Female	Male
Households with Children	73,586	39,949	33,637
Children Under 2 Years	14,151	8,079	6,072
Children 2-5 Years	27,156	15,220	11,936
Children 6-11 Years	34,115	18,608	15,507
Children 12-17 Years	33,599	17,385	16,214

Source: Selected from *Mediamark Research Multimedia Audiences Report, Spring 1990* (New York: Mediamark Research Inc., 1990).

Women as Caregivers: An Overview
Some statistics and predictions on the status of women as caregivers.

According to the Older Women's League, women can expect to spend **17** years caring for children and **18** years helping an elderly parent. **Eighty-nine percent of all women over age 18** will be caregivers to children, parents, or both.

Predictions are that between 1985 and 2020, the over-65 population will number more than 52 million, 1 in 6 persons. If present trends continue, caregivers will be their wives, daughters, nieces and granddaughters. Mainly due to caregiving responsibilities, women average **11.5 years** out of the paid labor force; men average 1.3 years.

Source: Maryanne Sugarman Costa, "Women Who Care Are Women Who Need Relief," *National Business Woman,* Summer 1989, p. 20. Primary Source: "Failing America's Caregivers: A Status Report on Women Who Care," Older Women's League, 730 11th St., NW, Suite 300, Washington, DC 20001. Also in source: a discussion of possible solutions to the long-term care situation, such as improving the working conditions of paid caregivers.

Working Mothers: Day Care Data

	Child Care Arrangements: Children Under Five	Care/Weekly Cost: Children Five to Twelve
Parent	29.9%	37.7%
After school activities	—	19.0%
Day care centers	26.5%	11.3%
Relatives	17.6%	17.2%
Family day care	18.6%	6.6%
At home with sitter	3.7%	3.4%
Other	3.6%	4.8%

Source: Marketing to Women, February 1993 (Boston, MA: About Women, Inc., 1993).

■ *Sports and Leisure*

Involvement in Charitable Activities

Questions: Do you happen to be involved in any charity or social service activities...? Number surveyed: women = 616; men = 614.

Characteristic of respondent	Personal involvement	
	Yes	No
U.S. Total	41%	59%
Sex:		
Female	46%	54%
Male	36%	64%
Age:		
18-29 years	30%	70%
30-49 years	44%	56%
50 and older	45%	55%

Source: George Gallup, Jr., *The Gallup Report*, Report No. 290 (Princeton, NJ: The Gallup Poll, November 1989), p. 19. Also in source; other characteristics of respondents; opinions on the involvement of others in the community; trends of personal involvement since 1977.

Women and Golf

Some statistics on women in golf, according to *Business Week*, October 1990.

1. "Upscale" women now make up **40%** of beginning golfers.
2. About **50%** of Mazda owners are women. Mazda sponsors the Mazda LPGA (Ladies Professional Golf Assn.) Championship.
3. LPGA prize money grew from $13 million in 1989 to $17.1 million in 1990.
4. Only 5 LPGA tournaments were televised on the three major networks in 1990, compared to 37 for the regular PGA Tour.

Source: William C. Symonds, "Golf: The Ladies Tour Slices Into the Rough," *Business Week*, October 1, 1990, p. 134.

Women in Sports

General opinions of female athletes on women in sports.

Statement	Agree Strongly	Agree Somewhat	Disagree Somewhat	Disagree Strongly
Women's sports should be kept separate from men's so that women are free to develop their own skills.	23%	46%	23%	8%
In this society, a woman is often forced to choose between being an athlete and being feminine.	20%	37%	21%	21%
Girls should be allowed to play contact sports like football if they want to.	36%	37%	17%	10%
Intense athletic involvement complicates romantic relationships.	8%	33%	26%	33%
Female athletes exhibit higher levels of aggression than their non-athletic counterparts.	16%	36%	26%	22%
A woman athlete's sexual orientation is no one's business but her own.	76%	17%	4%	3%
Participation in racially mixed sports/fitness groups often reduces prejudice.	49%	42%	6%	3%
Women have something to teach men about humane competition.	36%	42%	16%	5%
Participation in sports diminishes a woman's femininity.	3%	3%	12%	82%
There is too much pressure today for women to be just like men in sports and athletics.	10%	32%	36%	22%
American women athletes are going to have to take steroids and drugs to compete successfully internationally.	1%	3%	12%	84%
If young girls compete successfully on the athletic field, they will be better able to compete successfully in later life.	57%	36%	5%	2%
What a woman does is feminine.	40%	31%	20%	9%
Compared to other women athletes, women of color are less able to convert their athletic success into commercial success off the field.	12%	38%	30%	20%

Source: *Miller Lite Report on Women in Sports*, December 1985, p. 11. Based on a random sample of 7,000 members of the Women's Sports Foundation.

More Resources for

Your Reading Pleasure

■ *Books*

Auburdene, Patricia and Naisbitt, John. *Megatrends for Women.* New York: Villard Books, 1992.

Berry, Frances. *The Politics of Parenthood, Child Care, Women's Rights, and the Myth of the Good Mother.* New York: Viking Penguin Books, 1993.

Brennan, Shawn. *Women's Information Directory.* Detroit: Gale Research, Inc., 1993.

Auburdene, Patricia, and Naisbitt, John. *Megatrends for Women.* New York: Villard Books, 1992.

Berry, Frances. *The Politics of Parenthood, Child Care, Women's Rights, and the Myth of the Good Mother.* New York: Viking Penguin Books, 1993.

Brennan, Shawn. *Women's Information Directory.* Detroit: Gale Research Inc., 1993.

Bullen, Martha M. and Sanders, Darcie. *Staying Home; From Full-Time Professional to Full-Time Parent.* New York: Little, Brown, & Company.

Capek, Mary Ellen S. *A Women's Thesaurus: An Index of Language Used to Describe and Locate Information By and About Women.* New York: Harper & Row, 1987.

Coontz, Stephanie. *The Way We Never Were: American Families and the Nostalgia Trap.* New York: Basic Books, 1992.

Evatt, Cris. *Opposite Sides of the Bed: A Lively Guide to Significant Differences Between Men and Women.* Emeryville, CA: Conari Press, 1993.

Faludi, Susan. *Backlash: The Undeclared War Against American Women.* New York: Crown Publishers, Inc., 1991.

Goldscheider, Frances K., and Waite, Linda J. *New Families, No Families? The Transformation of the American Home.* Los Angeles: University of California Press, 1992.

Howe, Neil, and Strauss, Bill. *13th Generation. Abort, Retry, Ignore, Fail?* New York: Vintage Books, 1993.

Leong T. L., and Sekaran, Uma. *Womanpower: Managing in Times of Demographic Turbulence.* Newbury Park, CA: Sage Publications, 1991.

Lewis, Herschell Gordon. *Copywriting Secrets and Tactics.* Chicago: Dartnell, 1993.

——— . *Herschell Gordon Lewis on the Art of Writing Copy.* Englewood Cliffs, NJ: 1989.

Schmittroth, Linda. *Statistical Record of Women Worldwide.* Detroit: Gale Research Inc., 1991.

Schneider, Gretel. *The New Diversity: SELF Magazine Reports on Women.* Ithaca, NY: American Demographics, Inc., 1992.

Steinem, Gloria. *Revolution from Within.* Boston: Little, Brown, & Company, 1992.

Swiss, Deborah, and Walker, Judith. *Women and the Work/Family Dilemma.* New York: John Wiley & Sons, Inc., 1993.

Tannen, Dr. Deborah. *You Just Don't Understand, Women and Men in Conversation.* New York: Ballantine Books, 1990.

Thomas, Richard K. *Health Care Consumers in the 1990s.* Ithaca, NY: American Demographics Books, 1993.

TV Dimensions '93. New York: Media Dynamics, 1993.

Waldrop, Judith, and Mogelonsky, Marcia. *The Seasons of Business: A Marketer's Guide to Consumer Behavior.* Ithaca, NY: American Demographic Books, 1992.

■ *Directories*

Brennan, Shawn. *Women's Information Directory.* Detroit: Gale Research Inc., 1993.

Henry, Dawn. *A Directory of Women's Media, 16th edition.* New York: National Council for Research on Women. 1992.

A Women's Mailing List Directory. New York: National Council for Research on Women, 1990.

■ *Magazine and Journal Articles*

Altaner, David. "Baby Boom or Bust?" *Weekly Business* (March 1, 1993): 7-9.

Appelbaum, Cara. "For 'Relationship Marketing,' It's Hard to Beat Diaper Makers." *ADWEEK's Marketing Week* (July 2, 1992): 9.

Baldwin, Pat. "Consultant sees red over stereotype." *Dallas Morning News* (January 2, 1993): 1F.

Bernikow, Louise. "The New Activists: Fearless, Funny, Fighting Mad." *Cosmopolitan* (February, 1993): 62-65.

Blanke, Gail. "Notes on the Recent Reinvention of the Avon Wheel." *A.N.A./The Advertiser* (Summer, 1992): 28-31.

Boyd, Malia. "Generation X." *Business and Incentive Strategies* (May, 1993): 22-31.

"Boys and Girls Together . . . And Apart: Advertising and the Sexes." *Tested Copy* (October 1992).

Brause, Patricia. "Women of a Certain Age." *American Demographics* (December 1992): 44-9.

Buchanen, Rob. "Girls Night In." *ADWEEK* (November 25, 1991): 22.

Burka, Ken. "Generation X." *Direct* (January, 1993): 34-35.

Cox, James. "Newspapers Court Women." *USA Today* (November 24, 1992): 8B.

Deveny, Kathleen. "Blame it on Dashed Hopes (and Oprah): Disillusioned Dieters Shun Liquid Meals." *Wall Street Journal* (October 13, 1992): B1.

D'Innocenzio, Anne. "Emphasis on super-sizes, merger boost Catherines' plus-sizes share." *WWD* (October 28, 1992).

Donaton, Scott. "Boomers bringing buying power." *Advertising Age* (November 16, 1992): S-2.

——. "Magazine of the Year." *Advertising Age* (March 1, 1993): S-1-10.

——. "The Media Wakes up to Generation X." *Advertising Age,* (February,1, 1993): 16-17.

——. "Women hit 'sexy' ads, but say condoms on TV would be OK." *Advertising Age* (April 12, 1992).

"Easing pain of business travel." *Cincinnati Enquirer* (Sunday, May 17, 1992): G6.

Feldman, Amy. "Hello Oprah, good-bye, Iman." *Forbes* (March 16, 1992): 116-17.

Fitzgerald, Kate. "TV's hottest number?" *Advertising Age* (June 1, 1992): 30.

Gates, Anita. "The Best Hotels For Women." *Working Woman* (April 1993): 77-81.

Geer, Carolyn T. "Gender Gap." *Forbes* (March 16, 1992): 102.

Goldman, Debra. "Marketing's Biggest Myths." *ADWEEK* (January 27, 1992) 24-29.

——. "What do Women Want?" *ADWEEK* (June 25, 1990): 39-42.

Goldman, Kevin. "Sassy Talk Show Targets Young Women." *Wall Street Journal* (March 11, 1993): B1-3.

Horovitz, Bruce. "Brewers Raise Glasses to New Pals — Women." *Los Angeles Times* (March 24, 1992): D1, 6.

——. "Some Fuming, Few Surprised by Madison Avenue's 'Male Bashing' Ads." *Los Angeles Times* (August 8, 1989): 6.

Lane, Randall, and Yeager, Dorian. "Somewhere there's a car for you... (what women want in a car)." *Cosmopolitan* (December, 1991): 202-4.

Lazarus, George. "Aiming at women: Budget on the Ball." *Chicago Tribune* (February 8, 1993): 4.

Liesse, Julie. "Lean Cuisine ads get tasteful touch." *Advertising Age* (November 23, 1992): 37.

Lipman, Joanne. "Marketers of Luxury Goods Are Turning From Self-Indulgence to Family Values." *Wall Street Journal* (October 22, 1992): B1.

Lippert, Barbara. "Breaking the Bimbo Barrier." *ADWEEK* (November 4, 1991): 35.

——. "'90s Icon Man." *ADWEEK* (November 30, 1992): 24.

——. "Pinstripes and New Lace." *ADWEEK* (April 27, 1992): 30.

Lipton, Lauren. "A Woman's Place." *Los Angeles Times Magazine* (April 5, 1992): 7.

"Mail Order Madness." *Marketing to Women* (November 1992): 8.

Mandese, Joe. "Doug McCormick: Attuned to women's issues as Lifetime chief." *Advertising Age* (March 1, 1993): 34.

——. "Who sees 'Murphy Brown'" *Advertising Age* (June 1, 1992): 34.

Manly, Lorne. "Makeover Contest." *ADWEEK* (February 17, 1992): 30-1.

Miller, Cyndee. "Liberation for women in ads." *Marketing News* (August 17, 1992): 1-2.

Miller, Jonathan, and Skipworth, Mark. "Double Standards Claim in Agencies' War on Men." *The Business Australian* (June 26, 1992).

Newman, Judith. "The Year of the Woman's Magazines." *ADWEEK* (March 1, 1993): 11-15.

O'Neil, Kathleen, and Townsend, Bickley. "American Women Get Mad." *American Demographics* (August 1990).

Pearl, Daniel. "Newspapers Strive to Win Back Women." *Wall Street Journal* (May 4, 1992): B11.

Reilly, Patrick M. "Women's Service Magazine Advertising Revives as Design, Articles Grow Livelier." *Wall Street Journal* (October 21, 1992): B10.

Schiller, Zachary, and Flynn, Julia "Sex Still Sells — But So Does Sensitivity." (March 18, 1991): 100.

"The Sexism Watch." *U.S. News & World Report.* (March 27, 1989): 12.

Shapiro, Joseph P. "Just Fix It!" *U.S. News & World Report* (February 22, 1993): 50-6.

Sharkey, Betsy. "You've Come a Long Way, Madison Avenue." *Lear's* (March, 1993): 92-101.

St. James, Lyn. "Women tell automakers not to sell them short." *Detroit Free Press* (April 22, 1993).

Szathmary, Richard R. "Newspapers fight back!" *Sales and Marketing Management* (May 1992): 57.

Teinowitz, Ira. "Looking for women: Miller ads pay more attention to females." *Advertising Age* (March 16, 1992): 20.

Wright, Lydia. "Nation's dealers anticipate gradual upturn in 1993." *Automotive News* (February 8, 1993): 41.

Yankelovich Clancy Shulman. "Taking Control and Taking No Chances." *ADWEEK* (June 22, 1992): 36-38.

■ *Studies and Reports*

Advertising Options Plus. Wilmette, IL: Standard Rates and Data Service (SRDS), 1993.

Advertising: What Do You Find Offensive? Arlington Heights, IL: Telenation Reports, Fall 1992.

Annual Compendium of Trends. About Women, Inc. Boston: Marketing to Women.

Baby Products Tracking Study 1991: Diapering Products. New York: American Baby, 1991.

Best Hotels for Women. New York: Working Woman, April 1993.

Facts about Newspapers '93. Reston, VA: Newspaper Association of America, 1993.

Glamour's National Fashion Study. Walter K. Levy & Associates. New York: Conde Nast Publications, Inc., 1992.

Mantrack II: The Man Thing — Adapting to a Changing Culture. New York: The Roper Organization for Playboy Enterprises, 1991.

Mature America in the 1990s. New York: The Roper Organization, 1992.

Menopause Survey. New York: McCall's, June, 1991.

Motherhood Survey. New York: EDK Associates for Redbook, September, 1992.

The New American Family: Significant and Diversified Lifestyles. New York: Simmons Market Research Bureau, 1990.

Office Worker Retail Spending. New York: International Council of Shopping Centers, 1988.

The Oft Quoted 5th Annual Sassy Entertainment Poll. New York: Sassy Magazine, January 1992.

Oppenheimer Women and Investment Survey. New York: The Withlin Group for Oppenheimer Management Corporation, March, 1992.

Personal Safety Survey. New York: Self Magazine Survey, 1992.

Retirement Housing and Long-term Health Care: Attitudes and Perceptions of the Mature Market. Annapolis, MD: National Association for Senior Living Industries, Fall 1991.

Shopping for Health. Emmaus, PA: Food Marketing Institute, June, 1992.

Special Report Chore Poll. Knoxville: Special Report Magazine, March/April, 1993.

Summer Vacation Forecast. Washington D.C.: U.S. Travel Data Center, May 1993.

Survey of Business Travelers 1991. Washington D.C.: U.S. Travel Data Center, 1991.

Time Off: The Psychology of Vacations. Chicago: Research and Forecasts for the Hyatt Travel Futures Project, 1991.

Twentysomething: The New Individual. New York: The Roper Organization for Mademoiselle, January, 1992.

Valvoline Poll of the American Motorist 1991. St. Louis, MO: Valvoline, 1991.

Woman at the Wheel. New York: Yankelovich Clancy Shulman, August 1992.

Women Extended Stay Travelers: Taking It in Stride. Washington D.C.: Report by Marriott Residence Inn.

Women, Work, and Health Insurance. Washington D.C.: National Commission on Working Women of Wider Opportunities for Women, February, 1991.

Women's Voices '92: A Policy Guide. Washington D.C.: Ms. Foundation for Women, September, 1992.

■ *Newsletters and Publications*

Colloquy: The Quarterly Frequency Marketing Newsletter. Frequency Marketing, Inc. P.O. Box 3920, Milford, Ohio 45150 (513)248-9084.

Marketing to Women. About Women, Inc., 33 Broad Street, Boston, MA 02109 (617)723-4337.

Tested Copy. Starch INRA Hooper, Inc., 566 E. Boston Post Road, Mamaroneck, NY 10543 (914)698-0800.

Index

t